Promise and Betrayal

Promise and Betrayal

Universities and the Battle
for Sustainable Urban Neighborhoods

John I. Gilderbloom
and
R. L. Mullins Jr.

FOREWORD BY HENRY CISNEROS

State University of New York Press

Published by
State University of New York Press, Albany

For information, address State University of New York Press,
194 Washington Avenue, Suite 305, Albany, NY 12210-2384

Production by Diane Ganeles
Marketing by Michael Campochiaro

Library of Congress Cataloging-in-Publication Data

Gilderbloom, John Ingram.
   Promise and betrayal : universities and the battle for sustainable urban neighborhoods /
John I. Gilderbloom and R. L. Mullins Jr.
      p. cm.
   Includes bibliographical references and index.
   ISBN 0-7914-6483-0 (hardcover : alk. paper) — ISBN 0-7914-6484-9 (pbk. : alk. paper)
   1. Community development, Urban—United States.   2. Universities and colleges—
United States—Public services.   3. Community and college—United States.   I. Mullins,
R. L. (Robert Lee) 1955–.   II. Title.

HN90.C6G55 2005
307.1'416'0973—dc22   2004017160

10 9 8 7 6 5 4 3 2 1

Dedication

This was not just another project to us; rather, it was an intellectual labor of love for a topic we are passionate about. Both authors made equal contributions to this book. Many people were important to us during the production of this book and the research at its core. Local officials, university administrators, and businesses were very support-ive. Our family and friends were behind us, especially Dr. Mark T. Wright, who was part of the team and took this research into the com-munity and is developing affordable housing in Louisville and else-where. He is doing well by doing good. Sam Watkins and the late Frank Clay were instrumental in opening doors in the Russell Com-munity. Finally, we appreciate the support and energy of the residents of the Russell Neighborhood. We are glad they let us share their lives, hopes, and dreams.

If you would not be forgotten
As soon as you are dead and rotten
Either write things worthy reading
Or do things worth the writing
                    —Benjamin Franklin

Contents

Illustrations

Tables

Foreword

Our colleges and universities have always been the hope for our nation's future. As repositories and conservators of knowledge, they pass on the accumulated understanding and wisdom of one generation to the next. As centers of thought and research, they continually build on the work of previous generations, constantly expanding our horizons of understanding.

Our institutions of higher learning introduce young people to the wider world beyond the familiar confines of home and family—to new ideas, new ways of looking at things, and, most importantly, to other people from widely varying backgrounds—to the rich diversity of human experience. They instill values critical to the health of a democratic society, including lifelong respect for learning and openness to new ideas, concern for others beyond our immediate circle of family and friends, personal civic responsibility, a drive to make tomorrow better than today, and tolerance.

Colleges and universities are an invaluable resource for urban policy and planning, doing fundamental research, providing seminal analysis of urban problems, developing strategies for their solution, and supporting programs to train urban planners and scholars. Academic research has already made vital contributions to the understanding of urban issues and, through that understanding, to the well-being of American cities. But as important as they are, research and understanding are not enough. Articles, books, and conferences are not enough. Political capital is not of much use unless it is spent on leadership. By the same token, intellectual capital's value is diminished if it is not invested in action.

In that regard, the university-community partnership has been pioneered in Chicago by the University of Illinois (UIC), DePaul, and Loyola as a model for the nation—a vivid demonstration of what can be accomplished when major institutions combine resources with those of government, business, and community groups.

The UIC Neighborhoods Initiative is helping to create: (1) an affordable housing consortium; (2) commercial and industrial area design; (3) entrepreneurial programs for youth; (4) adult literacy and community health programs; and (5) linkage of neighborhood groups on the Internet through UIC's academic data network. The Department of Housing and Urban Development (HUD) has supported the UIC effort with a variety of grants, including HUD Academy (a joint project with DePaul) to train HUD staff ($160,000), the Community Outreach Partnership Program ($580,000), and the Joint Community Partnership Center ($2.4 million).

Additionally, the University of Louisville (U of L) has worked in partnership with businesses, government, public schools, and community-based groups to help inner-city residents lift themselves out of poverty. The U of L's HANDS (Housing and Neighborhood Development Strategies) program provided support for the conversion of 150 units of former public housing development—La Salle Place—to private homes for sale to low-income buyers. More recently, the university's Sustainable Urban Neighborhoods (SUN) program has worked closely with the Telesis Corporation (a Washington, D.C., developer), local and HUD officials, Mayor Jerry Abramson, and community organizations to save the 600-unit HUD Section 8 Village West Apartments from foreclosure and eventual demolition. They have also provided technical support to several nonprofits for building affordable homes and even converting an abandoned school into an assisted housing development.

As another example, the University of Pennsylvania Center for Community Partnerships was started in 1992, in part to create new and effective partnerships between the university and the community and to strengthen a national network of institutions of higher education committed to engagement with their local communities.

While I was at HUD, we created the Office of University Partnerships to help colleges fulfill their urban mission. Our goals were to recognize, reward, and build upon successful examples of universities' activities in local revitalization projects, create the next urban generation and encourage them to focus their work on housing and community development policy and applied research, and form partnerships with other federal agencies to support innovative university teaching, research, and service partnerships. Now, more than ever, universities are essential in helping HUD achieve its mission of creating communities of opportunity.

Of particular note was our work with local communities and their universities and colleges to create a "campus of learners" initiative to build partnerships between public housing developments and nearby schools. This initiative converted some developments into "learning campuses" similar to dormitories at universities. Family members study at home to learn skills, using computers hooked up to self-paced education and training courses devised by the schools.

A good example is the model community revitalization initiative incorporating the "campus for learners" concept that Trinity College has begun in Hartford, Connecticut. Trinity's plan links it with nearby hospitals through a new Allied Health and Technology Center and includes three new innovative public schools, a home ownership initiative that combines housing with education—and their own version of a campus of learners—and possibly a regional children's science center.

This initiative has the support of local officials, key private organizations—especially the hospitals—and the state government. By focusing on job-oriented economic development, education, and home ownership, the Trinity initiative holds great promise for the future of Hartford and for the college. HUD helped greatly through a Community Outreach Partnership grant and some technical assistance funds.

Tulane and Xavier, two prestigious universities, also brought about dramatic improvement to a most troubling public housing authority. Working together, the partnership implemented a "campus of learners" program for residents of some New Orleans public housing developments. The universities and HUD also inaugurated a community project to develop comprehensive solutions for problems in inner-city communities that have public housing.

This book, by John I. Gilderbloom and R. L. Mullins Jr., is about translating our understanding of the tough urban issues facing us today. It is about leadership and a call to action. It is about partnerships between the public and private sectors, profit-making businesses, and nonprofit organizations, between community-based groups and public agencies, and especially between the university and the community. Forging these partnerships is absolutely critical to the future of urban America. And it is a ten-year history of the University of Louisville program. While it celebrates its successes, it also discusses its mistakes so we can learn from them. It makes a major contribution to understanding the dynamics of university-community partnerships.

The nation's cities are an important focus of American life as major centers for commercial activity, housing, leading banks, community networks, and international trading companies. They are home to the basic infrastructure of trade and commerce—our roads, bridges, seaports, and airports. The central cities are megacenters for the arts, education, and scientific discovery. All of these amenities bring together people of diverse races, backgrounds, and religious persuasions.

Many American cities, however, are in a steep and steady decline for reasons both contemporary and historic. Current economic pressures on cities arise from global competition and technological innovation, which are fundamentally restructuring the U.S. economy. Having suffered through more than twenty years of job losses and fiscal stress, our cities are failing to generate robust economic opportunities and create good jobs for those with less than a college education.

Businesses have fled to the suburbs or overseas, leaving behind "brown fields" and empty buildings on contaminated lots that no one wants to develop. These communities can no longer sustain themselves. Sadly, this fundamental fact of life will not change with an upswing in the business cycle.

The American city, as the historic gateway to social and economic mobility, is becoming home to many of the most disadvantaged people in America. Labor force detachment, lack of education, welfare dependency, drug use, teenage pregnancy, a high infant mortality rate, and an increase in violent crime reflect a cityscape in which upward mobility and economic independence are virtually unknown. We are in danger of becoming two nations—one as highly skilled, well-paid workers and professionals, and the other as low-skilled, low-wage workers or a no-skilled, no-wage unemployed underclass.

The resources of our colleges and universities are critical to the fight to save our cities. Institutions of higher learning must join the effort to turn around their communities—not just for moral reasons—out of enlightened self-interest. The long-term futures of both the city and the university are so intertwined that each needs the other for survival—one cannot have longevity without the other.

The American institution of higher learning may, in the dawning of a new century, be entering one of its most challenging and productive eras. Among its tasks will be that of helping to reshape the city to become, once again, the driving force in the economic, social, and cultural life of this nation. HUD stands to make that task more doable and more likely to succeed. It has invited American colleges and universities to join in this worthwhile effort.

It is not Washington's role to pay for everything, regulate everything, or mandate everything. Its role is to marshal resources from all sectors of society and bring them to bear on the problems we face as a society. HUD's role is to catalyze, facilitate, mediate, and get out of the way and to let people of good-will and faith in our communities do their jobs.

My vision as mayor of San Antonio as well as HUD secretary was clear—make tomorrow better than today. Leave your piece of the world better for your children. We must take responsibility for the problems facing us today. All of us must contribute our time, talents, and resources to resolving them. We own these problems and have a collective stake in their solution. And, believe me, the only way we can solve them is together. They must be solved in communities, by communities, and through community partnerships. That is why this theme of partnership, of pooling skills, talents, and resources with other federal agencies, state and local governments, private industry, and community groups with colleges and universities, runs like a strong, steady current through everything we did at HUD.

In the end, there are really no words that can adequately describe how important one's work as a chancellor, president, provost, dean, board of trustee member, professor, student, and staff is to the future of this country. But these professionals have the power to make the university more responsive to the immediate needs of the community. I can only say: Keep it up. This book by Gilderbloom and Mullins is an important contribution to the field and should be read by university and community leaders, as well as by policy makers at all levels.

Henry Cisneros
Former Secretary of the U.S.
Department of Housing
and Urban Development

Preface

Universities can play important roles in partnership with the public, private, and nonprofit sectors. The University of Louisville turned a poor black neighborhood into a laboratory of innovation. Soon this once blighted neighborhood was rebuilt, reclaimed and revitalized. This neighborhood went from a laboratory to a model for the rest of the nation. University programs such as SUN make operational the concept of public-private partnerships in order to succeed in urban renovation and rehabilitation where many others have failed. The key is creating a sustainable partnership that can grow with the neighborhood. Urban universities with planning programs can bring tremendous creative and technical resources to community leaders and should take activist roles in helping their communities by supplying the knowledge and assistance.

Acknowledgments

We thank the following individuals and organizations: the Honorable Henry Cisneros, Sam Watkins, the late Frank Clay, Marilyn Melkonian, John Martin-Rutherford, Derek Bok, Donald Swain, Larry Muhammad, Armand W. Carriere, Kristy Salerno, the American Planning Association, the Urban Land Institute, Patty and Max Gilderbloom, Sarah Wortham, Jim Allen, Mayor Jerry Abramson, Scot Ramsey, Jennifer Fowler, LaTondra Jones, Jackie Alvarenga, Fitsum Kassie, Karthik Suresh, Dexter, Snoopy, Steve Zimmer, Jian Sun, Reg Bruce, Paul Bather, Abey Mulugetas, Muthusami Kumaran, Tom Donovan, Dan Hall, Bill Friedlander, Patrick Flanagan, the late I. Don Terner, Bill Rothwell, Vanessa Cunningham, Laura Chafin, Russ Barnett, Russ Simms, Jeanette Wilson, Warren Wolfe, Nancy Martin, Stephen Roosa, Kao Chiupink, Michael Brazely, Michael Rinella, Joseph Stopher and Jim Davis of the Gheens Foundation, the Association of Governing Boards, Rich Novak, John Nelson, Sam Bell, Scott Cummings, Mark Wright, Sharon Mullins, and Hank Savitch. We would also like to thank our colleagues at SUNY Press, Michael Rinella, Diane Ganeles, and Michele Liberti-Lansing. They provided support, guidance, and insight into the challenges of urban revitalization. In addition, the following organizations and individuals helped fund HANDS and SUN either by cash or in-kind contributions from 1992 to 2002: The United States Department of Housing and Urban Development, Community Outreach Partnership Center Award, University of Louisville Research, Gheens Foundation, Dupont, Telesis, U of L Partnerships for Urban Development, Plymouth Community Renewal Center, Innovative Productivity, City of Louisville HUD, Canaan Community Development Corporation, St. Stephens Community Development Corp., Neighborhood Development Corporation, Louisville Central Development Corp., United States Department of Education, Greater Louisville Building and Construction Trades Council, Neighborhood House, Lincoln Foundation, Kentuckiana Minority Supplier Development Council, George Montgomery, United States Department of Housing and Urban Development Assistant Secretary for

Policy, Development Research for International Conference on Revitalization of Cities, Environmental Justice funded by the United States Environmental Protection Agency, and the Association of Governing Boards, University Community Partnerships (principal consultant/private contract), funded by the MacArthur Foundation and the ARCO Foundation. Also, the Kentucky Housing Corporation, Kentucky Real Estate Commission, Neighborhood Development Corporation, Neighborhood Housing Services, Louisville Central Community Center, Louisville Central Development Corporation, Project One, Telesis Corporation, University of Kentucky School of Architecture, University of Louisville Foundation, Liberty National Bank and Trust, PNC Bank, National City Bank, Cumberland Bank, Homebuilders Association, of Louisville, Jefferson County Commissioner Darryl Owens, Mortgage Bankers Association: L&T Properties, Housing Authority of Louisville, Jefferson County Public Schools, National Center for Family Literacy, Housing Partnership of Louisville, University of Louisville faculty, Metroversity, University of Louisville Foundation, University of Louisville, Kentucky, Institute for Environment and Sustainable Development, and Fannie Mae.

Additional Resources

We have been funded to provide seminars and a DVD based on this book. The DVD that complements this book provides an eighty-picture slide show of before and after pictures of our target neighborhood, video clips of former President Clinton, former HUD Secretary Henry Cisneros, former Harvard President Derek Bok, Mayor Jerry Abramson of Louisville, Kentucky, and former University of Louisville President Donald Swain discussing the importance of the university-community partnership. Also included are various clips produced by the HUD and the University of Louisville that were developed for this project. The DVD is approximately two hours long. It is available at the following web sites: <http://www.gilderbloom.org> or <http://www.louisville.edu/org/sun>.

We also do a yearly seminar based on this book and on the DVD. We are available to present the information in this book and DVD, at your university or city.

CHAPTER 1

Promise of University-Community Partnerships

Collaborative processes, or bottom-up approaches, have not been tried extensively. When tried, many have not truly been bottom-up. One thing that distinguishes a bottom-up approach from a top-down approach is the scope of the project and sources of funds. Most of the failed, top-down approaches have employed large amounts of federal money and minimal local investment and have been geographically extensive, covering large sections of cities or regions. Bottom-up strategies are narrowly focused from an areal perspective, often concentrating on a single neighborhood or part of a neighborhood. While seed money may come from a federal program, there is usually a significant local investment component (25% or more), which gives local governments, nonprofits, and neighborhood groups more ownership of the program and its processes.

Neighborhood residents must, in concert with others in the community, reach out and form partnerships with those who can help revitalize their neighborhood. A broad-based coalition must be assembled to address problems; we can no longer be categorical in our approach. The categorical grant programs of the past have not been as effective as their developers had hoped. A holistic approach is required. The individuals working in the coalition must believe that they have the power to make a difference and to find, through themselves or their partners, people who can wield the necessary power to carry out their plans. Finally, these plans must be developed and carried out at the lowest level. If there is not a significant commitment by all parties, especially residents, then the effort will fail. If the plans are being directed from afar, then history shows that change will be either fleeting or non-existent.

Neighborhood planners working within the confines of an overall city plan are under a tremendous amount of pressure to remake the neighborhoods that comprise the cities. Attractive, safe, desirable, convenient neighborhoods in conjunction with economic opportunities and residents who can seize them may be the only things that can stem the tide of emigration from the cities to suburbia. Scholars almost forty years ago were not optimistic about the future of cities. According to Dahl (1967):

> Our cities are not merely non-cities, they are anti-cities—mean, ugly, gross, banal, inconvenient, hazardous, formless, incoherent, unfit for human living, deserts from which a family flees to the greener hinter-lands as soon as job and income permit, yet deserts growing so rapidly outward that the open green space to which the family escapes soon shrinks to an oasis and then it too turns to a desert. (p. 964)

Inner-city communities have severe problems with crime, homelessness, joblessness, illiteracy, drugs, and a host of other challenges. One might have thought that graduates from our outstanding professional schools, armed with the research of our social scientists, could have done more to help our govern-ment agencies and community organizations reduce the incidence of poverty, illiteracy, and stunted opportunity. Since these results have not occurred, it is fair to ask whether our universities are doing all that they can and should to help America surmount the obstacles that threaten to sap its economic strength and blight the lives of its people (Bok 1990, p. 6).

J. Martin Klotsche, former chancellor of the University of Wisconsin-Milwaukee, provides an appropriate frame of reference for this discussion of university involvement in the community. Klotsche (1966) writes:

> Our society is irretrievably urban. Since our cities are here to stay, the time is at hand to take a new look at them. It is urgent that a major ef-fort be made to reshape them. This will require serious reflection, and positive action. In all of these matters the urban university can play a central role. It can, in fact, become the single most important force in the re-creation of our cities. (p. 128)

Several cities, acting as laboratories of innovation, have proven programs that help revitalize inner-city neighborhoods. Universities can play important roles in partnership with the public, private, and nonprofit sectors. As the late Ernest Boyer (1990) noted, "[T]he work of the academy must relate to the world beyond the campus" (p. 75). Stukel (1994) states:

> The ideal of the urban university rolling up its sleeves and getting involved in urban affairs will spread because it is a tremendous op-portunity to deal with real issues—crime, taxes, the economy, and elementary and secondary education—the issues that are on people's minds every day of the year. This will generate public and political

support, which will be increasingly necessary in this era of diminishing resources. And it will actually be doing some good for this country. (p. 21)

University involvement in urban affairs is not a new idea. Forty years ago President Johnson provided a vision of university-community partnerships at a speech to open the University of California at Irvine. He argued that universities should try to provide answers to the pressing problems of the cities "just as our colleges and universities changed the future of our farms a century ago" (Klotsche 1966, p. 51). Six months later, President Johnson addressed Congress and urged universities to replicate their success with helping farms by addressing the needs of the city. He stated:

> The role of the university must extend beyond the ordinary extension type operation. Its research findings and talents must be made available to the community. Faculty must be called upon for consulting activities. Pilot projects, seminars, conferences, TV programs, and task forces drawing on many departments of the university should be brought into play. (Klotsche 1966, p. 60)

Noted educational leader Clark Kerr (1968), in an address to the New York City Chapter of Phi Beta Kappa, asked those assembled:

> Cannot the intellectual resources that created the new age of science now tackle the equally explosive problem of our cities? The threat is as real and the obligation surely as great. The university can come increasingly to aid the renovation of our cities, and in return the university can be inspired by the opportunities and strengthened by the participation. (p. 14)

During the ensuing period many creative, bold, and innovative university-community partnerships were developed. These efforts had mixed results. Cities continued to be overwhelmed by a whole range of social, political, and economic forces. Even today, the same problem remains. As much of the literature on the cycle of poverty indicates, urban issues are complex and interdependent. Because of this, initiatives that are not comprehensive in scope do little more than provide temporary relief. Recent federal programs have recommitted the federal government as a central player in facilitating urban/university partnerships (Gilderbloom 1996, p. 7). For example, in 1993, the U.S. Department of Education's Urban Community Service Grant Program funded twenty-three colleges and universities to ". . . work with private and civic organizations to devise and implement solutions to pressing and severe problems in their urban communities" (U.S. Department of Education 1992, p. 1).

The U.S. Department of Housing and Urban Development (HUD) has taken strides toward increasing university involvement in addressing urban needs. According to former Secretary Henry G. Cisneros, the five-year Community Outreach Partnership Centers (COPC) demonstration program awarded grants to institutions of higher learning " . . . to establish and operate centers for multi-disciplinary research and outreach activities in cooperation with community groups and local governments" (U.S. Department of Housing and Urban Development 1994a, p. 5). Schools such as the University of Illinois at Chicago, Yale University, Marquette University, Northwestern University, the University of Alabama at Birmingham, Marshall University, Duquesne University, the University of Wisconsin-Milwaukee, and the University of California at Los Angeles performed some exciting revitalization efforts under the auspices of HUD's COPC program (Cisneros 1995, p. 14; Stegman 1995, p. 98). Now that the federal government has provided incentives for universities to fulfill social obligations, there is no excuse for higher education not to respond. "As Oscar Handlin observed, our troubled planet 'can no longer afford the luxury of pursuits confined to an ivory tower. [. . .] [S]cholarship has to prove its worth not on its own terms but by service to the nation and the world'" (Boyer 1990, p. 23).

There are, however, many who have believed that the university should remain aloof and apart from the larger society in which it exists. They believe the academy should be a place for contemplation and a search for truth. They believe in knowledge for the sake of knowledge. Some of these historical figures such as John Henry Cardinal Newman and current figures are discussed in Bok (1990), Cisneros (1995), and Kerr (1972).

Literature Review

There is not a vast body of literature on university-community partnerships. In fact, there has been little effort to rigorously evaluate the successes and failures of partnership ventures (Harkavy and Wiewel 1995; Nyden and Wiewel 1992). "The academy has not yet devoted much thought to the study of partnerships and to its role in the social, political, and economic environment" (Harkavy and Wiewel 1995, p. 12).

The urban university is a much different entity than a business or government agency. The role or position of the university is unique in the pantheon of urban organizations. Many in the metropolitan university do not understand a crucial fact that Ruch and Trani (1995) make so well: "Metropolitan universities are not simply *in* the city but *of* the city, and the importance of activities with their surrounding environment is central to the life of the institution" (p. 231, emphasis added). Too often, the university has forgotten its foundation in the affairs of its community. Hathaway, Mulhollan, and White (1990) and Perlman (1990) make the same point in slightly different ways.

Universities play a variety of roles in their communities. They are economic entities, players in both the intellectual and cultural lives of the community, and they have the potential to touch all aspects of community life (Johnson and Bell 1995, p. 193). As an economic entity, Washington University in St. Louis, Missouri, formed a redevelopment corporation around its medical school that invested over $100 million in capital improvements in its neighborhood (Porter and Sweet 1984, p. 58). In Philadelphia, "the University of Pennsylvania is the largest private employer and education is the largest single industry" (Hackney 1986, p. 136). Early on, universities were cultural bastions, a means of transmitting the fruits of Western culture; they helped rapidly growing cities by contributing "to the development of the city and to the quality of life of a new and impoverished citizenry" (Hackney 1986, p. 137). These are just a few examples. There are also roles that are more traditionally associated with the university, such as research, which has been a hallmark of the major American university. "While the conduct of sophisticated research is a distinctive characteristic of a research-intensive university, this research informs and takes place within a framework of teaching and service; the three types of academic activity are integrated and intertwined" (Greiner 1994, p. 319).

Higher education has played a role in many research endeavors with entities outside the academy. This has been documented in a variety of sources. The following are just a few of the many examples. Illman (1994) discussed the role of the National Science Foundation in furthering basic university research in key commercial sectors such as chemicals, biotechnology, and software development. Horowitz (1990) also discussed the research partnerships in higher education and the funding of research. Individual colleges and universities and businesses have also joined together for mutually beneficial purposes. The Chronicle of Higher Education (1993) discussed the cooperative program between IBM and the University of California at Los Angeles for data processing research and development. Lissner (1980, p. 320) discussed the efforts of City University of New York administrators to establish urban research centers at various system campuses. Winthrop (1975) provided information on the establishment of interdisciplinary programs at colleges and universities to help "meet community needs" (p. 245). These ventures do not always result in solutions to community problems, and the solutions seem to come from a different type of venture.

The history of university involvement in community problems is a different story. The university has taken a directive role or provided a limited contractual service rather than working in true partnership with other entities. One example is found in Medoff and Sklar's (1994) work. They discuss the role that planning students at the Massachusetts Institute of Technology played in providing limited, one-time planning services pursuant to a contract with an educational agency. The following discussion captures the essence of the partnership literature.

An Overview of University-Community Involvement

The role of the university in the life of the city has changed over time. Before World War I, Hackney (1986) notes that:

> Universities were also starting to expand, although opinion as to their proper purpose was still divided between those for whom they appeared as a haven for pure research and knowledge and others who saw the value of academic institutions as vehicles for promoting a liberal culture that might soften the rough edges of a society absorbed in commerce and industry. (p. 137)

One of the earliest attempts made by a university to take an active role in a community partnership was in Boston. "In 1954, with a grant from the Ford Foundation, the Boston College School of Business started a series of Citizen Seminars in an attempt to initiate a new partnership between the city's closely knit Yankee business elite and its upwardly mobil [*sic*] Irish politicians" (Squires 1989, p. 38). University-community relationships have been marked by feelings of distrust, disinterest, and disdain (Kysiak 1986; Perlman 1990). The role of some universities in urban life has changed over time. Universities have moved from a detached dispenser of knowledge to an intimate economic partner without abandoning their central mission of education. This has not been easy, quick, or painless for the universities or their communities.

University involvement in the community has been wide-ranging in scope, but there has been little agreement on the nature of the players, their proper roles and responsibilities, and their impact on communities. In fact, according to Kerr (1972):

> "Involvement in the life of society" has grown greatly. The campus has even been drawn to the "city hall," and the predicted "Pandora's box" may well have been opened. How to serve the city, as the rural community has long been served, is now a perplexing problem for many campuses. New pressure groups are insisting that knowledge

really be for "everybody's sake." The campus still debates involvement while strong elements in society insist upon it. (p. 132)

Urban universities are markedly different from their land-grant counter-
parts. Land-grant universities were founded pursuant to the Morrill Act signed
into law by President Abraham Lincoln in 1862 (Kerr 1972, p. 46). They were to
provide a variety of technical and economic development services to large areas
of the countryside and open higher education to a broad cross section of the pop-
ulace. The initial goal of the land-grant university was to focus on economic development and lift the countryside out of poverty and move the region into a
more competitive stance vis-à-vis the urbanized areas. "The original land-grant
universities did a masterful job on agriculture and engineering. American farmers are the most efficient and productive in the world, and students from all over
the world come to this country to study engineering and science" (Stukel 1994,
p. 19). Wallerstein (1969) makes the same point. Urban universities have typically had a more restricted mission from both areal and functional perspectives.
Their goal was to not only focus on training knowledge workers but to enhance
the social, cultural, and intellectual life of the community that chartered it or in
which it was founded. Currently, many urban universities provide an economic
development component to their community; however, it is usually limited in
scope and application, unlike its land-grant counterpart.

The Roles of the University in the Community

Before discussing the roles of the university in the community, it is helpful to investigate the ultimate ". . . purpose for which it exists—the advancement of learning" (Klotsche 1966, p. 19). This is echoed by Hackney (1986),
who says, "the university's primary contribution to the betterment of the human
condition comes through education and the creation of new knowledge"
(p. 136). The roles of the university can be framed around its raison d'etre.
   One of the principal challenges in analyzing community partnership problems is the lack of a consistent, generally accepted paradigm in the urban affairs
field (Friesema 1971, p. 10). Even today, the same problem remains: universities
are seeking a role, unsure of what the community needs or wants from its intellectual center. What is the proper role of the university in urban affairs?
   Many have tried to define the role of the university in the urban environment. The producers (faculty) are rewarded for three different things: teaching,
research, and service. Service is a common feature of most definitions of a role
of the university. "The university as producer, wholesaler, and retailer of knowledge cannot escape service" (Kerr 1972, p. 114). The following are three

representative samples from the literature. Hester (1970) described three roles: ". . . serving the people and institutions of the city, doing research in the problems of the city, [and] using the city as a teaching laboratory [. . .]" (p. 89). Stukel (1994) notes that the primary role of the university is to provide an education to the people; however, they are also being asked "to apply their research expertise to the very real, day-to-day problems of the city [. . .]" (p. 19). Cisneros (1995), after reviewing literature from John Henry Cardinal Newman (isolation of the university in the search for truth) to John Dewey, "who emphasized that school and society are one" (Cisneros 1995, p. 6), said:

> The American university embraces both the research and the service dimensions. The American university is supposed to focus on building character, promoting general education, and developing civic responsibility; it best serves society by producing competent, self-reliant adults who form a solid core of involved citizens. [. . .] In the broadest sense, the American university system functions to preserve, disseminate, and advance knowledge for the improvement of society. [. . .] [T]here is general agreement that the American university is designed to encompass the broad range of human knowledge and is dedicated to the preservation and advancement of that knowledge to help make the world a more civil and decent place. (p. 7)

While Secretary Cisneros's view is expansive, the literature indicates that there are three different roles for the university in its community that are distinct from its historical primary mission of teaching. The three roles for the community at large include: (1) a facilitator or an unbiased third party; (2) an equity partner or an action partner in ventures; and (3) a technical resource. The first two are not widely discussed in the literature, since the university is now growing into these roles. The third is most common and is discussed at length in a variety of publications. Each of these roles will be discussed briefly.

The University as Facilitator

One of the greatest obstacles to urban revitalization is political partisanship: the games people play (Farbstein and Wener 1993, p. 96; Peirce and Guskind 1993, p. 2). So many entities play political games because of power, money, status, or other concerns, that it is difficult at times to determine where anyone stands on a particular issue. "The city is [. . .] a uniquely political universe of its own" (Bookchin 1986, p. 6).

There is a need for honest brokers[1]—those organizations whose integrity is unquestioned and who can remain unbiased throughout a decision-making process. There are several examples of universities becoming involved as process facilitators rather than being a part of the outcome. Their neutrality was an asset to an overarching community goal. Klotsche (1966) notes that, "The university can provide a common meeting ground for the divergent elements of the community [. . .]" (p. 30).

Mazey (1995) describes Wright State University's role as a facilitator in the CHALLENGE 95 strategic plan process in Dayton, Ohio. The community was developing a plan to make itself competitive with other regions. "The two main threats to the economic development of the Miami Valley were identified as 'turfism,' i.e., promoting the self-interests of one political entity over another, and lack of leadership" (p. 196). The community had a difficult time finding someone or some organization that did not have an economic interest in self-promotion and could remain neutral—an honest broker. It turned to Wright State University to provide that service, and

> [President Mulhollan] demonstrated the university's commitment to a regional agenda and ensured the university's independence of any one particular entity in formulating and facilitating the plan. The latter point is extremely important, because the university's neutrality was an asset throughout the process. As a neutral entity, the university was able to minimize the political turf battles that could have destroyed the process. The university faculty and staff continually had to emphasize that the threats and competition were not within the region but rather with other regions. (p. 203)

This is an excellent example of the university playing the role of the honest broker. The community could rely upon Wright State's independence, and the administration ensured that independence through its internal processes.

The University of Louisville (the "University") played a similar role, albeit on a smaller scale, in helping organizations in the city of Louisville to try to determine priorities for grant opportunities to help revitalize inner-city neighborhoods (U.S. Department of Housing and Urban Development 1994b). The University brought varied segments of the community together for hundreds of hours of meetings. These people determined program priorities for grant opportunities. The University continuously provided information and sought feedback to make sure that all parties understood priorities and could "buy-in" to the decisions being made. The University played a similar role in its Sustainable Urban Neighborhoods (SUN) initiative in the Louisville Enterprise Zone. By working with a number of different organizations, the University developed a proposal that addressed human and economic development, home ownership, community design/urban planning, and crime prevention. The University played this role in grants that it would administer, and other grants were to be administered by the city or nonprofit agencies.

Charles Diggs, deputy director of the city of Louisville's Department of Housing and Urban Development, noted, "People have a mind-set that the university can be outside the process and mediate." There are some who would take issue with this characterization and believe the university cannot step "outside its box." Dr. Donald C. Swain, president emeritus of the University of Louisville, in a separate interview with the author, summarized the thoughts of many: "The university is a neutral ground to help people find common ground."

The University as an Equity Partner

Revitalizing our communities is an expensive proposition. There is no single institution or business that can afford to turn around the inner city. Shore ". . . propose[s] that each American city try to form a consortium of a few corporations, housing developers, and institutions of higher education, health, the arts, and social services together with all levels of government" (1995, p. 502). Others have also described this equity role (Goldstein and Luger 1992; Kysiak 1986; Cisneros 1995). These investigators recognize the crucial role that universities can play in the revitalization process.

There are many instances, particularly since the "go-go" decade of the 1980s, where the university has stepped outside its traditional role of service to take an equity interest in a venture that produces funds, goods, services, or other vendible outputs. While there have been many consulting arrangements between the university faculty and business and industry, this new role goes beyond that. It is institutional rather than individual. The university has a financial stake as an investor in the outcome of a venture rather than helping facilitate a process as described in the preceding section. Following are a few examples of the university in this equity partner role.

Kysiak (1986) describes two examples of university-community partnerships that had their beginnings in poor relationships between the university and community. His examples are the relationships between Yale and New Haven, Connecticut, and Northwestern University and Evanston, Illinois. As Kysiak points out, both universities were founded before the cities in which they are located. In addition, they have international reputations and, as they grew, "found themselves increasingly removed from the mundane administrative and political issues of city life that developed over time" (p. 49). They became isolated, cut off from the problems and deterioration around them (Boyer 1994).

As discussed in the preceding section, one of the biggest problems in the relationships between these universities and their cities was fiscal pressures. The cities needed more tax revenue and looked to the universities as sources of income. The universities, however, thwarted the cities at every turn. The situation escalated until outside parties stepped in to mediate and find a way to resolve what was fast becoming a crisis.

In Evanston, the city administration, university, and local businesses formed a nonprofit development corporation: Evanston Inventure. In addition, Northwestern University also joined the city in establishing a research park. Yale took a similar path and joined with the city and one large local business to form a research park. Yale also started building apartments and other facilities in New Haven as a way to do some good and secure its own real estate investments. "Both universities wanted to [. . .] stabilize the neighborhoods around them [. . .] creating an atmosphere of development that would enable them to expand their research and development partnerships with the private sector" (Kysiak 1986, p. 53). In both cases, most of the profits from these ventures will be reinvested in the partnership. However, both nonprofit organizations have for-profit, spin-off businesses that could net the universities significant income over time. They are helping to improve the economic position of the communities in which they are located. In addition, they have opened up opportunities and markets for their faculty and students through these ventures.

Kysiak makes a very interesting point about these developments. All partners are doing what they do best. None is trying to move outside their own expertise to make things happen. The universities offer "land, buildings, cash, and expertise [. . .]" (p. 57). Businesses offer their management expertise and ability to market the enterprise to the economy at large. The city provides "public improvements, some funding for the operating corporation, and support for some of the peripheral activities. In addition, its power of eminent domain allows the complete site to be pulled together, an absolute necessity for marketing purposes" (p. 58).

There are other instances of university participation in economic ventures. For instance, "Rutgers put its art school and a gallery into a defunct department store and brought a new medical school downtown, alongside an addition to the downtown hospital that the county built" (Shore 1995, p. 502). Perlman (1990) discusses the role of Suffolk University in helping revitalize a shopping district in Boston in partnership with the city, local businesses, and residents. Stukel (1994) discusses the role of Marquette University in reshaping the built environment of Milwaukee by expending over $9 million in partnership with local business and industry to revive the area around the university.

The University as a Technical Resource

The university has long been a repository of technical expertise that has been lacking elsewhere. Grigsby and Corl (1983), in discussing this topic, said,

"Whether federal, state, and local governments have the will, knowledge, and understanding necessary to develop such [redevelopment] plans and implement them is the question. On the whole, we think they do not have these qualities at the present time" (p. 97). From another point of view, former HUD Secretary Henry Cisneros (1995) notes:

> We at HUD know that Washington cannot pay for everything, should not regulate everything, and must not mandate everything. The Department's role is to marshal resources from all sectors of society and bring them to bear on these priority problems. HUD should catalyze, facilitate, mediate—and get out of the way [. . .]. (p. 13)

There have always been questions about how practical that knowledge was and whether it could be turned to an economic or a public good. The literature contains a number of references to the varied technical roles of the university. The types and extent of these roles are presented next.

RESEARCH

The university is a vital source of expertise in a variety of fields. Research is one of the most visible and least understood outputs of universities. There are those who dismiss this valuable work as the product of a select number of people who look at problems of no consequence to most of society and write about it for a small audience with neither the power nor interest to do anything with it! In the words of Bengtson, Grigsby, Corry, and Hruby (1977), "[A]nother academic study was to be conducted [. . .] by white, ivory tower researchers— a study which would bring few if any benefits to the people" (p. 82). A former governor of the Commonwealth of Kentucky, the Honorable Wallace Wilkinson, referred to this as the publication of research results in "itty bitty journals" that no one ever reads. In actuality, many university research products, especially those in the basic sciences and some in the social sciences, result in profitable applications by business and industry.

In the 1960s, the Ford Foundation funded numerous grants for universities to provide technical assistance to their communities (Ford Foundation 1965, p. 111; Bender 1988, p. 284). The foundation hoped to improve the quality of life in various communities across the country. The types of services were typified by Florida State University providing applied research and consulting services to local governments.

Friesema (1971) expressed a concern about pushing too far past research and into advocacy. He believes that the more action oriented the research, the poorer the theoretical development (p. 5). He does not think that is a reason to shy away from action-oriented research; it is something to be cognizant of in developing programs. He cites the problems associated with programs designed to train municipal professionals. However, others have sounded a clear warning about taking research beyond the walls of academia and moving into applications (Eulau 1968).

There are many uses for university research. A synopsis follows of some of the more interesting applications from the literature.

Hall (1989) discusses the value of universities focusing their planning schools on providing "feasible solutions" to the problems of the city (p. 282). Gilderbloom and Mullins (1995) also discuss the possibility of universities focusing and directing their planning programs on the problems of the inner cities.

Former HUD Secretary Henry G. Cisneros (1995) described the high-technology research efforts of American universities and their ties to businesses. He noted:

> [In fiscal year 1993], inventions developed at 117 of the Nation's leading research universities produced some $242 million in royalties and a total of 1,307 new patents, often directly benefiting local companies. For example, faculty at the University of Pennsylvania have made approximately 90 invention disclosures per year for the past 3 years, resulting in many collaborative research and license agreements with Pennsylvania businesses. (Cisneros 1995, p. 8)

Cisneros and others (i.e., Kysiak 1986) discuss the role of research in advancing economic agendas, as discussed in the preceding section.

Bengtson et al. (1977) discuss the role of university research in helping key decision makers by conducting policy-oriented social service research. They looked at aging in American society in one research project. An outgrowth of their research project was an interesting discussion of the conflicts among affected stakeholders in the community they were studying. This was another application of the politics described in Stone and Sanders' (1987) work on regime paradigm theory.

There is a split in academic and nonacademic circles about the usefulness, applicability, and need for research. "[I]n leading universities, research is valued over teaching, and pure research gains more respect than applied research aimed at solving problems in the real world" (Bok 1990, p. 50). This situation is likely to remain as long as academic rewards systems are set up to encourage scholarly as opposed to applied research. When equal weight is given to service and action-oriented research, the debate may either cease or be reduced. It will depend, to a great degree, on what is being valued in the academic marketplace.

EDUCATION AND TRAINING

A traditional role for the university through its liberal arts curriculum is that of cultural memory. It is responsible for passing on from one generation to the next a method of critical thinking and an appreciation for the heritage of the literature, art, and beauty of Western culture. Cisneros (1995) notes this traditional role of the university "to preserve, disseminate, and advance knowledge for the improvement of society" (p. 7). He goes on to note the positive impacts of professional training (i.e., teachers, engineers, doctors, lawyers, etc.) on society as a whole in addition to the broad liberal arts education provided to others.

Perlman (1990) presents a differently focused view of the education and training roles. In addition to the initial training that professionals obtain through their undergraduate years, Perlman discusses the continuing education role of the university in modern society. It is a way of getting out into the community without a full-fledged commitment to be a major external player. The university can help these individuals hone and maintain their skills while seeking assistance from these very groups in the training of their current student body and in seeking funds and donations for the institution. It is a reciprocal relationship, each getting something from the other.

There is another view of the city, and that is one of a classroom. This goes back to the late nineteenth and early twentieth centuries and the "Chicago School" of sociologists at the University of Chicago (Glaab and Brown 1983, p. 244). They looked at the city as a laboratory, a place to experiment. Popenoe (1969) presents a twist on the role of the university in education. He discusses the need "to bring the community to the classroom, and new and relevant knowledge to the community" (p. 145). Hester (1970) makes a similar point that the university needs to make use of the "'living laboratory' that surrounds the classroom" (p. 89). Bartelt (1995) expressed concern with the "laboratory" attitude. He noted that "[universities] have viewed their surrounding communities as objects of investigation, specimens of quasi-anthropological interest, from which institutional and personal reputations can be extracted, with little being returned in kind. It is unusual for schools to see communities as true partners in joint revitalization efforts" (p. 16). Ruch and Trani (1995) state that "[t]he boundaries between the classroom and the community can be made permeable, and the extent to which the flow of ideas and people is accelerated is to the mutual benefit of both" (p. 233). Stukel (1994) also investigates the educational opportunities afforded those in the health care field, for example, in being trained in an urban locale. In an unbroken line of thought, John W. Shumaker, former president of the University of Louisville, succinctly stated this view:

As a metropolitan research university, the University of Louisville must invest in making this community a better place for all of its citizens. This community has become for us an extended classroom, an extended laboratory for bridging the gap between theory and practice. We cannot achieve our full promise as a metropolitan university unless and until Greater Louisville is able to realize its full potential. Our future as a university thus remains intertwined with the future of the people and institutions of Greater Louisville and the Commonwealth.

A vital community is one in which all citizens are well educated, healthy, adequately housed, economically productive, and safe. The University of Louisville will continue to play an important role in helping our city, county, and metropolitan areas throughout the Commonwealth attain this kind of vitality. [. . .] We should approach this special component of our mission with an entrepreneurial spirit. We must have the courage to take responsible risks—and to learn from our failures as well as triumph in our successes. We assume this responsibility not in a prescriptive way—but as a partner. Our philosophy must be one of co-operation, collaboration, and responsiveness. (Shumaker 1995, p. 13)

BUSINESS INCUBATOR

Universities, particularly through their schools of business or management, can provide a great deal of expertise to the entrepreneurial sector of the community. Many schools are now providing some type of business incubator (Stukel 1994; Ruch and Trani 1995; Kysiak 1986). In this role, the university provides a number of different services, either on its own or, more often, in conjunction with others, to nurture small businesses. Lyons and Hamlin (1991) state:

The purpose of an incubator program is to promote the success of small businesses by helping them minimize overhead, find necessary financing, avoid typical managerial pitfalls, and ultimately, move out into the world to function on their own. This support is offered in the first two years of a new firm's existence, the most crucial period in its ultimate survival. (p. 118)

The types of services offered in an incubator vary. The following discussion briefly covers the types of services offered through university-affiliated incubators.

One approach to university involvement in business incubators is called the "proof-of-concept" funding (Tornatzky et al.1996). Often a faculty member or outside inventor has an idea but needs funds to make a working prototype to obtain development funding. A number of programs provide this assistance, including the Georgia Research Alliance, consisting of five colleges and universities, Iowa State University, the University of Arkansas, the University of British Columbia, and others. Boyer (1990) notes that a university president "often controls discretionary funds that can work as 'pump primers' for creative projects" (p. 78).

Another vital service that university-affiliated incubators provide is access to cutting-edge technology. As Kerr (1972) states, "Sometimes industry will reach into a university laboratory to extract the newest ideas almost before they are born" (p. 89). Faculty in the more esoteric sciences such as genetic engineering can be a tremendous knowledge source. As Tornatzky, Batts, McCrea, Shook, and Quittmon (1996) note, there can be problems when the incubator and university are too closely integrated—especially "if the culture and organizational practices of the latter impede the former" (p. 41).

University incubators also provide a number of other services to start-up businesses. These services can include-low cost office or production space and shared services (e.g., clerical or reception services, access to equipment), managerial assistance and mentoring programs, business planning and marketing assistance (e.g., research, testing), reduced-cost legal services, and access to low-cost capital (Lyons and Hamlin 1991; Tornatzky et al. 1996). Schools view this as an opportunity to actually create economic opportunities in the community, to engage faculty in "real world" problems, and to provide students with opportunities to deal with actual problems and seek employment opportunities.

OTHER SERVICES

An innovative program at Northwestern University in the 1970s was the Community Service Voucher Program (Pitts 1977). It was a cooperative venture funded by state and federal sources that allowed specific nonprofit organizations to purchase services from the university. The organizations had accounts and were allowed to purchase any service the university, could offer. They purchased a variety of services from across the university including work by the sociology, economics, management, social work, and architecture departments. They included items such as multiviewpoint policy analysis and economic analyses of proposals.

Problems of University-Community Relations

In spite of the potential good that could be done through cooperation, why is the history of community-university interaction so checkered? There is a long list of problems associated with university-community relationships. The problems have been economic, political, and social, and they have touched many other spheres. For example, the city of Evanston, Illinois, experienced severe financial pressure in the 1970s. It tried many different "revenue-enhancing" measures but still needed more money to meet its obligations. One way Evanston tried to increase revenues was a tax on student tuition at Northwestern University. It tried this approach because the university refused to pay any fees in lieu of taxes for services it received from the city (Kysiak 1986, p. 50). This confrontation drove the city and the university to communicate with one another more from necessity than from a desire for cooperation.

Why Partnerships?

The preceding literature review provides a background on university involvement in the community. Why should the university become a partner in community revitalization efforts? Young (1995) directly and succinctly addresses this question. "A university's goal of improving the quality of life and achieving high quality research, education, and service can be enhanced by working directly with affected communities in a relationship of shared authority and responsibility and mutual respect for each other's expertise" (p. 72). She also offers five specific reasons, from the university's perspective, for university-community partnerships to come into being:

1. To overcome our own ignorance. University faculties do not have the solutions for the problems of rejuvenating urban areas. But they can offer suggestions and a rigorous method of testing their efficacy. By working together, new ideas will emerge, be tried out, fail or succeed, and generate a forum for continuing to look for new ideas.

2. To focus additional minds on urban problems, even if some of those minds lack formal academic training. Where [. . .] collective engagement occurs, groups have been able to transcend the temptation toward quick fixes and search for new integrated solutions [. . .].

3. To provide a reality check for our ideas.

4. To diminish our deserved reputation as exploiters. Events that occurred in the past remain alive and fuel the skepticism [. . .]. [The University of Illinois at Chicago's] neighbors also remember that much of an immigrant community [. . .] was bulldozed

to make room for part of our campus. These are difficult images to erase.

5. To ensure the long-term viability of the university. We are not going to get many future students from an impoverished, illiterate, crime-ridden, unemployed, homeless community. Nor can the funds to operate a university be generated from failing communities. (Young 1995, p. 72)

Existing University-Community Partnerships: Louisville and Beyond

Urban revitalization is an immense undertaking and is beyond the scope of any single institution to solve. Partnerships can provide a coordinated approach to solving these problems. Robert Astorino, president of the Housing Partnership, has worked in the urban revitalization field in Louisville and elsewhere. He made the following observation:

> Part of the problem with solutions to affordable housing in Louisville today is that there are so many good people with good intentions all doing their own thing. The banks, in particular, feel that they are being nibbled to death by ducks. I don't think that makes for a credible synchronized solution. I think it makes for many wonderful small success stories. I often wonder how much grander the success story could be if all those ducks got together and nibbled at once. [. . .] I think that is a real problem in Louisville. [. . .] Corporate partners are confused. (personal interview with author)

Every university, including faculty and staff, performs many service activities for its surrounding community. This service can take a number of forms. At the University of Louisville, for example, faculty members donate their time serving on nonprofit and corporate boards, providing data analysis services; some faculty are loaned on a temporary basis to local government entities; some help with facilitating particularly thorny processes (i.e., local government restructuring process), and so on. These are service activities, not true partnership initiatives, because they fail to recognize that a partnership ". . . is a relationship between individuals or groups that is characterized by mutual cooperation and responsibility, as for the achievement of a specified goal" (Microsoft Corp. 1995). In the examples cited previously, the University is providing something of value and is getting, at most, goodwill in return. There is no mutuality in the relationship.

University-Community Partnerships around the Country

This section focuses on just a few of the outstanding university-community partnerships around the nation. It provides brief sketches of what is being done as well as what is working. It is difficult to find much in the literature that discusses the failures of particular programs.

As previously discussed, part of Yale's motivation for involvement with the surrounding community was the extent of its landholdings in New Haven, Connecticut (Kysiak 1986). It needed to help stabilize the neighborhood around the university to secure its holdings. The university came to realize that it was an integral part of New Haven—whither one went, the other would go. Yale set about to develop a comprehensive program addressing its relationship with its city. The program was broken down into three components: ". . . economic development, human development, and neighborhood revitalization" (Gilderbloom 1996).

Money talks. Too many universities are willing to invest "soft money" in projects (i.e., writing down overhead rates on grants, etc.). They are not generally willing to put up their own cash as part of a project. Yale invested $9 million in housing and commercial ventures in the city. "To encourage Yale faculty and staff to live in town, the university started the New Haven Home Buyers Initiative. Any university employee who works more than 20 hours a week is eligible for $2,000 per year over ten years to go toward the purchase of a home near campus" (Stukel 1994, p. 20).

Yale developed a broad-based partnership with New Haven leaders and community pacesetters in the Dwight-Edgewood-West River neighborhood for neighborhood revitalization. The following is a list of revitalization goals:

1. Establish mechanisms for collaborative financing, governance, implementation, and accountability.

2. Create or redesign open spaces to support community development.

3. Promote home ownership.

4. Promote responsible behavior by landlords and tenants.

5. Improve security.

6. Mobilize citizen engagement and opportunity.

7. Increase employment opportunities through targeted and coordinated access to job training, recruitment and placement, and development of micro-enterprise and small businesses.

8. Promote optimal development of children and youth, in and out of school.

9. Create a partnership among city departments and between them and the neighborhood to build on community policing capacity of the city to support community development.

As discussed earlier (Kysiak 1986; Stukel 1994), Yale is also investing money in a number of ventures as an equity partner or is providing venture capital to budding businesses. In addition to these initiatives, Yale is giving these entrepreneurs access to university resources to help build and sustain their momentum. The wide-ranging nature of these ventures and the willingness to use its own capital make this one of the most aggressive university-community partnerships in the country.

The University of Pennsylvania

The Center for Community Partnerships of the University of Pennsylvania was founded on the notion that the vast range of resources of the American university, appropriately and creatively employed, can help us figure out how best to proceed. At Penn, over the past number of years, they have been working on the problem of how to create modern, cosmopolitan, local communities.

BACKGROUND

The Center for Community Partnerships was started in 1992 to achieve the following objectives: improve the internal coordination and collaboration of all university-wide community service programs; create new and effective partnerships between the university and the community; encourage new and creative initiatives linking Penn and the community; and strengthen a national network of institutions of higher education committed to engagement with their local communities.

Much of the center's work has focused on the public school as the educational and neighborhood institution that can, if effectively transformed, serve as the concrete vehicle for community change and innovation. Penn has tried to help create university-assisted community schools that function as the center of education, services, engagement and activity within specified geographic areas. Focusing on improving education and health in particular, Penn has helped develop significant service-learning programs that engage young people in creative work designed to advance skills and abilities through servicing their school, families, and community. Penn students and faculty are also engaged in service learning that requires the development and application of knowledge to solve problems as well as active and serious reflection. This Deweyan approach might be termed learning by reflective doing and active problem solving.

Community Outreach Partnerships and Strategies

CENTER FOR COMMUNITY PARTNERSHIPS

- Through the center, the university currently engages in three types of initiatives: academically based community service; direct traditional service; and community and economic development.

- The center's director reports to both the vice president for government, community and public affairs and the provost.

WEST PHILADELPHIA IMPROVEMENT CORPS (WEPIC) originated in the spring of 1985 from an honors history seminar co-taught by Penn's former president, Sheldon Hackney, and historians Lee Benson and Ira Harkavy on "Urban Universities-Community Relationships: Penn-West Philadelphia, Past, Present and Future, as a Case Study." The research of four students on the issue of youth employment resulted in a proposal to create a youth corps that would use existing agencies and resources.

- Beginning as a youth corps program, it is currently a year-round program that involves over 3,000 children, their parents, and community members in educational and cultural programs, recreation, job training, and community improvement and service activities.

- Producing comprehensive university-assisted community schools that serve, educate, involve, and activate all members of the community is the WEPIC's main goal.

Functioning simultaneously as the core building for the community and as the educational and service delivery hub for students, their families, and other local residents, it intends, ultimately, to develop schools that are open to the public twenty-four hours a day, 365 days a year.

The WEPIC works in partnership with unions, job training agencies, churches, community groups, city, state, and federal agencies and departments, Volunteers in Service to America (VISTA) volunteers, local health institutions (including Misericord Hospital, Penn Medical Center, and Greater Philadelphia Health Action), and other community agencies and services.

The WEPIC is coordinated by the West Philadelphia Partnership—a mediating, nonprofit, community-based organization composed of institutions (including the University of Pennsylvania) and community groups—in conjunction with the Greater Philadelphia Affairs Coalition and the Philadelphia School District.

The University of Illinois at Chicago (UIC) started its Great Cities initiative in late 1993. The purpose of the initiative is to channel the university's "teaching, research, and public service toward improving the quality of life in Chicago and other metropolitan areas" (Stukel 1994, p. 19). The Great Cities Initiative is a minimum ten-year commitment on the part of the University. The goal is to approach the intractable problems of the city from an interdisciplinary as well as a multiorganizational perspective in hopes of bringing all resources required to bear on the challenges confronting urban areas.

The UIC is trying to focus on being a member of a partnership, contributing what it does best rather than trying to address multidimensional problems on its own. It is taking a project focus rather than a problem focus. Rather than trying to address the overarching problem of teen crime in the city, for example, it is trying to identify projects that will make a difference in attacking a manageable piece of that overall problem. One project, Incubators for Youth, is providing young males in a housing project with training and assistance in taking advantage of entrepreneurial opportunities in the Chicagoland area. It will give them marketable business skills and provide training in self-development, self-esteem, and problem solving. Related projects are trying to improve the transition of students from an academic environment to the workforce.

The UIC has a number of other initiatives underway with community partners to improve life in its city. Some of these include improving the existing housing stock, increasing the amount of affordable housing, providing economic opportunities for businesses to work with the university, providing design and architectural services to community businesses to improve the built environment, and improving health care. All projects are being undertaken in an integrative way to ensure the best use of university resources in concert with its partners.

One of the advantages of this program over the University of Louisville's Housing and Neighborhood Development Strategies (HANDS) program is its institutional commitment. At the UIC, there is a university-wide commitment to a comprehensive partnership program. At the University of Louisville, HANDS was just one of hundreds of grants.

The systemic problems of the inner city can only be remedied through a holistic approach involving education; job placement and training; leadership; and entrepreneurship training; home ownership; community planning and design; and related programs. The cornerstones of the HANDS partnership involve attracting moderate- and middle-income families back into the neighborhood by providing home ownership opportunities and giving residents the means to move up the economic ladder.

The University of Louisville's HANDS program has helped residents in a variety of ways. Nonprofit developers have built affordable, energy-efficient, moderately priced housing for residents with mortgage payments lower than area rents. In the first twenty-four months of operation, over 350 residents were provided with some combination of education, esteem, leadership, job training, or home ownership counseling. The HANDS program helped build economic capacity in the neighborhood by providing minority contractor and small business training as well as supporting a micro-loan program. These long-term initiatives created the sustainable development necessary for the inner-city neighborhood to be reborn.

For many inner-city residents, the American dream of home ownership, economic opportunity, work, and a good life is not possible. Good, affordable housing is essential to any family. If we want to promote family values, then we must first provide families with decent homes in which to practice those values. Vacant or abandoned lots and homes are more than empty houses. They are magnets for the urban plagues of litter, trash, rats, and drug dealers and users. They speak of a breakdown, not just of shutters and doors and windows, but of the strength that binds a community together. Faith in the American dream needs to be restored by making a commitment to renew the inner city. People without hope for a better future become destructive to themselves and others. The Russell Partnership in Louisville demonstrates a viable role for institutions of higher education and a humanistic approach to renewing a blighted inner-city neighborhood. When a partnership unites under a singular vision, lives and communities can be transformed.

Taxpayers are becoming increasingly frustrated by the lack of results produced by money spent on urban problems. Expressing this sentiment, former Ohio Governor George Voinovich said in his 1990 inaugural address, "Gone are the days when public officials are measured by how much they spend on a problem. The new realities dictate that public officials are now judged by whether they can work harder and smarter, and do more with less."

From 1978 to 1991, the HUD budget was slashed from $32 billion to $12 billion. Not surprisingly, it was during these same years that homelessness began to take on new faces: women, children, and even educated intact families. As our infrastructure deteriorated, as our affordable housing stock evaporated, as jobs moved to the suburbs, as high-paying manufacturing jobs were traded for low-paying service jobs, and as more and more people felt the sting of poverty and homelessness, Washington turned a deaf ear. The results manifested themselves in the anger, frustration, and despair expressed in urban unrest in Los Angeles and in the lyrics of gangster rap, but even these examples are mere shadows of the much larger problems existing in our nation's inner cities.

In an era characterized by fiscal austerity and increasing social challenges, the university is a sorely needed resource. Can the university be a player in solving our most pressing urban problems? Currently, universities are in crisis: political correctness (PC) wars, shrinking budgets, declining public confidence, scientific fraud. How can universities regain public confidence? University professors need to get out of the ivory tower and back on the streets.

The coupling of fiscal austerity and increasing social challenges demands the creation of new paradigms. As we talk about reinventing government, we must begin to consider reinventing the university. In the words of former HUD Secretary Cisneros (1995):

> All of us have to take responsibility for the problems facing us today. All of us must contribute our time, talents, and resources to resolving them. Universities are not exempt. Students should have the opportunity to roll up their sleeves and get their hands dirty before they enter the job market. More attention should be placed on teaching partnership strategies and teamwork. Young scholars should be encouraged to celebrate cultural diversity.

Though visible at the highest levels of the university, the HANDS program could not claim to be a broad-based university program and has therefore not sufficiently met the needs of the community.

Milwaukee, Wisconsin, faces many of the problems that old industrial cities in the Rust Belt suffered. Marquette University was seeing the community deteriorate around it. Enrollment was falling, crime was rising, and the quality of campus life was falling precipitously. As the Reverend Albert DiUlio, president of the university, said, "We could wall ourselves in or we could weave ourselves in" (Boyce 1994, p. A1). One of the unique things about Marquette that distinguishes it from other private schools, such as Yale University, discussed earlier, is its religious affiliation. It is named after a Jesuit missionary and is still run by members of the Society of Jesus. However, it had done little to assist the neighborhood or ingratiate itself with the residents in the years of its expansion (it tripled in area over a thirty year period).

The "straw that broke the camel's back" came in July 1991, when Jeffrey Dahmer, murderer and cannibal, was arrested in an apartment "just 10 blocks from Marquette" (Boyce 1994, p. A1). In late 1991, Marquette University committed $9 million to start the Campus Circle initiative to help revitalize its neighborhood, the Avenues West area. The motivations behind this initiative were pragmatic but complemented the mission and philosophy of the school's leadership. The university recruited local government, businesses, neighborhood organizations, and residents in developing a comprehensive approach to neighborhood revitalization. The partnership established the following six goals:

1. Create and maintain affordable family housing for neighborhood residents by rehabbing [*sic*] existing housing and constructing new units;

2. Provide quality off-campus student housing through new construction and rehabilitation;

3. Establish walk-to-work and retirement housing for area employees;

4. Acquire and renovate buildings which do not contribute to a positive neighborhood environment;

5. Foster commercial development, both upgraded and new;

6. Advocate community involvement. (Campus Circle 1994, p. 3)

The various players brought their particular expertise to the partnership. For example, the city "established a tax incremental financing district, which provides a low-interest loan to be repaid through income created by the project" (Stukel 1994, p. 20). The university contributed many different types of technical expertise in addition to its cash endowment. Businesses were brought in for additional financing and management expertise.

What are the results? Because of the significant up-front financing and the commitment of the partners, after a couple of years of operation, Campus Circle owned and/or managed almost 140 properties, had spent almost $55 million on purchasing and rehabilitating or constructing new housing and other facilities, and started a number of human development and community improvement programs (Boyce 1994). Stukel (1994) reports that the combination of the establishment of a community-oriented policing program and crime prevention-awareness program had reduced crime by 30 percent. A fact sheet provided by the organization indicated that it had established goals for minority, women-owned, and disadvantaged business participation in its projects. Whether or not this level of effort can be sustained remains to be seen.

Marquette University is showing that a commitment to its community, a willingness to reach out to others, and an ability to rally disparate groups of people to a common cause can make a difference. If other universities would heed the call and follow Marquette's and Yale's lead by similarly investing in their urban communities, then all urban communities would be revitalized, and there would be growing economic opportunities for all.

Conclusion

The university can offer a wide variety of services to the community at large to complement its traditional roles of teaching, research, and service. These services can be offered asymmetrically (university has control) or in partnership (an environment of shared decision making and control). The primary roles that the university plays are facilitator, equity partner, and technical resource. The most common role is technical resource. The university is most often called upon to apply its expertise to help solve urban problems. "University-community partnerships offer great potential for improving the vitality of both partners. Communities have the opportunity to acquire the empowerment necessary to rejuvenate themselves. Universities have the opportunity to be active participants in a natural learning laboratory [. . .] while improving its image with its neighbors" (Young 1995, p. 77). According to Bartelt (1995):

> It is important that universities not lose sight of an important, persistent reality. In each of the efforts noted, from urban renewal to community partnerships, the essential power and asset relationships have been essentially asymmetrical: communities are largely viewed as being "in need"; in turn, they are provided for by an asset-rich (comparatively) college or university. This creates a relationship that, in times of institutional largesse, can be seen as charity, and in times of fiscal crisis, unimportant to the institution. It is not surprising to see communities approach such a relationship with suspicion, nor to see institutions of higher education questioning the imposition of yet another set of performance guidelines. It is vital for both universities and communities to grasp the nature of community development, on the one hand, and of the social context of institutions of higher education, on the other. Communities develop self-sufficiency as they are successful in amassing a resource base [. . .]. In this context, higher education is a potential resource for community development. It is not an abstract form of the "general good" that we should be addressing, but the specific needs of neighborhoods and communities that form the location and context of colleges and universities. (p. 23)

CHAPTER 2

Universities Providing Human Services

A U.S. Department of Education Urban Community Service Grant funded the University of Louisville HANDS (Housing and Neighborhood Development Strategies) proposal. At the time, the HANDS program was a fresh, innovative, bold and pragmatic partnership of business, government, local universities, the public school system, and community-based organizations. It was a multifaceted effort and commitment to assist a low-income, African-American neighborhood in lifting itself from poverty into self-sufficiency. Low-income neighborhood problems can only be remedied by a combination of programs involving education, job and leadership training, home ownership counseling, financial investment, non-profit community organizations, and strategic design. Reaction to the HANDS program was overwhelmingly positive from African-American community leaders, elected officials, bankers, and developers.

The 100-year-old Russell Neighborhood in western Louisville (see Figure 2-1) was chosen for this opportunity. It was a once-proud neighborhood that was home to Muhammad Ali as a youth and was a vibrant community of shops, businesses, and homes. Over time, as economic and population patterns changed, out-migration occurred, and the neighborhood went into a severe decline and remained there until the early 1990s. It was the neighborhood with the greatest economic need and offered the most opportunity for change because of the commitment of neighborhood, community, and business leaders. There are a number of churches in the area, and the spiritual leaders were working in very small, targeted ways to resurrect the neighborhood, but the needs were too great.

The overall neighborhood was 95 percent African American, with low educational attainment, literacy rates, and home ownership percentages. Over 30 percent of the households were on some form of public assistance, three-fourths of the families lived below the poverty line, and unemployment was several times the average for the community as a whole (U.S. Department of Housing and Urban Development, 1994b). The HANDS program gathered up the various strands of commitment, building and training programs, and other activities and worked with

Figure 2-1 The Russell Neighborhood

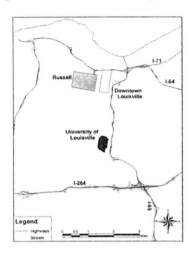

a number of partners to weave them into a fabric reflecting the people and energy of Louisville.

More detail on the Russell Neighborhood follows.

The Russell Neighborhood

The Russell Neighborhood contains approximately 10,000 residents and is split into both east and west portions. Each half of the neighborhood encompasses over 100 city blocks (see Figure 2-2). It was one of the most economically disadvantaged areas in the city of Louisville, characterized by excessive poverty, unemployment, crime, and homelessness, along with relatively low levels of educational attainment and training. Table 2-1 contains more detail about the socioeconomic conditions of the neighborhood.

"Mixed use" best describes the land patterns. The neighborhood includes single and multifamily residences, commercial and industrial uses, and public uses such as community services and churches. Many structures have been razed, abandoned, or boarded up. Several blocks have been without any viable structures (see Figure 2-3). Pawnshops, liquor stores, and taverns abound, whereas supermarkets and pharmacies were almost nonexistent (see Figure 2-4).

The Russell Neighborhood was among the city's poorest. For example, in 1989, the poverty rate for households was 59 percent. Median household

Figure 2-2 Location of HANDS Activities in the Russell Enterprise Community

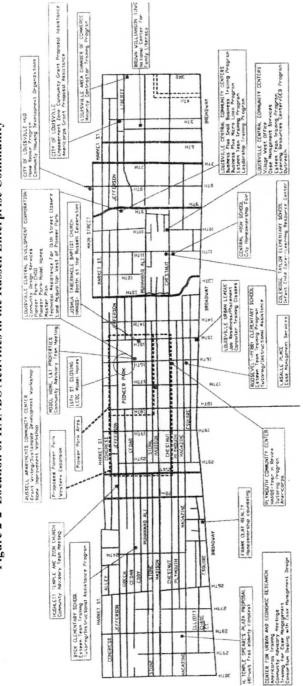

Promise and Betrayal

income in Russell was only 32 percent of the city of Louisville as a whole. According to the 1990 census, the unemployment rate was almost 10 percent. The most disturbing information concerned the number of individuals, ages sixteen and over, who were not participating in the labor force (56%). Lack of education and training added to the economic distress in the area, which had a high school dropout rate of 32 percent (U.S. Department of Commerce 1990).

There was a clear shortage of affordable housing in Russell. Census data indicate that less than 25 percent of residents were home owners. For 34 percent of owned units, residents spent 30 percent or more of their income on owner costs. For renters, it was worse. Fifty-two percent of renters spent more than 30 percent of their incomes on gross rent (U.S. Department of Commerce 1990).

Table 2-1
Extent of Need in the Russell Community by Census Tract

Description	Census Tract 6	Census Tract 20	Census Tract 24	Census Tract 30	Total
Income					
Median HH Income	14,727	11,303	8,835	4,999	8,946
Per Capita Income	6,808	7,444	7,260	2,559	5,559
HH in Poverty (%)	63.7	37.6	41.5	83.8	59.1
HH on Public Assistance (%)	22.6	11.3	26.5	47.9	30.5
Housing Characteristics					
Number of Units	813	943	1,573	1,651	4,980
Vacancy Rate (%)	15	19.8	25.7	15.7	19.6
Mean Rooms/Unit	5.1	4.9	4.3	3.8	4.4
% Units Built before 1940	54	49.1	62.2	31.1	48.1
Median Monthly Gross Renter Costs	313	265	268	114	193
Median Monthly Owner Costs	364	368	341	629	536
Gross Rent >=30% of Income	43.1	64.7	48.0	52.1	51.9
Gross Owner Costs >= 30% of Income	29.2	45.1	32.3	0.0	33.7
Median House Value	23,800	17,500	14,999	67,500	20,429
Population Characteristics					
Number of Persons	1,873	1,668	2,420	3,737	9,698
White	210	93	88	324	715
African American	1,652	1,560	2,317	3,413	8,942
Number of Households	680	753	1,160	1,404	3,997
Number of Families	444	379	580	887	2290
Unemployment (%, 16 & over)	9.2	5.6	9.3	16.4	9.7
Labor Force Participants (%, 16 & over)	52	47	43	39	44
High School Dropout Rate	31.0	22.5	27.1	44.2	32.3

Source: Markham and Gilderbloom 1996 (1990 Census of Population and Housing, STF 3A, Kentucky State Data Center).

Figure 2-3
Photographs of Abandoned Housing

Photograph by John I. Gilderbloom.

Photograph by John I. Gilderbloom.

Figure 2-4
Photographs of Undesirable Uses

Photograph by John I. Gilderbloom.

Photograph by John I. Gilderbloom.

Many residents did not associate themselves with the Russell Neighborhood. The head of one nonprofit service agency indicated the lack of association with a defined neighborhood. The city and the census bureau defined the boundaries of the Russell Neighborhood. In workshops, residents were asked to draw the boundary of their neighborhood on a map. Most circled one or two blocks. Their concept of neighborhood was not related to the official boundary. This was an anecdotal indication of the weakness of the community fabric. This weakness was manifested in another way as well. One thing that was difficult to convey with numbers was the depth of despair among residents of the Russell Neighborhood. Many residents were without hope. A contributing factor was the relatively high rate of crime in the neighborhood (see Table 2-2). While most of the crime was property related, there was a distinct increase in the seriousness and volume of crime over a six-year period. Particularly worrisome were increases in minor assaults and auto thefts.

The HANDS Program and the Russell Partnership

What is the Russell Partnership? It is not a coordinated effort; rather, it is a multitude of programs, services, and activities working in and for residents of the Russell Neighborhood. It encompasses the programs of dozens of churches, the activities of the city of Louisville, neighborhood schools, private development and rehabilitation, local businesses, and thousands of residents striving to achieve a better life. It is also the University of Louisville and the HANDS program. A list of the partners in the HANDS grant, and the extent of their participation, is included in Table 2-3.

The HANDS program was funded by the U.S. Department of Education in conjunction with local groups throughout the Louisville metropolitan community. Most of the work was completed in 1995. Evaluation and some administrative tasks were funded at a limited level in 1996. The program included a comprehensive case management system, educational assistance, job, minority contractor, leadership, and home ownership training, community design assistance, and evaluation. The hope behind the grant was to develop effective ". . . neighborhood revitalization strategies" (Gilderbloom 1992, p. 45).

One goal of the HANDS program was to help create a sustainable base in the neighborhood that would allow revitalization to continue after the grant was terminated. "[B]y project's end, HANDS will have established an infrastructure for community development. [. . .] This infrastructure will help sustain the gains achieved" (Gilderbloom 1992, p. 45). This will be important in later discussions of the accomplishments of the HANDS program. Others (Haughton and Hunter 1994) have noted that one of the greatest challenges to the continued

Table 2-2

Crime in the Russell Neighborhood

Crime in Russell: Census Tract 24, 1990–2001. Number of Crimes and Percentage Change

Crime	1990	1991		1992		1993		1994		1995	
	Units	% Change	Units	% Change	Units	% Change	Units	% Change	Units	% Change	Units
Homicide	4	0%	4	-25%	3	-67%	1	0%	1	N/A	0
Rape	4	-25%	3	67%	5	-20%	4	0%	4	-75%	1
Robbery	30	17%	35	23%	43	-16%	36	8%	39	-13%	34
Assault-major	31	-10%	28	25%	35	-9%	32	31%	42	-57%	18
Burglary	121	-16%	102	-6%	96	2%	98	26%	123	-46%	67
Theft	100	8%	108	-18%	89	12%	100	15%	115	-3%	111
Auto theft	37	41%	52	38%	72	-3%	70	16%	81	-35%	53
Assault-minor	11	118%	24	-29%	17	112%	36	22%	44	-43%	25
Other sex offenses	2	-100%	0	N/A	3	0%	3	-67%	1	N/A	0
Criminal mischief	51	6%	48	69%	81	-26%	60	32%	79	-23%	61
Misc. offenses	17	-47%	9	67%	15	0%	15	67%	25	-4%	24
Total	408	-20%	413	11%	459	-1%	455	22%	554	-29%	394

Crime in Russell: Census Tract 30, 1990–2001. Number of Crimes and Percentage Change

Crime	1990 Units	1991 % Change	1991 Units	1992 % Change	1992 Units	1993 % Change	1993 Units	1994 % Change	1994 Units	1995 % Change	1995 Units
Homicide	0	N/A	0	-100%	0	N/A	2	N/A	1	-50%	1
Rape	2	300%	1	-88%	2	100%	2	0%	3	50%	2
Robbery	19	42%	27	0%	14	-48%	10	-29%	15	50%	3
Assault-major	35	-9%	29	-9%	23	-21%	13	-43%	23	77%	3
Burglary	75	-21%	40	-32%	25	-38%	29	16%	69	138%	3
Theft	71	-24%	45	-17%	56	24%	42	-25%	89	112%	2
Auto theft	22	9%	25	4%	18	-28%	14	-22%	50	257%	2
Assault-minor	35	-3%	25	-26%	37	48%	29	-22%	18	-38%	
Other sex offenses	2	50%	5	67%	2	-60%	3	50%	2	-33%	
Criminal mischief	75	5%	40	-49%	21	-48%	26	24%	28	8%	
Misc. offenses	4	400%	9	-55%	7	-22%	3	-57%	10	233%	
Total	340	1%	246	-28%	205	-17%	173	-16%	308	78%	14

Source: After Markham & Gilderbloom (1996) - (data is from the City of Louisville Division of Police, Research Office).

Table 2-3
Participants in the HANDS Grant

Participant	Cash/In-kind	$ Amount	%
City of Louisville	Cash	165,000	7.83
Cumberland Bank	Cash	5,000	0.24
Gheens Foundation	Cash	94,000	4.46
Homebuilders' Association of Louisville	Cash	2,750	0.13
Housing Authority of Louisville	In-kind	88,000	4.17
Housing Partnership of Louisville	In-kind	19,400	0.92
Jefferson County, Commissioner Owens	Cash	1,500	0.07
Jefferson County, Public Schools	In-kind	34,204	1.62
Kentucky Housing Corporation	Cash	18,827	0.89
L&T Properties, Inc.	Cash	500	0.02
Liberty National Bank and Trust	Cash	10,000	0.47
Louisville Central Community Centers	Cash	7,000	0.33
Louisville Central Community Centers	In-kind	38,900	1.85
Louisville Urban League	In-kind	15,000	0.71
Metroversity	In-kind	5,973	0.28
Mortgage Bankers Association	Cash	500	0.02
National Center for Family Literacy	In-kind	16,500	0.78
National City Bank	Cash	5,000	0.24
PNC Bank	Cash	10,000	0.47
U.S. Department of Education	Cash	1,520,238	72.12
University of Louisville Faculty	In-kind	9,731	0.46
University of Louisville Foundation	Cash	40,000	1.90
TOTAL		2,108,023	99.98

viability of our cities is creating sustainable political, social, and institutional structures around which "sustainable urban development can be framed" (Haughton and Hunter 1994, p. 285). Table 2-4 contains a summary of HANDS goals and accomplishments for the entire grant.

The U.S. Department of Education Urban Community Service Grant programs fund higher education institutions to form collaborative relationships with government, business, and community groups to address significant urban problems. In 1992, the University of Louisville was awarded a three-year $1.5 million grant (with a half-million dollars local match) for the HANDS program, a multifaceted approach to turn around Louisville's most impoverished neighborhood.

One of the early actions was to establish two advisory committees. The Community Advisory Committee represented the broad constituency of the neighborhood and the city. It provided insight into the thoughts and feelings of

the residents as to what did and did not work. It helped make the program le-
gitimate and accountable in the neighborhood. A National Advisory Committee consisting of subject matter experts and prominent academicians brought a
broader perspective to the program and helped shed light on other national initiatives that could help in Louisville.

Table 2-4
HANDS Project Goals and Accomplishments

Objectives	Level of Accomplishment	Comments
Enroll, provide referral, placement, and counseling services to 400 clients.	1,462 individuals served	
Provide job development training services to 90 clients (40% of whom receive public assistance).	201 individuals served	Percent receiving public assistance is unknown.
Of the 90 clients assisted with job development and training, 45 to obtain employment after training.	51 obtained jobs or began small businesses.	
Provide leadership training to 60 clients.	35 individuals trained	
Provide grant writing training to 15 people.	60 individuals attended	
Be a *participant in the process* of 180 low- and moderate-income families becoming home owners.	(See comment.)	Meaning of "participant" is ambiguous. The process included individual and family development, employment creation and achievement, and home purchase preparation. The only way to objectively assess this measure would be with a long-term follow-up.
Provide home ownership orientation to 75 clients.	109 received counseling; 41 reported an interest in purchasing a home in Russell.	

(continued)

Table 2-4 (*continued*)
HANDS Project Goals and Accomplishments

Objectives	Level of Accomplishment	Comments
Bring 50 housing vendors together with potential home owners/clients.	57 different vendors participated in the first two Home ownership Fairs.	Vendors from 1995 and 1996 fairs not included, since HANDS successfully turned this program piece over to a community-based organization in 1995.
Make available home ownership counseling and support services to 150 past and present La Salle residents.	While counseling was "made available" to all La Salle residents, 59 chose to participate.	
Provide homeownership orientation to 400 individuals interested in home ownership.	Goal was far exceeded (see comment).	1993 Home ownership Fair drew an estimated 300–400 individuals (exact number not available). The 1994 Home ownership Fair drew 338 individuals—only 34 of these 338 individuals reported attending the 1993 fair.
Complete 9 prototype housing designs for Louisville Central Development Corporation (LCDC) that meet the mandates of the Historic Preservation District.	13 prototype designs approved.	
Complete a neighborhood design plan.	(See comment.)	A "complete" plan was not developed; however many components of it were. Completion of this objective was deemed possible only if the COPC grant had been received. Removal of this goal was recommended at the end of 1995.
Develop a plan and cost estimate to upgrade Western Cemetery to a passive park.	Partial completion with approved Russell master plan closing 16th St. (See comment.)	Because of resources, the design team focused their efforts on the 16th St. closure. This goal was recommended for removal at the end of 1995.

(continued)

Table 2-4 (*continued*)
HANDS Project Goals and Accomplishments

Objectives	Level of Accomplishment	Comments
Prepare a report to obtain approved developer designation for another tract in the Russell urban renewal area.	Completed. Team prepared report for an area bounded by Congress Alley on the north, 18th St. on the east, Chestnut St. on the south, and 21st St. on the west.	
Work with L&T Properties on the Phase I-B development.	Accomplished. Team worked extensively with L&T Properties.	L&T is not presently pursuing new housing development in the Pioneer Park area.
Participate in the Bruner Foundation competition.	Accomplished. Helped prepare the nomination package for the Rudy Bruner Award for Excellence in the Urban Environment; presented by the Bruner Foundation.	While the HANDS submission did not win the competition, the team was encouraged to apply for the award in the future.
Refer 60 clients through the Metroversity Educational Opportunity Center. 20 to have received higher education scholarships. 20 to have received a high school general equivalency diploma (GED). 20 to have been enrolled in a family literacy/Adult Basic Education (ABE) program. Half of those enrolled in family literacy/Adult Basic Education program (10) to have received a high school equivalency diploma.	At least 70 clients were referred; 51 received partial higher education scholarships and financial assistance. A total of $21,978.71 was spent; 76 individuals were enrolled in Jefferson County Public Schools (JCPS) ABE/GED/Family Literary Training.	Number obtaining GEDs is not available.

(continued)

39

Table 2-4 (*continued*)
HANDS Project Goals and Accomplishments

Objectives	Level of Accomplishment	Comments
Enroll 100 children in Esteem Team training.	198 students enrolled in Esteem Teams from 1993 to 1995.	Esteem Teams component not continued as part of HANDS for 1995–1996 school year.
Attempt to obtain an external grant to support HANDS educational activities.	Accomplished with award of Gheen's Foundation grant.	$100,000 awarded for two years.
Work to obtain an environmental education program.	Accomplished under the Center for Sustainable Urban Neighborhoods.	Considered duplication of effort for a separate HANDS initiative to occur.
Implement a family literacy center at Coleridge-Taylor in Village West (with JCPS).	Accomplished.	Due to low enrollment, the center was discontinued, effective 1/13/95. Students were transferred to other ABE/GED sites coordinated by JCPS.
Help create and provide assistance to a nonprofit housing corporation.	Accomplished with the creation of LCDC.	
Assist the city of Louisville with the preparation and submission of at least two grant proposals that would benefit the Russell Neighborhood.	Accomplished.	Enterprise Community Grant and the AmeriCorps Grant
Assist two nonprofit organizations with grant proposals that would benefit Russell.	Accomplished.	Fifth St. Baptist Church and St. Augustine Catholic Church
Write and submit at least three articles for national publication.	Accomplished.	*Journal of Housing and Community Development* (1995); *Center for Urban and Planning Research Report* (1995); *Metropolitan Universities* (1995); *Harvard Journal of African American Public Policy* (1994).

(*continued*)

Table 2-4 (*continued*)
HANDS Project Goals and Accomplishments

Objectives	Level of Accomplishment	Comments
Encourage other departments of the university to become involved in the community.	(See comment.)	The exact impact HANDS has had in this area is truly not measurable. However, from the perspective of the Principal Investigator, various neighborhood leaders, and the evaluator, there has not been an increase in the number of faculty working actively to assist this area of Louisville. One reason may be that the reward and incentive structure of the university does not encourage this kind of activity by faculty members.
Help implement micro-business development at LCCC.	Accomplished.	
Institute a micro-business loan program.	Accomplished.	
Recruit 30 clients for the micro-business program. 20 to have completed training 10 to have received business loans	75 enrolled; 47 completed training; nine first-time loans of $1,500 each were made; six second-time loans of $3,000 were made.	
Identify and target 20 retail- and service-oriented companies to approach and discuss the possibility of locating their businesses in Russell.	Accomplished.	45 individuals participated in a forum in November 1995.
Help convince four businesses to locate an operation in Russell.	Not accomplished.	Repeated attempts to establish new businesses failed. It is difficult to tell what the long-term impact of these efforts will be.
Approach four banks to create innovative loan programs for business development. One innovative loan program to have been implemented.	The Mortgage Bankers Association was approached in 1995.	At this time no new innovative loan programs have been implemented.

(*continued*)

41

Table 2-4 (*continued*)
HANDS Project Goals and Accomplishments

Objectives	Level of Accomplishment	Comments
Recruit 8 clients for minority contractor development training.	37 enrolled.	A study is being planned to follow up on what happened to these participants.
Accomplish integrated model for university to respond to community.	A Community-University Partnership Center located in the West End has been proposed, and plans are underway to make this center a reality.	Not able to measure or assess this objective in any quantifiable manner.
Develop matrix to identify categories of clients and tie specific demographics to each specific component of HANDS.	Not accomplished.	
Develop and implement a Strategic Management Plan to facilitate direction and purpose to the HANDS organization.	Accomplished.	
Develop a work plan for soliciting private companies and other organizations to provide matching funds to HANDS.	The direct contributions and in-kind match exceeded the 25% requirement of the grant.	
Negotiate and execute a written agreement with LCDC for a set contribution to HANDS on a per home basis.	Accomplished.	LCDC rejected this agreement of a per home basis; instead, it gave a single, lump-sum payment.
Submit a proposal to the city of Louisville for matching funding for a UofL/City "Center for Community Partnerships."	Proposal submitted in 1995.	Formal announcement on the creation of a Community-University Partnership Center, summer of 1996.

(*continued*)

Table 2-4 (*continued*)
HANDS Project Goals and Accomplishments

Objectives	Level of Accomplishment	Comments
Prepare for submission to the Department of Education a grant for a 5-year extension of HANDS.	(See comment.)	Department of Education would not fund an extension of HANDS—it required a new grant proposal. This proposal led to the awarding of the Sustainable Urban Neighborhood (SUN) Grant to the University of Louisville.
Submit a request to the university for ongoing core funding for the HANDS project, which would have included permanent funding to support core administrative staff positions.	Not accomplished.	While HANDS will not continue, the direction in which it took the university will continue with the establishment of the Community-University Partnership Center in the West End.
Identify and submit grant applications for annual funding of at least $100,000 to four funding sources.	Not pursued.	This effort to take place under the proposed Community-University Partnership Center.

Source: Reginald Bruce, Evaluator for HANDS.

Community Advisory Committee

The Community Advisory Committee was an eclectic mix of people representing all walks of life in the Russell Neighborhood, from political figures to residents. One of the most interesting stories involved Mattie Smith, a hard-working African-American grandmother who worked as a domestic. She never asked for anything from anyone. She lived in rental housing all of her adult life because she could not afford to buy a house. Because of the mix of home ownership programs, she was able to buy, through the HANDS program, at almost sixty years of age, her first house—not through handouts, but because she earned it. She wanted to show her grandchildren that they would get what they wanted in life if they worked hard enough. Hers is just one of many success stories.

The committee members follow:

Rhonda Richardson, former alderman, city of Louisville

Charles Diggs, associate director, city of Louisville Housing and Urban Development

Mary Hackley, president of the Russell Neighborhood Advisory Committee

Kathleen Davis, Russell resident

Robert Taylor, police officer working in the Russell Neighborhood

Benton Hawkins, police officer, working in the Russell Neighborhood

Omari Rankin, building contractor living in the Russell Neighborhood

LaGlenda Reed, business owner of Models and Self Esteem, Inc.

Carl Mitchell, owner of local catering business

Mattie Smith, new Russell Neighborhood home owner

Sam Watkins, president of the Louisville Central Development Corporation

Patti Bowles, bank officer, Fifth Third Bank

LaTondra Jones, administrator of the HANDS program

National Advisory Committee

The National Advisory Committee was a fascinating mix of scholars, writers, and practitioners. Derek Bok provided the vision that helped this committee guide the HANDS effort. Marilyn Melkonian believed so much in what was happening in Russell that her company helped renovate the decrepit Village West complex, discussed later. Each member contributed to the effort. The list of members follows:

Derek Bok, former president of Harvard University and noted education author

Mark Dowie, muckraking book author and faculty member at the Massachusetts Institute of Technology

Vincent Lane, president, Chicago Housing Authority

Marilyn Melkonian, president, Telesis Corporation and former deputy for the federal HUD

Don Terner, president, Bridge Housing Corporation and housing author (deceased)

Roger Hamlin, Michigan State University and author of books on small minority business development

The HANDS program helped build economic capacity in the neighborhood by working with government and private agencies to sponsor a minority contractor training program. The surge in construction activity also gave rise to minority entrepreneurship training. According to the Homebuilders' Association of Louisville, only a tiny percentage of African Americans in Louisville are registered homebuilders. The HANDS program responded by participating in a partnership with former Jefferson County Judge Executive David Armstrong through the Louisville and Jefferson County Office of Economic Development and the Kentuckiana Chapter of Associated Builders and Contractors (ABC) to provide a minority contractor training program.

The intense, ten-week training program covers topics including, but not limited to: business plan development; developing business relationships; business licenses and permits; establishing an office; marketing, preparing, and delivering a bid; estimating; job performance; cash management; operational insurance; workforce development; and safety requirements. Following classroom training, program graduates are matched with contractors to foster networking skills. Contractors act as mentors to minority protégés to offer experience and direction.

Through the HANDS program, a class instructor and experts for class panels were provided, and administrative duties were performed. Additionally, it worked with area churches to recruit participants.

Case Management

Family Advocate Skill Teams (FAST) were formed under the auspices of the HANDS program to perform comprehensive family assessments and counsel 400 families in the HANDS target area. These teams were coordinated by a certified social worker and were comprised of a social work intern, an early childhood specialist and/or a gerontologist, and a nursing student. Three area higher education institutions (University of Louisville, Spalding University, and

Southern Baptist Seminary) pooled their social work programs to implement internship programs providing comprehensive family assessments counseling to 400 families. Case management placed program participants in one or more of the HANDS component programs. Each team leader served as a case manager. The designation of the lead person depended upon the health, education, or social-economic needs of the client family. The FAST case manager directed residents to support services, including wellness, employment, child care, education and home ownership. The role of the case manager included surveying families, planning with them, and brokering and networking with existing community resources and/or HANDS program components.

A student team was assembled with four social work students from the University of Louisville's Kent School of Social Work, one each from the University of Kentucky and Jefferson Community College, and a total of eighteen nursing students from the University of Louisville and Spalding University. Family members were referred to the HANDS leadership training program, with computer training available through the Louisville Urban League and educational assessments conducted by the Educational Opportunity Center of Kentuckiana Metroversity, a coalition of local colleges and universities.

Households were contacted to determine their interest and eligibility for home ownership in renovated La Salle Place condominiums. Without credit stability or an adequate income, home ownership is not possible. For this reason, case managers assisted in connecting people to job training and educational counseling. For example, one student was interested in attending a small Kentucky junior college on a basketball scholarship. The family's case manager accompanied the student and his mother to the campus. Tutoring for the American College Test (ACT) entrance exam was arranged for him in order to ensure his success on the exam.

The case management teams did not wait for clients to come in. Each team made appointments at the convenience of the families to visit their homes. At that time, a complete assessment was made to determine the family's interests in jobs, educational opportunities, and home ownership. The HANDS case management field office was located in the heart of the Russell Neighborhood, thus HANDS case managers were close to the families being served.

Leadership Training

The leadership training program was intended to draw together individuals who demonstrated the inclination and capacity for leadership within the

Russell and La Salle target areas. A partnership between the University of Louisville's College of Business and Public Administration, Jefferson County Public Schools, Louisville Central Community Center, and Louisville Community Design Center put together a leadership program to train thirty residents in the HANDS target area. Through the HANDS program, participants were instructed in community organizing strategies, entrepreneurship, and positive career, financial, and lifestyle choices. The goal of the training program was to reinforce and enhance the leadership capabilities of individuals. Child care workers, home owners, and a chef were chosen to make up the first of six leadership classes.

In order to establish permanent change in the community, the community's leaders must take ownership of and direction for the type and quality of activities they select. When trained, these community leaders become instructors for subsequent groups of residents, thus perpetuating leadership skills within the community. The importance of entrepreneurship was stressed in training sessions. A spirit of self-sufficiency must be instilled to break an often intergenerational pattern of dependency on public support. Economic empowerment through entrepreneurial business concerns can provide resources to help implement the strategies developed to solve community problems and reinforce efforts to build collective self-esteem. Through HANDS, a community speakers program was arranged to stress African-American business-building skills. A program of internships for students earning a masters degree in business administration was developed, and interns worked with African-American business owners to learn marketing, accounting, management, and leadership skills for newly developing business enterprises.

Through HANDS an "esteem program" also was developed for Russell and La Salle youth directed by the Jefferson County Public Schools. An esteem program provides a positive approach to leadership by using performing arts, life skills activities, and community service and parental involvement to encourage youngsters to believe in themselves, their parents, and their community.

Job Training

Roughly two-thirds of the residents in the HANDS target area were unemployed and needed job-related assistance. Therefore, job training was an essential component of the program. Persons entering the program had no work history or history of employment in minimum-wage jobs. Two levels of training were provided to the participants: entry and remedial. Entry-level training involves efforts to inculcate job skills in new labor market applicants. Individuals in this program who lack basic skills to compete at the entry level have fallen so far behind in job-related skills that they need special help. Remedial training enables these individuals to compete in the current labor market, because minimum-wage laws often make employers reluctant or unable to provide general training to unskilled workers. The Louisville Urban League administered the program.

Trainees began an eight-week course in computer skills training as a part of the HANDS project. The course was designed to familiarize students with business computer systems, computer terminology, word processing (Word-Perfect), typing speed development, spreadsheet use and application (Microsoft Excel), alpha and numeric data entry, and current trends in the use of computer software. Trainees found employment in local firms such as insurance agencies, Louisville Gas & Electric, the American Red Cross, and Cumberland Bank.

Job training covered basic workforce skills, including self-actualization, human relations-interpersonal communications, employer expectations, employability skills, and job search techniques. The University of Louisville Labor Management Center provided a training segment on effective communication skills in the workplace, which utilized role-playing and other hands-on techniques to illustrate the importance of meaningful communication in the work setting.

Another important part of job training was a mentoring program to assist unemployed or underemployed adults to become successful in the workplace. The unique quality of this program involved creating a necessary bridge to employment opportunities in the community. Each job trainee was assigned a mentor, a leader in labor or management relations who could give one-on-one attention to the trainees and who were aware of the appropriate skills needed to help job trainees succeed in the world of work.

Education

Like job training, education is central to the success of revitalizing an inner city. The more one learns, the more one earns. Educational programs can turn the unemployed into the employable and give those in minimum-wage jobs the means to earn higher salaries, allowing them greater home ownership opportunities. The School of Education at the University of Louisville contributed ideas, talent, and training through a new teacher education program using student teachers and certified teachers. Working with the University of Louisville's School of Education, a comprehensive program was established to advance the educational achievements of residents. This comprehensive effort included the following four components:

Adults and Children Coordinated Education (ACCE)

The ACCE component provides education services for youth and adults who needed help to complete their high school education. Accredited classes in local community centers prepare residents to obtain the GED. High school and other continuing education courses are available through the Jefferson County Public Schools, Adult and Continuing Education Program.

Pooling Assets for Continuing Educational Development (PACED)

When youths and adults complete the requirements for a high school diploma, higher education becomes possible. The PACED component continues where ACCE ends. An outreach program under the Kentuckiana Metroversity assists in providing financial aid to area residents seeking to attend college or other educational or vocational training programs. The staff of Metroversity provides ongoing educational counseling and workshops for residents at community centers located in their own neighborhood. Scholarships are solicited from private corporations and foundations.

Literacy Is a Family Affair (LAFA)

With the assistance of the National Center for Family Literacy, the HANDS program assists in combating illiteracy. Using family literacy programs, LAFA ties two generations together in a unique educational opportunity. Parents and children learn together and attend school together. As parents identify their strengths and develop literacy skills, essential messages about the importance of education are passed successfully to their children. Parents and children become partners in learning. The National Center for Family Literacy is working with the residents of the Russell and La Salle target areas in implementing this program. Early research indicates that 90 percent of the children who have participated in family literacy programs improved school performance.

Community Teaching and Tutoring (CTT)

The CTT program utilizes University of Louisville School of Education students as tutors and teachers for the residents of the target areas. A weeknight community study hall is available. The study hall is equipped with computers for training in basic job skills, remedial education, and grade school and high school programs. University of Louisville student interns work directly with residents on their homework. Older students are encouraged to work as mentors to younger students. The education program requires pre-service or student teachers to complete a specified number of community service hours as a requirement for graduation. The HANDS program uses education as the foundation for building a vision of paths toward the development of a sense of community.

Summary of the Accomplishments
of the Goals and Objectives Set[1]

The worth and merit of a program such as HANDS must be assessed both in terms of the quantitative accomplishment of goals and objectives and in terms deemed more qualitative. Indeed, because of the nature of some of the goals and objectives (e.g., "for HANDS to become a model of community partnerships"), it would be meaningless to attempt a purely quantitative assessment of goal accomplishment. The HANDS personnel created and supported services in the following areas: case management intake and referral, small business development, home ownership counseling, education, job training, and community development and planning. Additionally, the HANDS staff worked to help create community-university partnerships.

An important aspect of this partnership development was the initial contact most residents in Russell had with the HANDS program—case management. The role of case management included surveying families, planning with them, and brokering and networking with existing community resources. Indeed, case management's overarching purpose was to help create partnerships directly with Russell residents. The case management teams often did not wait for clients to come to them. Each team made appointments at the convenience of the families to visit their homes. An assessment was made to determine the family's interests in jobs, educational opportunities, and home ownership. An important aspect of this intake and referral process was the creation of a HANDS case management field office located in the East Russell Neighborhood in the two census tracts with the greatest poverty. The HANDS case managers were close to the families served.

A multidisciplinary team designed and implemented a computer information system to document HANDS services to residents of the Russell and La Salle neighborhoods. The database served three primary purposes: (1) it provided information as to who was served and which services were provided; (2) it was a management tool to let HANDS leadership know if the program was meeting goals and objectives as stated in the strategic plan; and (3) it assisted in the evaluation of HANDS programs by providing information about client characteristics and service history that could be (to some extent) linked to service outcomes.

At different times, case managers collected information about families and services. These case managers were interns from the Kent School of Social Work, Southern Baptist Seminary, and Jefferson Community College. Another important source of information about services provided was the service provider. While case management provided information about program referrals, the service provider (e.g., the Louisville Urban League, in terms of job training and development) supplied information concerning actual program enrollment and completion. Thus the handoff of information between case management and the service provider was an important link in the completeness of the database. This handoff of information was met with some difficulties. The original database developed specifically for the HANDS program turned out to be a rather cumbersome program used for evaluation and tracking purposes. The HANDS leadership should have asked why it spent all the money it did on a system that did not work as needed, when a simpler program could work to everyone's best interests. Eventually, the database was transformed into a system that could be used relatively easily and with confidence as to its completeness.

Households Served

The HANDS program served 664 *households* and 1,462 *individuals* since its inception in January 1993. A brief profile of those served reveals that: (1) nearly 94 percent of those served were African American; (2) of those who were of working age (eighteen or greater), 48 percent worked full time and 27 percent were unemployed; (3) of those who were of working age, approximately 46 percent had a high school education or less; (4) the mean monthly income (from all sources) of all households served by HANDS was $795.41, with half of all households earning less than $692.50 per month; and (5) almost 75 percent of the households were headed by women who, for the most part, were single or separated parents. (See Table 2-4 for a summary of the accomplishment of objectives.)

The HANDS program also was a participant in services not directly a part of the Strategic Management Plan. Some additional activities include conducting two home maintenance programs in 1994 and 1995; enrolling children in a summer children's leadership program at Western Middle School in 1995; enrolling individuals in an apprenticeship preparatory class during 1995; enrolling individuals in a community writing workshop; conducting a "Youth Law Day"; conducting a "Law School for Non-Lawyers" program; and enrolling individuals in a workshop on making homes more accessible to those with special physical needs.

A Qualitative Assessment of the HANDS Program

PROGRAM ACHIEVEMENTS

The initial objectives for the HANDS program were quite broad—covering the areas of case management counseling, job training, education training, leadership training, home ownership, and community-neighborhood design. So too were the stated objectives and impact. For example, when first conceived, HANDS promised to help 108 students achieve their high school equivalency certificates, to provide higher education scholarships to 225 individuals, and to give 150 families literacy training. Further, HANDS sought to turn 180 low-income families into home owners and to create a neighborhood master plan around which new development could occur.

Earlier mid-project evaluations identified certain areas of strength within the HANDS project. Specifically, the areas of community design, home ownership counseling, and the home ownership fairs were seen as being quite successful. Community design brought to those interested in neighborhood development a skill and an expertise base previously nonexistent within the Russell Neighborhood. The home ownership fairs, on the other hand, brought together housing vendors with low-to-moderate income individuals interested in home ownership. Indeed, one of the underlying missions of HANDS was to develop "strategies" for promoting home ownership within the Russell Neighborhood. With the home ownership fair, HANDS facilitated the community (vendors and interested home-buying citizens) through a process that, hopefully, will lead to home ownership. After two years of successful fairs, the home ownership fair was turned over to a community partner in 1995. Thus an implicit objective of HANDS, the development of sustainable strategies within the community, was partly met.

The same mid-project evaluations identified areas where success was less than clear. Within the area of education, it was apparent that there was little that HANDS could do directly to help a large number of residents achieve their GED. Much of this was due to the low educational level of the clients when they began training. Furthermore, the infrastructure required for a successful family literacy program was found to be beyond the scope of HANDS.

While a large number of students enrolled in the Esteem Teams component of HANDS, and indeed reported happiness with the program, the long-term impact of this training is unknown. One area of the education components that seemed most appropriate for the HANDS project was the provision of instructional assistance to individuals wishing to attend Jefferson Community College (JCC) and Kentucky Technical Vocational School (KTVS) for specific training related to obtaining jobs. While the success of JCC and KTVS courses was beyond the extent of this evaluation, the *strategy* of HANDS helping to facilitate partnerships between residents and these institutions was clearly a primary charge of the project.

Within the area of job training, HANDS also experienced mixed results. After the first year, it became apparent that an eight-week computer training program was insufficient to take individuals with few clerical skills and train them in the areas of basic workforce skills, computer literacy, and office skills. As a result, the emphasis began to shift to helping individuals prepare themselves mentally and emotionally for jobs. While there were generally favorable perceptions from the Job Readiness Training Program for those who attended, many Russell residents stated that they were not interested in the program because it did not offer specific skill training. In the third year of the project, specific training in the construction trade was provided. Only five individuals graduated from this program. Of those five who graduated, only one got a job in construction. However, staff time in this project was extremely high. In retrospect, money for this project component (and some of the other human service project components) could have been better spent in other ways.

The mid-project development of Small Business Training and the Micro-Loan programs was a strategy that showed a fair potential. One of the major impediments of Russell residents purchasing homes is that few current incomes were sufficient for mortgage payments. The creation of new businesses based in the neighborhood not only directly helps the business owner but helps create jobs in the neighborhood.

Finally, while leadership training began with promise, it was difficult to sustain sufficient numbers of new training registrants. At the same time, past graduates of this program remained, for the most part, interested in learning more about how to make a positive impact on the Russell Neighborhood. Thus focus shifted to further developing the leadership and organizing skills of past graduates—with discussions on the development of grassroots leadership projects. This shift of strategy—focusing on a few individuals who may effect changes within Russell—continues. While the long-term impact is unknown, previous leadership training graduates should be followed in the future for their contributions to the community.

PROCESS ACHIEVEMENTS AND GROWTH

The initial approach for the HANDS program was not only to facilitate coalitions and partnerships in the community to achieve revitalization but also to be a direct service provider—helping residents improve their conditions in life through leadership, job, and education training. As a result, the project components often proceeded in different directions and without awareness of what other project components were doing. Perhaps this was due, in large part, to the pressures the project leadership team placed on itself to "hit the ground running" when the project first started. With so much to do, and so little time in which to do it, too little attention was given to such things as goal and objective clarification, realism (or lack thereof) of objectives, ensuring adequate communication across project staff, and documentation and evaluation of project components. As accurately portrayed in an article in the *Courier-Journal* on May 29, 1994 (by Nina Walfoort), a lack of records made assessing the effects of HANDS hard to establish.

Partly due to the aforementioned newspaper article, and partly due to project leadership changes, the next nine months took HANDS staff on an extensive search for where the project had been and where it was heading. This internal assessment culminated in the initial strategic management plan for HANDS. The plan that was developed identified measurable objectives for project components. A further development was that through this internal assessment process, the flow of communication across project components greatly increased.

CHANGES IN THE RUSSELL NEIGHBORHOOD

That the Russell Neighborhood has changed much since January 1993 is without question. For example, with the exception of census tract 20, where there has been a significant increase in crime, Russell's other three census tracts have shown an actual decrease in the total number of crimes committed (see Appendix B). The reason for this drop goes far beyond the actions of HANDS (or any single effort). Nonetheless, it does illustrate that change was on the way. Indeed, renovation has taken place at an increasing rate. For example, according to James Allen (former director, city of Louisville Department of Housing and Urban Development), through the efforts of four organizations (Project Rebound, thirty-eight; LCDC, eleven; Habitat for Humanity, forty-six; and Canaan Baptist Church, two), ninety-seven new single-family homes were built over a four-year period, with more homes under construction. In addition, 170 new apartments were developed through the energies of Hampton Place, Clark Development, and LDG Properties. Further, approximately sixteen single-family homes and forty multifamily homes were rehabilitated since 1993. There has also been commercial development in the construction of Jay's Restaurant, the rehabilitation of the old Jay's Restaurant site, and the rehabilitation of the Village West Mall. Also, two churches in Russell (Plymouth Congregational Church of Christ and West Chestnut Street Baptist Church) have undergone land development and improvements.

With such a large number of individuals and organizations effecting changes in Russell, it could be suggested that a more centralized and controlled approach would be more effective. However, according to Allen, "I'm not sure that all the efforts in Russell have to be centrally controlled. It's better having a bunch of people doing something different. You get much more innovation and initiative."

On Tuesday, June 18, 1996, Mayor Abramson announced that construction would begin soon on the complete restoration of Village West. The total cost of the redevelopment effort was $33.7 million. When the revitalization efforts in Russell are completed, there clearly will be a "Russell Miracle" to share with the rest of the country. As Mayor Abramson stated, this restoration of Village West is due "to the dedication and hard work of so many people. The banking industry in this community, the non-profit sector in this community, the private sector in this community, the education community, and people at the federal, state, and local levels of our government." In many ways, this development in the revitalization of Russell was an outgrowth of partnerships within the community. Mayor Abramson reflected this notion when he stated: "I don't think there is another city in America that would possibly have been able to organize the partnership, the public–private partnership that came together in order to carry out this very unique urban renovation."

Was HANDS the reason behind such an outgrowth? It was a significant partner in a team of organizations. The general partner in the new ownership is Telesis Corp. of Washington, D.C.—a company specializing in rebuilding neighborhoods and building affordable housing. Marilyn Melkonian, the president of Telesis, was on the National Advisory Committee for HANDS. A coincidence? One role HANDS played was facilitating the creation of additional partnerships in the community. Another role played by HANDS in this effort was providing a variety of additional services and activities. Through a new program made possible by the work of HANDS, the University of Louisville's SUN program, Mayor Abramson noted that John Gilderbloom "will continue to provide assistance to Village West with crime prevention, community planning, and other needs."

An important way in which SUN differs from HANDS is in the organization of the project members. The HANDS program quickly developed into a rigid hierarchical organization that was, in many ways, inefficient and nonresponsive. To get something done in job training, the director would have to go to the project manager who would, in turn, go to the job training leader, who would, in turn, go to job training staff who would, in turn, go to the clients. This cumbersome maze was eliminated with SUN. It is fast and efficient, and SUN saved over $100,000 by eliminating and consolidating the positions of jobs team leader, project manager, and program assistant positions. Now more people are in the field instead of on campus.

The HANDS program proved that it was possible for the University of Louisville to enter a depressed neighborhood and help create partnerships with

private and nonprofit organizations. At the same time, HANDS also demonstrated that playing such a facilitative role was not without its difficulties. For
many HANDS staff, it was hard to adopt the role of change agent, rather than
of service provider. This inability to adopt a new role led HANDS into program
components that it probably should have left alone (e.g., education, case management, and job training programs). For many in the community, it was difficult to see the University of Louisville in a help-giving role—since little
previous university assistance had been focused in the Russell Neighborhood.

The HANDS program experimented with multiple solutions, and this was
probably the greatest success of the program. Few private or nonprofit agencies
can afford to fail with a project component. However, a university-based project
can experiment—and succeed or fail. Through its experiments, HANDS learned
that some things work quite well, and others less well. That a new, and more focused effort (the SUN program) resulted from many of these previous experiments is a testament to the efforts of the HANDS staff and their tenacity to
continue to work through project components that were not initially successful.

Some HANDS initiatives duplicated existing successful programs. As
part of the ongoing evaluation process, resources were reallocated to take advantage of those programs rather than "reinventing the wheel." The following
section discusses the most successful component as determined by measurable
accomplishments: community design. As Professor Roger E. Hamlin, Michigan State University, of the HANDS National Advisory Committee said,
"[D]uring its final year, HANDS should focus on promoting home ownership."

Table 2-5 illustrates some of the possibilities in our assessment of potential value-added activities from the HANDS program. The assessment is a sub-
jective one based on the need for faculty and student involvement and the
potential benefits, if any, that each of these groups will receive as a result of its
participation. A + (plus) indicates a positive impact, a − (minus) indicates a
negative impact, and a 0 (zero) is neutral.

Using case management as an example, having teachers guide social service students through case management situations in the community can be an
invaluable teaching tool. But taking theory into the streets may or may not have
value for research: much depends on the quality of the data and the controls on
the students. Some data collected by the HANDS student case managers proved
not useful or suspect. If the work is more than an educational experience and
supports, for example, a nonprofit service group trying to improve service delivery to their customers, it may also act as an excellent service function for the
university (Gilderbloom & Mullins 1995, p. 81).

The education component provided a number of opportunities for positive
teaching experiences. It was not seen as either a positive or negative for

Table 2-5
Assessment of Value-Added Activities by the HANDS Teams

Category	Teaching	Research	Service
Case Management	+	0	+
Education Assistance	+	0	+
Job Training	−	−	0
Leadership Training	−	−	0
Home-ownership	+	+	+
Planning/Design Assistance	+	+	+

Source: Gilderbloom and Mullins, 1995.

research. It was not expected to yield research articles. The education component provided significant opportunities for service and raised the university's profile in the African-American community.

The job training component was a failure from a teaching standpoint, since vocational education is not a true function of the university. Again, it did not expect to yield any significant scholarly contribution. Limited service opportunities for specialized faculty members were available.

Leadership training was very similar to job training. It is not a mainstream function of the university and is not a true focus for either teaching or research service activities. Providing this service did usefully apply some university resources but was not a high-profile activity.

The home ownership component provided chances for university and community specialists to teach empowerment strategies and practical economic skills to potential home owners. The way home ownership dovetailed with the planning and design component provided research opportunities particularly with economic follow-up and related items. Helping people move into owner-occupied housing was seen as a significant service opportunity on the part of the university.

The planning and design assistance component was clearly a winner from a teaching standpoint. Two special classes were taught at the University of Louisville that focused on this component. Several refereed journal articles were published, as well as book chapters, and one monograph on research results was published. As a service activity, this component received significant praise from the community. The focus has been on the use of students. Sam Watkins, president and CEO of the Louisville Central Development Corporation, commented by saying that the "university needs to encourage [students] to get out and live the urban mission."

Social Impacts

Children are the key to the long-term future of the neighborhood. Will they want to remain and help it evolve into a great place to live again? Research has shown that early intervention to provide a positive self-image leads to a more successful adult life. Over 100 elementary school children have participated in the HANDS Esteem Team Program to boost their self-image. The HANDS personnel designed and were instrumental in gaining local regulatory approval and funding for the first new park in decades in the Russell Neighborhood. It was planned as a low-cost, low-maintenance gathering place for all ages, which should, in conjunction with traffic changes, enhance the quality of life, increase safety, and provide a focal point for residents, street fairs, and reduced traffic problems. In addition, HANDS personnel provided assisted-living designs, showing how to make houses accessible to the disabled and elderly at a modest cost.

Summary of HANDS Programs

The HANDS program was a partnership where success was based on cooperation with business, community, and government groups. Mayor Jerry Abramson and the city of Louisville Board of Aldermen played major roles in the revitalization efforts of Russell. The mayor and board of aldermen provided extensive resources to help the Russell and La Salle neighborhoods. Millions of dollars in public and private funds were invested in the HANDS target area. The city of Louisville planned to spend over $2 million to revitalize Russell, $1.1 million in public improvements, and $900,000 for neighborhood rehabilitation. Another $10 million was spent developing the 150-unit apartment complex, Hampton Place, which is the anchor for Russell. Russell, along with two other neighborhoods, became eligible for grants up to $600,000 for community housing development corporations to build new single-family housing for households earning up to $27,000 a year. In addition to these programs, Louisville acquired funding for a citywide homestead program ($1,350,000), programs for elderly aging in place (repairs for elderly and disabled persons totaling $512,000), and a rehabilitation investor program ($450,000). The HANDS program hoped to organize residents so Russell and La Salle could take advantage of these citywide neighborhood and housing programs.

While the city provided much of the bricks and mortar, HANDS, according to Mayor Jerry Abramson, "help[ed] rebuild lives." Activity stimulated interest from the private sector. One multimillionaire developer, in conjunction with a minority nonprofit organization, announced plans to build 100 cottage-style homes ranging in price from $48,000 to $58,000. Another development planned to renovate historic buildings in the area for rent. The HANDS program attempted to match African-American investors who wanted to learn how to build affordable housing with established Louisville developers committed to the Russell Neighborhood.

Louisville mirrors many of the nation's urban ills, with high homelessness rates, excessive rent-to-income ratios, neglected inner-city neighborhoods, and a large number of impoverished persons who are without the training and education skills to be employable. The HANDS program developed a partnership with the university, community, government, and businesses. It helped develop and secure the necessary resources to support the aspirations of residents in the target areas.

Many colleges and universities across the nation are reaching out to their communities, either as part of their mission or out of necessity, and forming partnerships for urban revitalization. The University of Louisville is an institution that reached out to its city as a result of its unique, Commonwealth-directed urban mission.

The goals of the University of Louisville for the HANDS proposal included providing expert faculty technical assistance, monitoring projects, conducting program evaluations, providing administrative assistance, and conduct training seminars for the Russell area. Community and government leaders with demonstrated track records of success carried out this project.

The University of Louisville's pilot project, the HANDS program, resulted in successes and failures. Some of its human development functions did not achieve significant gains over its short life. The physical development program met with some success in helping to change the face of the neighborhood through housing and park development, but it failed to develop a sustainable base from which involved nonprofit community development corporations could grow and prosper without direct university involvement and funding. Nevertheless, despite the problems, the program did show that locally controlled development programs could work, unlike some of the top-down, federally funded programs of the 1960s. All in all, the HANDS program, even given its flaws and limitations, provided an object lesson and a starting point for other university-community partnerships.

Our hope is that HANDS demonstrated that it is possible to revitalize impoverished neighborhoods, provide housing ownership for low-income persons, create job opportunities for the unemployed, and teach empowerment strategies to the poor. We believe the partnership that HANDS facilitated is a model for the entire nation. In many ways, HANDS was akin to the agricultural component of traditional land-grant universities that provides state-of-the-art information to farmers on the best kinds of seeds for crops and food for animals (Klotsche 1966).

The HANDS program represented an important pioneering effort to offer help to impoverished neighborhoods. With higher-education institutions under increasing public scrutiny, HANDS also represents the future—where universities should be heading. When universities become viable community partners, this will help solve some of our most pressing societal problems.

Sustainable Urban Neighborhoods

The University of Louisville's Sustainable Urban Neighborhoods (SUN) program was funded, by HUD from 1998 to 2002. HUD funding is partially matched by local churches, nonprofit organizations, industries, businesses, local foundations, and community groups. The goal of the SUN program is to make operational the concept of public-private partnerships in order to succeed in urban renovation and rehabilitation where many others have failed. As Marilyn Melkonian, president of Telesis Corp., observed, its vision goes " beyond just the physical improvements of the bricks and mortar." The SUN program carries out its vision through outreach-oriented partnerships with community development organizations, business firms, government agencies, community groups, and universities. It promotes human and economic development in the impoverished neighborhoods of West Louisville, with a resulting impact on the entire city. Its effort to save the Village West, one of Louisville's historic African-American neighborhoods, from foreclosure and eventual demolition was a comprehensive one toward multifaceted growth achieved through partnering with the community, the government, and the private sector. Louisville's West End (the Russell Neighborhood in particular) was a familiar portrait of inner-city American poverty, unemployment, crime, and despair.

The SUN Directive

The mission of the SUN program is to explore all strategies that foster a sense of community while empowering individuals in the community and promoting neighborhood revitalization, individual self-sufficiency, and self-reliance. These goals are achieved through community partnerships. Former University of Louisville President John Shumaker remarked in 1996 that "SUN, through its sheer tenacity, helped turn an eyesore of blocks and blocks of boarded-up buildings into a development that the entire city can be proud of."

The SUN project has had success in all of its programs. It encourages national banks' involvement in community and economic development activities to fulfill the goal of ensuring access to credit. To accomplish this goal, it provides policy guidance on community and economic development. It also serves as an outreach resource for banks and their community development partners, while providing technical assistance to organizers of community financial institutions.

As part of its comprehensive approach, the SUN project provides oversight, monitoring, technical assistance, and advocacy for low-income West Louisville residents. It works closely with local officials on budgetary and policy issues affecting the neighborhood. Revitalization of old urban neighborhoods is crucial to preserving Louisville's cultural heritage. Strengthening existing neighborhoods helps reduce sprawl, helps safeguard green spaces, and helps create healthier environments. The SUN project offers assistance to housing developers and small business owners in locally designated revitalization areas, stimulates community revitalization activities that protect and enhance historic resources, and improves existing residential and commercial structures. The SUN program and its partners support initiatives to revitalize neighborhoods through programs such as redevelopment assistance, business training for individuals, education, and community crime prevention. The SUN program also works to identify, evaluate, preserve, and protect significant historic sites, structures, cultural landscapes, cultural artifacts, and tangible community traditions of Louisville's West End.

The SUN project's successful programs illustrate the impact that university and community and public and private partnerships can have on target areas. Documented results have been produced. The processes that have developed and are being utilized are tools to successful urban rehabilitation. The SUN program celebrates its successes and learns from its mistakes.

Community Outreach Partnership Center

The University of Louisville's Community Outreach Partnership Center's (COPC) goal is to develop partnerships that succeed in urban renovation and rehabilitation. Through out-reach oriented partnerships with community development organizations, business firms, government agencies, community groups, universities, and churches, the COPC promotes community organization and economic development in West Louisville. Populated predominantly by African-American residents, it is the most economically disadvantaged area of the city, plagued by economic disinvestments, physical blight, crime, excessive poverty, unemployment, and homelessness.

The COPC project was designed to serve as a change agent in promoting revitalization in West Louisville. The overall mission of the COPC is to improve the quality of life for residents. Its three-year goals and strategies focused on four functional categories: housing, economic development, community organizing, and neighborhood revitalization. Strengthening the existing neighborhoods helps create healthier environments in which better futures for its residents can be built. East Russell, an inner-city Louisville neighborhood, has seized the nation's attention by creating a renaissance in the central city, bringing new life and vitality.

As a result of the COPC project, SUN was recognized by Harvard University. The John F. Kennedy School of Government chose SUN as a semifinalist in its "2001 Innovations in American Government Awards Program."

The University of Louisville's outreach community partnership initiative through the SUN program received the Sierra Club National Best Practices Award. The SUN project has been selected by Industrial Economics, a U.S. Environmental Protection Agency (USEPA) funded group, as one of the most outstanding examples of "Smart Growth Practices in the United States."

Housing and Neighborhood Revitalization

The University of Louisville (U of L) and the University of Kentucky (UK) forged a unique partnership that helped invigorate the greater Louisville metropolitan area. This relationship between the state's largest universities created the Louisville Urban Design Center (LUDC). The UK College of Architecture spearheaded this and is responsible for the overall leadership and daily operation of the LUDC, which serves as a classroom and a forum for ideas related to urban redevelopment strategy. U of L's College of Urban and Public Affairs plays a role in the formulation and achievement of the center's projects. It is modeled after the downtown urban design center in Lexington, Kentucky, which was run by a HANDS consultant, Michael Pride-Wells. The Louisville design center is now run by former SUN staff member and architect John Martin-Rutherford. The design center has been institutionalized by the University and is independent of the SUN program.

Working on the LUDC projects offers UK and U of L architecture and urban design students the opportunity to work together in a real-life design environment with some of the top professionals in the field of urban design. The center directs university academic resources and research capabilities to the solution of critical urban issues in Kentucky while supporting real world LUDC objectives, which include: (1) promoting the role of design in the livability and vitality of urban spaces; (2) identifying opportunities to improve conditions within urban neighborhoods through design; and (3) analyzing implications of zoning, development regulations, and public policy. As a result of its being a center of expertise, the LUDC is key to supporting the development of low-income housing. It is a meeting place for developers, planners, architects, government leaders and the University.

The SUN program provides direct assistance to the neighborhoods and institutions through community design work such as architectural services and helping developers adhere to the Urban Renewal Commission's rules and regulations. It also provides technical assistance ranging from resurveying lots, redesigning houses, creating design plans, and providing site visits to oversee construction to nonprofit developers, with the objective of improving the availability, affordability, and quality of housing in the Russell Neighborhood and surrounding communities. This resulted in several new rehabilitated units.

The COPC was retained as a consultative and mediatory partner in the development of a HUD Section-232 backed project to construct a 156-unit retirement residential center for the underserved, which will be replicated in other parts of Louisville. The project is anchored by a for-profit Limited Liability Company (LLC), which is made up of three cooperative partners. The project includes the landowner, the builder, and a local labor organization, which is providing predevelopment financing. The project demonstrates how unions can realize superior investment returns by investing in housing.

The project, if built, would yield units that rent profitably at approximately 30 percent below current market rents for similar housing as a result of LLC partnership and HUD financing. Financing, land, and construction cost savings are pooled to create a long-term investment opportunity for the company and needed housing for the elderly. Hopefully, the COPC will see this model replicated by other labor organizations, nonprofits, and faith-based organizations in the future.

The Traveling Affordable Housing Fair's target population is potential home owners. The goal of the program is to provide information about affordable housing opportunities and the various components that are associated with home ownership. The fair promotes affordable housing in areas close to the locations where individuals work near the Russell Neighborhood. One slogan is, "Why commute when you can walk?" The fair promotes housing in the targeted area as well as sustainable development while complementing existing efforts to revitalize the area.

Economic Development

The goal of this facet of the program was to improve the economic environment of the area and foster the development of new local business enterprises.

An entrepreneurship program consisted of two-hour sessions held on Saturdays.

The aims of the program were: (1) to develop participants' knowledge of business theory and practice and their application to a variety of situations; (2) to develop participant's understanding of the public policy context in which community activities take place; (3) to provide an opportunity for participants to reflect on and share with others their practice as business owners in order to improve their skills and understanding; and (4) to build relationships with potential partners and clients. Approximately twelve people successfully completed this course.

The program context of the course included how to establish businesses, how to develop a business plan, how to manage accounts, and how to become a successful entrepreneur. Students were also provided with a successful introductory business skills course for two years, and attendees continually ask about other opportunities for business training and qualifications.

Entrepreneurship was further encouraged through the Women and Minority Contractor Training (WMCT) program, created as a response to the need to train women and minorities with skills to develop their own construction or related businesses. This program was a joint venture among the Neighborhood Development Corporation, the University of Louisville's Center for Sustainable Urban Neighborhoods, the National Institute of Aging (NIA) Center, the Kentucky Minority Supplier Developer Council, the Office of Economic Development, the Greater Louisville Building and Construction Trades Council, the AFL-CIO, and local contractors. Over 432 people successfully graduated during the SUN program's involvement.

The WMCT program began in 1996. Many of the students are already journeymen or masters who want to take the next step and become contractors on their own. The various speakers for the sessions represent a wide cross section of the construction industry and related fields. The WMCT program is comprised of individuals interested in beginning a career in contracting, subcontracting, or a related field. The program is aimed at those who have some experience within the contracting industry and need the additional tools to venture into businesses on their own.

Community Organizing

The goal of this aspect of the program was to increase the level of participation of residents of the area in community policy making and community leadership.

The University of Louisville's SUN program has been working with the Gheens Foundation and Innovative Productivity, which became the McConnell

Technology and Training Center (MTTC) to build a community where all residents have easy access to information, services, and businesses. The Empower-Net program, which began in 1998, provides low-income residents of an inner city with home access to business and service networks. At the same time, this program builds the ability of small businesses and nonprofit organizations to serve a community through the Internet.

EmpowerNet is a unique approach to encourage residents to change the future. People with home access to services, business opportunities, and global information resources will be more successful than those lacking access. This program tests that supposition. The target area is a land of decay—nearly half live below the poverty level. As a state, Kentucky is near the bottom in computer ownership and Internet use. Of the fifty largest cities, Louisville is last in the percentage of residents with Internet connections. Through the combined efforts of the Gheens Foundation, the COPC, and the University of Louisville's SUN program, twenty-seven fully functional computer centers in nonprofit agencies were started and provided many scholarships to residents of the designated area, enabling many to obtain computers and receive literacy training at a minimal cost. An evaluation of this program showed that after one year, twenty-five centers were still operational.

Reports compiled by the SUN program indicate that since EmpowerNet's inception more than 500 computers have been distributed to program participants. Community computers and Internet access were provided along with basic computer skills training, academic exercises, word-processing deftness, and an introduction to the Internet.

A majority of individuals reported that they had been motivated to become involved with the SUN computer program because it represented an opportunity for them to obtain computers at a minimal cost. Only one of the participants had ever owned a computer prior to his involvement with the SUN program. Parents commonly explained that they took the training class in order to acquire a computer for their children, something they otherwise would not have been able to afford. Participants who were older students viewed the program in a similar manner.

The SUN program has developed and maintained a World Wide Web site, which is highly sophisticated, innovative, and user friendly. This site includes the listings for and/or links to minority businesses, city offices and services, legislative representatives, information on COPC programs and events, and other pertinent policy issues.

Users visit the Web site from countries worldwide. This Web site is an example of a successful, integral program that has grown in importance—enough to warrant more intense attention—and has developed into an integral COPC component. The site may be visited at <http://www.louisville.edu/org/sun>.

Service Learning Program

The Service Learning program is an illustration of an integrated partnership among university faculty, students and university staff, community partners, and residents. The SUN project provided service-oriented opportunities for University of Louisville students volunteering to work in the area. Students from the School of Education provided tutoring and instructional assistance for elementary and high school students. Used computers were made available to students in the community through a SUN program, which encouraged skills enhancement and educational opportunities.

Evaluation and information tracking or referral services were conducted by students from Jefferson Community College and the University of Louisville Kent School of Social Work. It was an open door for information and involvement in the research and learning process. The Service Learning program encouraged professors to incorporate hours of service learning or service-for-paper in the course curriculum, giving students the option to explore hands-on application of course concepts. It encouraged nonprofit community partners to hire students as assistants in various projects, or as tutors and mentors for children with special needs.

The SUN staff conducted a comprehensive study to identify "hot spots" of criminal activity and created a Louisville and Jefferson County Information Consortium (LOJIC) map for community groups to use in combating criminal activity within the neighborhood. The data and map illustrated a concentration of three-to-one more crimes relative to nearness to public housing and schools than in any other quadrant. Auto theft, wanton endangerment, burglary, and theft by unlawful taking were the most prevalent crimes in these hot spots.

The Crime Prevention program provided education for home owners on crime prevention strategies. Crime prevention through urban design workshops was provided in addition to GIS maps identifying hot spots of criminal activity. Neighborhood cleanup programs and block-watch neighborhoods were developed. The SUN project sponsored neighborhood residents, activists, and leaders to attend the National Crime Prevention Institute's training course focusing on prevention through environmental design. This is based on the principle of defensible space and techniques for creating a natural surveillance. The information acquired through this course was the base structure for another course in housing development.

The extent to which the number of participants increased (70 percent in the second year) is an indication of the success of this activity. The community residents, leaders, and activists are determined to assist the SUN program and its partners in the process of changing the physical and social characteristics of their neighborhood.

Conclusion

The SUN program's approach is holistic rather than piecemeal, enhancing problem-solving capacities by linking residents with systems that provide resources designed to increase productive self-sufficiency. Community education coordinated through partnerships with educational institutions, nonprofit organizations, and faith-based groups increases the depth and breadth of information available to the residents. These partnerships promote a positive outlook to overcome initial skeptical neighborhood attitudes. New business and investment in the neighborhoods, vital to their redevelopment and growth, came about through the coordination of enterprises outside of the neighborhoods and those struggling within the neighborhoods.

Service to the community has always been a vital part of the University of Louisville's mission. Partnerships with local government and business have resulted in a nationally recognized urban revitalization program.

The University's history within the community is a testament to its dedication to addressing local urban issues. The link between the community and the University strengthens each participant.

CHAPTER 3

Universities Helping to
Rebuild Neighborhoods

One of the positive things about university involvement in the community
is the culture of experimentation and the freedom to do it. Much of this chapter focuses on the most successful aspects of the HANDS program—community design and home ownership. This is the chronicle of what worked and what
did not work in the physical redevelopment effort. It is also a record of unreal-
ized dreams (i.e., development of vest-pocket parks).

We will start with a discussion of how home ownership was encouraged
and what was done to prepare potential home owners for their responsibilities.

Home Ownership

The HANDS program referred low-income residents with a demonstrated
interest to the intensive home ownership program of the Housing Authority of
Louisville. Interested families contacted the HANDS program to apply for participation in the program. Completed applications were reviewed, and appointments were scheduled for families to meet with counselors. A completed
financial analysis was conducted to determine what might prevent a family from
obtaining mortgage loan approval. Then a plan of action was designed specifically to meet a family's particular need. Each family was placed in one of four
groups on the basis of similar financial and credit characteristics. A counselor
also prequalified a family to determine the house value it could afford, based on
income and debt.

Once a family, with the assistance of a counselor, resolved the identified
problems (i.e., established a savings account showing adequate funds for a
down payment, closing costs, and a reserve, sufficiently reduced debt load, improved credit standing, and acquired good money management skills), it was
ready to be enrolled in the educational phase of the program.

The potentially qualified home buyers attended seven educational class lectures, which addressed every aspect of the home-buying process. Topics of the class included credit, basic home inspection, parts I and II, selecting a realtor and understanding a sales contract, mortgage financing and vocabulary, home owners insurance, loan application, and loan closing.

Families continued to meet with counselors throughout the process to enhance budgeting skills, build reserve accounts for replacement items, and avoid foreclosure. They continued in this manner for six months, after receiving their Certificates of Program Completion. All graduates were allowed to reenter the program if the need arose.

The HANDS program worked closely with the Housing Authority of Louisville in its conversion of the La Salle Public Housing Project to La Salle condominiums. In this successful, federally funded $7 million condominium conversion grant application, the Housing Authority of Louisville was able to cite the HANDS leadership, job, education, and home ownership training components as part of the match combination. This two-year rehabilitation project transformed the outdated, fifty-five-year old La Salle Place Public Housing Development into new condominiums, providing attractive and affordable homes for first-time, low-income buyers. The development offered one-, two-, three- and four-bedroom homes, complete with new kitchens and baths. The homes feature central air, patios, wall-to-wall carpeting, major appliances, and dishwashers. Also offered are off-street parking and on-site playgrounds for children. Many of the homes have washer-dryer hookups, and others have on-site laundry rooms.

Perhaps the best feature of the new La Salle Place condominiums was the purchase price. La Salle Place quickly sold 150 attractive, up-to-date, low-priced housing units, which ranged in the mid-1990s from $18,000 for one-bedroom units to $36,000 for four-bedroom, two-bath cottage units. These prices allowed households with very low annual incomes to qualify for home ownership. Monthly mortgage payments for a one bedroom were as low as $187 a month. Or, put another way, a two-person household working full time at minimum-wage jobs could afford these units. Ten years later, these units are still well maintained and attractive. Buyers must also be first-time home buyers. However, for the homeownership program to be a success, a multifaceted effort such as HANDS must be put into place (Stegman 1991; Rohe and Stegman 1992).

One component of the HANDS program involved developing linkages with local banks and financial institutions so that residents had access to the best possible financing. As part of this strategy, a housing fair was organized for the Russell and La Salle housing developments to encourage African-American middle-class persons to move into these historic neighborhoods. Builders, bankers, and community leaders were brought together to help "reframe" Russell/La Salle from a poor, unattractive, crime-ridden neighborhood to a place that is "on the rebound" with attractive middle-class homes and community amenities (Capek and Gilderbloom 1992).

A portion of the Russell Neighborhood was renamed "Pioneer Park" by the Louisville Central Development Corporation (LCDC) as it was preparing to build new homes in the area. In addition, it was hoped that residents would see themselves as leaders of revitalization. Residents accepted the name change as part of the new development. The name change did not supplant the existing name or neighborhood fabric. Home ownership became a success. The demand for single-family, detached housing was accentuated when the HANDS program sponsored the City Homeownership Fair at a high school in the heart of the Russell community. This event drew representatives from thirty-eight firms from Louisville's housing production community and attracted to the two fairs over 700 individuals who wanted to learn how to become home owners.

Community Design

The HANDS community design resource team prepared design guidelines for barrier-free living, created a neighborhood development plan, and assisted nonprofit community development corporations. These programs helped ensure a stable home owner market and thus a stable neighborhood.

The first part was structured to assist residents and developers in planning, design, code compliance, obtaining required regulatory agency approvals, and producing energy-efficient and affordable housing designs. Advice was given to residents who wanted to bring properties into code compliance or make improvements on existing structures. Special attention was given to the needs of disabled and elderly residents, helping them make their homes barrier-free to avoid premature institutionalization. Advice and assistance were available for the renovation and construction of new, affordable housing.

The second part dealt with empowering neighborhood groups to become developers and contractors by helping them meet agency processing requirements, putting together financing packages, and meeting ongoing procedural requirements as construction progressed.

A third part was preparing a detailed neighborhood development plan for Russell. The Russell Neighborhood Development Plan was to be a comprehensive analysis of neighborhood needs and concerns covering public improvements (sewer, street and sidewalk repairs, abandoned buildings and houses, and recreation and commercial use). While not fully realized, it helped create a vision of what Russell could look like in the future.

A fourth part was providing technical assistance and training regarding defensible space design to significantly reduce neighborhood crime. It is not possible to revitalize a neighborhood or encourage home ownership if the target area is not safe. The University of Louisville's National Crime Prevention Institute helped provide training for community leaders in building renovation and crime prevention through environmental design as well as other aspects of crime prevention.

Community Design Team Efforts

The community design team, after consulting with Louisville HUD, began gathering information to address the best role it could play in revitalizing the Russell area. HUD's main concern was a "too many soldiers and no generals" situation. Jim Allen, former director of Louisville HUD, was worried that the new interest in the Russell area would prompt builders to construct dwellings randomly without a master plan. HUD's initial solution was to drive the Russell urban renewal area into development sectors controlled by the planning commission. In this way the city could control the level of development and be selective with the developers. This was helpful, but the sectors were large, still approximately ten-block parcels, and they required careful planning and even more careful execution.

Allen suggested that the design team might help the LCDC design a master development plan for one of the sectors. This was the crucial beginning, allowing the team to identify a client and define the scope and goals of the project.

The design team began work with the LCDC, a Kentucky nonprofit corporation dedicated to addressing a broad range of housing, economic development, and social service issues. The initial goal of the partnership was to help the LCDC obtain approved developer designation for a ten-block section of the Russell urban renewal area. Developer designation would grant the LCDC exclusive developer rights in the specified area.

The requirements for designation were to

1. describe the development area with a development plan and a narrative description;

2. provide a broad outline of the proposed development area;

3. provide a development schedule showing the preliminary start date for beginning development;

4. obtain approval from the Russell Neighborhood Advisory Committee made up of residents from the area; and

5. present the plan to the Urban Renewal Commission.

Figure 3-1
Community Design Team's Integrative Role

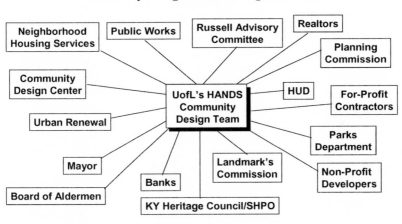

Source: Mullins (1996), p. 62.

In January 1993, the LCDC formally requested technical assistance from the HANDS design team with the initial planning meeting set for February 2, 1993. The design team evaluated the scope of work and established a time line schedule in order to meet the deadline of March 23, 1993, for the presentation to the Urban Renewal Commission. The team then started the coordination process (see Figure 3-3). On March 9, 1993, the LCDC board approved the proposal unanimously. On March 16, 1993, the design team submitted the proposal to the Russell Advisory Committee for review and comments. Not only did the committee unanimously approve the proposal but it asked the design team to prepare a development plan for the entire Russell urban renewal area (quickly expanding the role of the design team). On March 23, 1993, the Urban Renewal Commission unanimously approved the LCDC's proposal and granted developer designation.

Components of the Community Design Team Development Plan

The design team identified the following three components to investigate in designing the development plan (see Figure 3-2):

1. new housing and rehabilitated housing

2. green space/passive recreation space

3. commercial and service development

Figure 3-2
Phase I Development Plan for the Russell Neighborhood—
15th to 18th Streets and Muhammad Ali Boulevard to Congress Alley

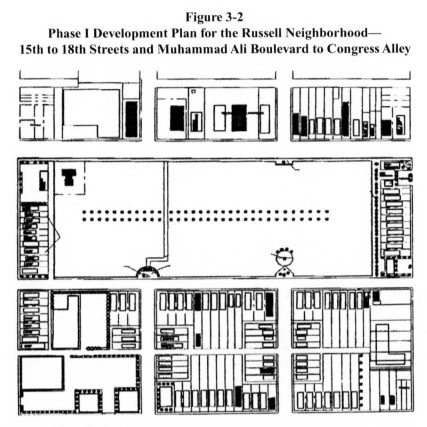

Source: Mullins (1996), p. 67

The design team reviewed the previously prepared master plans as a basis for their design strategy. The plans were general land-use assessments that lacked imagination and conceptualization. The master plans also obscured the development process precluding effective community involvement. The team built upon the previous master plans by concentrating on the proposed development area to test concepts before seeking wider application.

The intent was to maintain and enhance the character of the structures. In addition, security design was an important consideration. The most important security feature was, of course, a healthy and vital neighborhood that was attractive to people with varied incomes (Louisville Central Development Corporation 1993). The plan development and approval process is shown in Figure 3-3.

Figure 3-3
Development Plan Approval Process for an Urban Renewal Area

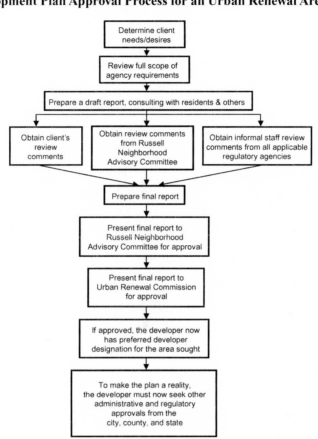

Single Family Housing

Traditional planners encouraged racial, social, economic, ethnic, and religious homogeneity (Silver 1985; Capek and Gilderbloom 1992; Feagin 1998,
Tannenbaum 1948). This was in complete contrast to the Russell plan, where
the intent was to integrate the neighborhood with middle-income residents
while preserving the housing of low-income families. The design team's vision
was to create a neighborhood at a human scale that reflected the intimate quality of the urban fabric. Housing was integrated with commercial property to
avoid the "strip mall" disease of suburban sprawl. Providing a variety of new

housing styles and prices, from $38,000 to $65,000, and not displacing residents already living there but rehabilitating their housing through money from forgivable loans and grants will create a stable neighborhood through diversity. Affordable housing does not have to be faceless, monumental, ice tray-like architecture that breeds fear, anonymity, alienation, and anomie. The HANDS program was determined to show that affordable housing can be attractive, individualistic, and human scale, which can help foster community.

As new housing is constructed, sidewalks are improved, streets are landscaped, and new buildings are constructed, the quality of the neighborhood and the lives of its residents improve.

Green Space and Passive Recreation

A wonderful opportunity existed in the plan for a passive recreational green space park in the Western Cemetery, the focal point of one affordable housing development. The cemetery was abandoned years ago, and the records of burial have been lost. It is a beautiful, elevated green space located in the center of the development area. Coordinating efforts with the Louisville design team, which has done extensive archaeological work to locate the grave sites, the team proposed planting new trees in strategic places that would not disturb the graves. In addition, the team proposed meditation areas in the cemetery, access ramps for the physically challenged, and a memorial fountain for unidentified grave occupants. Funding could not be found to complete this plan.

Commercial and Service Development

The design team encouraged businesses compatible with the quality of the neighborhood, such as a branch bank, barbershop, restaurant, and so on, to set up operations. Service businesses, such as multigenerational development centers, could make valuable contributions to the quality of life. These businesses would provide services not only to the immediate neighborhood but also to the areas beyond. The HANDS project also provided start-up businesses with expertise in management, employee relations, marketing, accounting, and customer service with University of Louisville graduate interns from its MBA program.

Difficulties and Ways to Succeed

Political posturing between minority organizations, minority nonprofits, politicians, and for-profit developers and infighting and competing interests in the neighborhood are political fences the design team straddled. In Russell, different groups have different motives that vary from money and power to philanthropy. These factions unite under one issue: housing. Housing is the common thread that unites profit with good intentions. It allows the design team the extra balance to stay on the political fence. The team helped entrepreneurs make a profit while doing the right thing. Further, the team's concept avoided gentrification and extensive demolition and preserved the architectural character of the site while also avoiding the political, social, and economic failures and stigma of previous urban renewal efforts. By understanding the political pros and cons, the design team guided the different factions toward good planning and design. As a nongovernmental agency, the design team was concerned with doing the right thing rather than with political considerations.

Perhaps the biggest challenge was the difficulty in bringing together and educating nonprofit groups, academic institutions, city agencies, builders, and the public in the design and development process. In most cases, this is a slow process, but the design team believed this approach was the most fruitful path and the future of planning.

Encouraging residents to own homes or start their own businesses is a powerful way to bring economic advancement to an impoverished community. In an attempt to facilitate these activities, an inner-city bank, such as South Shore Bank of Chicago, was built as part of an independent effort to help serve the needs of low-income neighborhoods as a partnership between the city and various businesses. Normally a dollar circulates only once in an inner-city neighborhood. Economic empowerment programs encourage the dollar to be recycled several more times within the neighborhood. This is the kind of holistic approach that is necessary for a sustainable community.

Community Design

One of the community design team's (the "team") primary goals was to help neighborhood leaders attract moderate-income families to live in the neighborhood by providing home ownership opportunities. "To break the cycle of poverty, we need to address housing first. And if we use housing as an entree, it's the nonprofit sector that has the desire to make it work" (Garr 1995, p. 76). Home ownership provides stability to the neighborhood population. It has a number of positive impacts on the neighborhood, including wealth creation. The psychic impact of home ownership, while not unimportant, is difficult to quantify. For example, Rohe and Stegman (1994) indicate that home ownership does not, in itself, increase self-esteem but can lead to increased life satisfaction and greater community involvement. Rossi and Weber (1995) echoed these findings. Gilderbloom and Markham (1995) found that home owners are more likely to be better citizens by voting more in elections. If the community can attract family owned rather than rental housing and bring in the income, then businesses and other commercial enterprises should be inclined to locate in the neighborhood. Home ownership adds stability to the neighborhood and gives businesses a better sense of safety in their investment and market. "After a critical mass of new middle-class residents has been created at the center, growth will feed on itself" (Grigsby and Corl 1983, p. 91).

The team's mission was to help neighborhood leaders implement their vision of the future-built environment of Russell. Secondary goals were related to the university's urban mission. Students on the team gained practical planning experience, learned the value of and problems associated with teamwork, learned more about the issues and politics of neighborhoods and local government, and helped raise the university's profile in the African-American community.

How the Community Design Team Worked

The design team was interdisciplinary in nature. It brought together individuals with diverse backgrounds in architecture, engineering, urban planning, sociology, and law. Many perspectives allowed the team to see the multiple facets of neighborhood problems and bring cross-functional skills to bear on them.

Team members adopted a consultant-client attitude in helping neighborhood leaders. The focus was on what the client wanted, not what team members believed was best. Team members provided advice and gave the client options and an analysis of impacts. It was the client's ultimate decision since the client had to live with the outcome. The team provided planning and related services that lowered entry barriers to small and nonprofit builders and developers. This approach allowed these small developers to compete with more established developers and builders in the local construction market.

Each project was approached in a similar manner: What does the client want? The team reached out to individuals, agencies, and other organizations and drew them into a partnership to flesh out the vision and develop options and impacts for the customer to consider. Once the client chose a course of action, team members helped the client widen the partnership to draw in those parties with the resources to turn the vision into a reality. Finally, all of this happened at the lowest possible organizational level, whether neighborhood or block.

Team members demonstrated that cooperation rather than confrontation is the key to success. Many people look at government agencies and regulatory bodies as obstacles to be overcome rather than as partners in action. Members of these organizations were very willing to share their wisdom, advice, and resources when asked.

The team, through innovative thinking and imaginative action, provided limited planning services and an integrative function that spanned the gaps among the professional world, developers, nonprofit corporations, government funding and regulatory agencies, academia, and neighborhood organizations.

Community Design Team Accomplishments

Community design activities moved the University from the sidelines to the field into a nontraditional role as a player-coach in the neighborhood, as Hall (1989) might have noted. In three years of operation as part of the HANDS project, the team accomplished a number of things. Some of its more notable achievements will be described.

Many community improvements made in the name of efficiency have injured inner-city neighborhoods. Examples include elimination of two-way streets with tree-lined sidewalks, thereby turning a quiet neighborhood into the Indianapolis Motor Speedway at rush hour. Another example is routing expressways through vibrant, often poor, neighborhoods, carving them up, and leaving them to decay and die like great carcasses in the sun. Planning that is sensitive to the needs and circumstances of individual neighborhoods is essential if real change is to be achieved.

The team worked hard to be sensitive to the needs of the neighborhood. It completed numerous planning reports in addition to providing various technical services to neighborhood agencies and organizations. It also worked to integrate the efforts of many agencies (see Figure 3-1) into the neighborhood redevelopment strategy.

Phase I Development Plan

The first project completed by the team was a development plan for part of the Russell Neighborhood. The plan included residential, commercial, light industrial, and recreational components. The client was a new nonprofit developer, the LCDC, a subsidiary of the Louisville Central Community Center (LCCC), a well-established, nonprofit human services agency. The LCDC had no technical capability and no money. What it did have was a board of directors with a desire to make a difference in the neighborhood.

The first step in any development process is to get control of the land. A land bank authority, a joint effort of the city, Jefferson County, and the Commonwealth of Kentucky, held the land. The Urban Renewal Commission is the agency that grants the coveted "preferred developer" designation. This designation allows the commission to hold land in reserve for the preferred developer for a specified period of time. This gives the developer time to implement its plan without worrying about another developer trying to obtain a key part of the required real estate.

Beginning in January 1993, the team worked extensively with the staff of the Urban Renewal Commission and its neighborhood advisory group, the Russell Neighborhood Advisory Committee, to ascertain the agency's requirements, the first of many administrative and regulatory requirements. The committee was truly a group of neighborhood residents, dedicated individuals who performed an urban planning "watchdog" duty on behalf of their neighbors nights and weekends. They did not have any real technical expertise in urban planning but knew what they wanted their neighborhood to be in the future. The team spent time with the committee trying to understand its vision, developed some concepts for its review, and then put its plans into place. Committee members indicated that many developers came in, laid a plan on the table, and expected approval. The committee viewed the team's collaborative approach as refreshing, which helped crystallize the vision and expectations of the residents in the body of the plan.

The LCDC obtained preferred developer designation from the commission in late March 1993 on the strength of the plan that the team prepared (see Figure 3-2). This gave the LCDC exclusive development rights in the area. If other developers wanted to build in the area, they had to come to the LCDC for permission. This would result in some type of development fee to the LCDC. The Urban Renewal Commission did not give the LCDC title to the land but merely granted it the right to develop it. Land was released in its own process involving multiple agencies and approvals. (See Figure 3-3, a flowchart for the development plan approval process.) An additional product in this phase was an AutoCAD® database containing existing and projected future conditions in the neighborhood.

In addition to approval by the Urban Renewal Commission, approval is also required from the Louisville Development Authority (an umbrella agency containing the staff of the Urban Renewal Commission, the Landmark's Commission, and the Urban Design Division) and the State Historic Preservation Officer, because of a historic district in the neighborhood. The provisions of Section 106 of the National Historic Preservation Act of 1966 applied to this proposed development. The team prepared a separate report to obtain approvals from these bodies. This process took several months.

The next step was obtaining approval from the local Board of Zoning Adjustment (BOZA), a component of the Louisville and Jefferson County Planning Commission. The BOZA's approval was required because a number of parcels of land within the master plan area required re-platting to make the lots economically efficient and aesthetically viable for a developer. Some of the existing lots were less than twenty feet wide, making development almost impossible, or more than forty feet wide, making them inconsistent with the character of local housing. The team assisted the LCDC in this effort as well by preparing the required documentation and assisting in presenting it to the board. In fact, the team represented the LCDC at the BOZA hearing. In addition to these efforts, coordination with local permit agencies was needed, and final approval was required from the Urban Renewal Commission before beginning construction. The Team prepared the documentation and negotiated these approvals on behalf of the LCDC.

It was a long path to build housing and to develop other areas. Many developers have neither the expertise nor patience to negotiate this tortuous path. For developers accustomed to building in virgin greenfield sites, the amount of red tape involved with developing housing in the inner city, especially in urban renewal areas, is discouraging.

If the desired land had been under the control of the Land Bank Authority, but not part of a designated urban renewal or historic area, then the process would have been much simpler. All of the steps relating to the Russell Neighborhood Advisory Committee, the Urban Renewal Commission, and the State Historic Preservation Officer would have been eliminated. The developer could have made a proposal to the city's Department of Housing and Urban Development and negotiated its best deal with that agency to gain control of the land.

This plan was dubbed "Phase I," with the expectation that there would be additional phases. This did not occur within the three-year period of the HANDS grant for a variety of reasons, including limited university resources (people and funds) and the long approval processes described later. The greatest problem to overcome was the inability of the nonprofit developer, the LCDC, to focus its limited resources on executing the master plan developed by the team. This problem had to be overcome to demonstrate to agencies controlling the land and to potential funding sources that the LCDC was capable of building not just reports but houses. No progress in the mutually agreed upon development time frame could mean "de-designation" and loss of preferred developer designation as well as loss of control over the land.

Vest-Pocket Park

The team also prepared a conceptual development plan to close a portion of 16th Street through the Western Cemetery, the oldest cemetery in the city, as part of Phase I (see Figure 3-4). This is what Goldsteen and Elliott (1994, p. 38) note has been called a "vest-pocket park," or small, urban spaces, generally under three acres, that have been developed to provide a measure of open space within the city proper, a haven in the midst of the noise and tumult of the city.

The team talked to residents, local nonprofit developers, and the Russell Neighborhood Advisory Committee about the kinds of items they would like in this type of park. It took this input and went to the drawing board, coming up with several conceptual plans. After more consultations, the team developed a final concept and presented it to the Advisory Committee, since it was the first step in the approval chain. The Advisory Committee liked the concept and the team's approach so much that it asked the University to allow the team to serve as its technical advisor to review the final plans developed by an architectural firm hired by the city.

The design is for a gathering place that uses sitting, viewing, and walking venues, public art, and planting areas to encourage a sense of community and provide a visual focal point in the neighborhood. This gathering space reconnects two separated portions of the Western Cemetery that were unceremoniously divided in the 1950s to facilitate traffic flow from Market Street to Broadway. Since the cemetery had not been used as an active burial site for over fifty years, it had been used, in part, as a passive park. Funds were not available to complete the entire plan, thus the western portion was partially completed. One advantage of the team's plan was that it was small enough to be funded locally yet large enough to potentially make a difference in the lives of the residents.

A side benefit of closing this portion of 16th Street will be a reduction in the number of automobiles speeding through a new housing development along 16th. At present, cars move through the cemetery portion of the street at high rates of speed that alarm some of the new home owners. Construction of the park would close off the critical portion of the street, forcing detours onto streets that have significant commercial and industrial development.

The team estimated the construction cost of this project for budgetary purposes and worked with local funding and regulatory agencies to bring the plan to fruition. After the plan was approved, a local architectural firm under contract to the city completed the design; funds were identified, and the design was started in 1996. A lack of construction funds resulted in the project's termination.

Figure 3-4
Small Urban Park Using a Street Closing

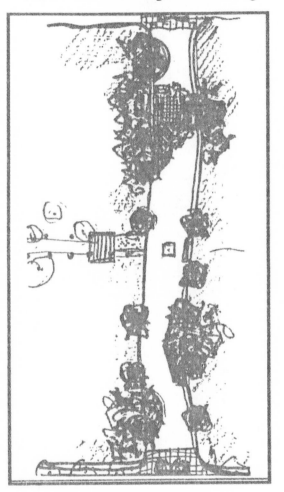

Source: Mullins (1996), p. 71.

As a companion to this project, at the far eastern edge of the Western
Cemetery, the team designed a promenade along Graves End to complement the
passive park and the housing development along Graves End. The team estimated the cost and coordinated the project on the LCDC's behalf with funding

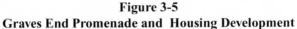

Figure 3-5
Graves End Promenade and Housing Development

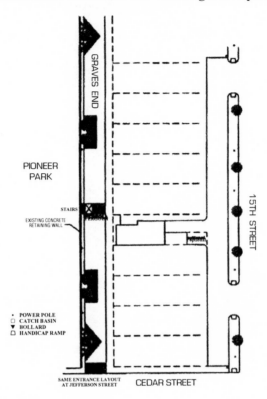

Source: Mullins (1996) p. 72

and regulatory agencies (shown in Figure 3-5). Again, funding constraints pre-cluded construction.

Housing Design and Construction

Eighteen affordable houses were initially built with the team's planning as-sistance. All were sold before construction was complete. Most designs had a "shotgun" layout, with three bedrooms and one and one-half baths. Some had two-to-four bedrooms with up to two and one-half baths with varying amenity levels. All houses were built to be energy efficient with low or no maintenance exteriors to reduce life-cycle costs to the owners. Most conformed to existing lot sizes, allowing builders ready access to the land for development without having to go through the time-consuming re-platting process. Land was purchased from the city for one dollar per lot as part of the overall strategy to reduce costs to the buyers. The houses were sold at a monthly mortgage payment of $375 and up. Many buyers were able to qualify for special below-market financing. Ten market-rate houses under contract were built in 1996. (See Figure 3-6 and 3-7 for photographs of some new houses built with HANDS assistance.)

Figure 3-6
Housing

Figure 3-7
Housing: Conversion of Notorious Liquor Store to Housing

Before (1992: John Gilderbloom)

After (2003: John Gilderbloom)

The team developed several conceptual housing designs for use by developers. A sample streetscape with house plans is shown in Figure 3-8 (these are the same houses shown in Figure 3-7). All designs were coordinated through and approved by all appropriate regulatory agencies because the neighborhood is subject to the provisions of the National Historic Preservation Act of 1966. A larger-scale sample house plan is shown in Figure 3-9. The elevation for it is included in Figure 3-10. Small-scale developers and builders can add details such as foundation plans and typical wall sections to these plans at minimal cost and then use them for construction purposes, thus minimizing the front-end costs of development. Since the plans have been approved by state and local regulatory agencies, the total time to get to market is reduced. This lowers entry barriers and costs in the local construction market. The team also demonstrated that these models could be made accessible to the elderly and disabled, again at minimal cost. The team provided many other services to help spur development, including planning and coordination with regulators and funders.

Figure 3-8
Sample Streetscape

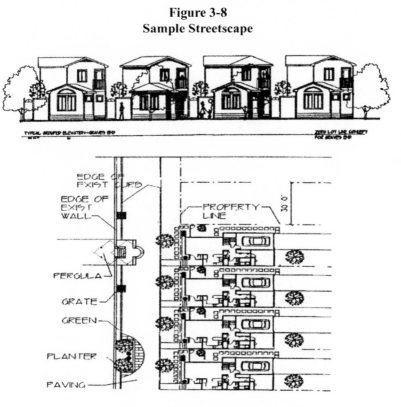

Note: This streetscape and house plans were designed by Dr. Mark T. Wright, AIA. The walkway was jointly designed by Dr. Wright and Dr. R. L. Mullins, Jr., PE, AICP.

The team's efforts were guided by the county's comprehensive plan as well as by the neighborhood urban renewal plan. Using these as source documents, the team was able to offer planning and design solutions for the neighborhood.

Figure 3-9
Sample Floor Plan of House "I"

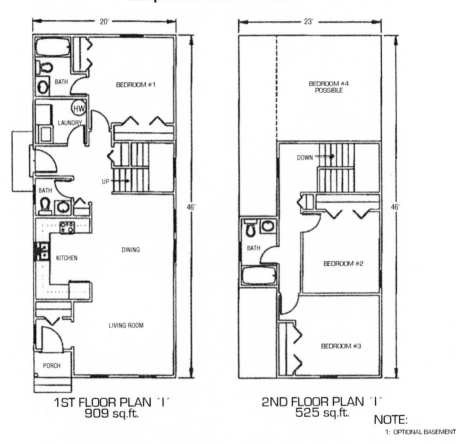

Note: House plans were designed by Dr. Mark T. Wright, AIA, Warren D. Wolfe, and Dr. R. L. Mullins, Jr., PE, AICP.

Figure 3-10
Sample Elevation of the Front of House Plan "I"

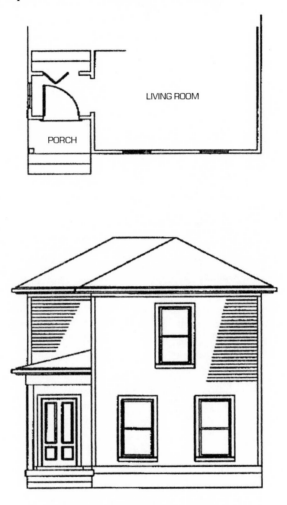

LIVING ROOM

PORCH

ELEVATION PLAN ´I´

Note: House elevation was designed by Dr. Mark T. Wright, AIA. Mr. Warren D. Wolfe, and Dr. R. L. Mullins, Jr., PE, AICP.

Hidden HANDS

The HANDS program was a backstage player in several other significant developments in the Russell and adjacent neighborhoods. Its work in this area has been largely hidden from the public eye and was, in certain cases, a political necessity. The goal was not necessarily who got the credit but to get affordable, accessible, and attractive housing built in the most pragmatic and responsive manner. The lack of public credit can hurt an institution in the eyes of local funders who want to see their funded groups getting proper credit. This is what Capek and Gilderbloom (1992) call the "backstage" of politics, which is often more important than the "front stage."

The HANDS program played a key role in helping save from foreclosure and eventual demolition the HUD Section 8 Village West Apartments in the Russell Neighborhood. This apartment complex was a public eyesore. Half the units were boarded up, and crack cocaine was a major problem (see Figure 3-11). Because Village West was the "gateway" to the Russell Neighborhood, other development efforts were being hampered by the presence of this eyesore. The HANDS program worked with an ad hoc coalition of groups from the Legal Aid Society, the Village West Residents Council, the mayor, the American Housing Communities, the Louisville Central Development Corporation, the Louisville Community Design Center, the U.S. and Louisville HUD, a major bank, and a well-known housing developer to help revitalize this large apartment complex. One way or another, each of these groups played a critical role in helping to save this development and renovate it. For example, without the mayor's support or the organizing efforts of Village West residents, this project would have been foreclosed a long time ago. In addition, a nationally known housing developer stepped in to save the tax credits and to acquire the necessary credit to start renovation.

The HANDS program, in conjunction with the University of Louisville's Center for Sustainable Urban Neighborhoods, helped convince the Telesis Corp., whose president, Marilyn Melkonian, was on the HANDS National Advisory Committee, to be the general managing partner for the over $30 million Village West development plus $2 million in other related developments. The HANDS program helped organize at least ten community presentations to various interest groups to help rally support for the renovation of the complex. Moreover, it performed critical liaison work between the Washington, D.C., developer and various local entities, from the mayor to financial institutions to the resident's council. Finally, it helped collect critical primary information on the residents and neighborhood demographics for the developer. It was seen by many as the interface between the developer, the community, and the government to make the project happen. It continued to work on the project by conducting surveys, coordinating environmental impact reviews, assisting in design, providing needed job and educational programs, and helping with management. A contract was signed in

December 1995, and the deal closed in April 1996 to renew Village West. This success story is detailed later.

Figure 3-11
Photographs of Village West Apartments Before and After

Before (1992: John Gilderbloom)

After (2003: John Gilderbloom).

The presence of HANDS human service programs, however successful they may have been with educational opportunities, job training, leadership develop- ment, and case management, also helped satisfy government concerns that proper human services would be available to help the needy. This proved critical for the tax credit approvals by the Kentucky Housing Corporation. The U.S. Department of Education grant was used as leverage to successfully convince the federal HUD to approve funds to convert a public housing project into affordable condominiums at La Salle Place, discussed earlier in this chapter. This conversion provided pub- lic housing tenants with opportunities to purchase one-bedroom condominiums priced at $18,000, with mortgage payments less than $200 a month for thirty years. The HANDS project was not involved in the La Salle conversion, only in assisting residents with the aforementioned programs.

Another positive function of the HANDS program has been the public availability of its "approved" housing designs, which have been used by other nonprofit housing groups. In one case, a former member of the community de- sign team "recycled" a team report and designs and was the lead person to get a ten-unit housing development approved for a church-based, nonprofit commu- nity development corporation.

Finally, members of the HANDS community design team helped resurrect a defunct, nonprofit development corporation and obtained city approval to renovate forty-five housing units in the Russell Neighborhood. The nonprofit housing de- veloper teamed up with a minority developer and a real estate salesman to make the rehab a success. They are now building more single-family housing develop- ments in the Russell area and in adjacent neighborhoods. Without the HANDS program's exposure to the Russell Neighborhood and the knowledge of various government programs, this rehabilitation effort might not have occurred.

The neighborhood has had little building activity in the past thirty years. In the mid-1990s Russell witnessed a 150-unit, middle-income rental housing apart- ment complex, twenty-four houses built by Habitat for Humanity, 100 houses built or rehabbed by the Louisville Central Development Corporation, 550 City View Park units renovated by Telesis Corporation, thirty or more housing units completed by the Louisville Urban League's Urban league, and more than forty housing units built by Archie Dale. The team and the University have been an im- portant part of this effort—especially in the beginning part of this overall effort.

Community Development Programs

The HANDS program assisted community leaders with the develop- ment of a plan for the entire neighborhood and a site development plan for specific blocks and lots, and it provided technical advice to builders and developers on the nature and intent of the design and site plans as well as information on meeting the requirements of the Americans with Disabilities Act (ADA). It made provisions so there would be support from architects, engineers, and other professionals and made available information on design issues for the elderly.

The University of Louisville helped community groups organize a non-profit community development organization along with neighborhood outreach, consensus-building, and leadership programs. Area churches worked with the partnership to find funding for a proposed 65 unit, frail elderly housing facility in the neighborhood. This development was started at SUN and completed when Bill Friedlander left to run a non-profit (see Figure 3-12).

The HANDS program aided the LCDC in achieving developer designation from the Louisville Urban Renewal Commission. In partnership with the LCDC, one of the most respected developers in the Louisville area (L&T Properties) proposed building many attractive single-family cottage-style houses with prices ranging from $49,000 to $69,000 in the mid-1990s. The HANDS program also worked with the LCDC to attract two other developers to build affordable housing in the Russell Neighborhood.

Community Design Team Failures

Failures can be put into two different categories: Type-1 failures associated with individual products and type-2 failures associated with the purposes of the overall grant. Although most products prepared by the team resulted in some positive change to the built environment, there was one failure of the first type.

The only type-1 failure was the Phase II development plan. It was not a failure of product development by the team; rather, it was a failure of implementation by the developer, the LCDC. The plan was prepared in response to a request for proposals by the City of Louisville's Urban Renewal Commission. The commission received three proposals for consideration. The plan the team developed involved the rehabilitation of three existing structures for rental and commercial space. The balance of the development was single-family housing. Competing proposals deemphasized single-family houses for a mixture of rehabilitation, duplexes, and single-family structures. The plan was prepared in strict conformance to all local planning and zoning requirements.

The commission did not select the plan; therefore, the LCDC did not get preferred developer designation for this two-block area. The commission wanted to diversify the number of developers in the urban renewal area. This was one reason the LCDC was not chosen. This failure was also attributable,

Figure 3-12
Senior Housing Development Street Scape

Senior Housing

Other Houses Design by SUN Team

in part, to the inability of the client, the LCDC, to present a realistic financing package and to commit to commencing construction within the time specified by the commission (thirty days). The plan the team prepared was the only one that actually met all of the requirements of the city, the Planning Commission, and the Urban Renewal Commission. An interesting postscript to this story concerns the designated developer chosen by the Urban Renewal Commission. The chosen developer did not start construction for over two years because of litigation with the third competitor, the collapse of the financing package (loss of investors), and problems with zoning and code issues!

The second type of failure is much more serious, because it affects the sustainability of the HANDS project as a whole. As presented earlier, one of the primary goals of the grant was to develop an infrastructure to "help sustain the gains achieved" (Gilderbloom 1992, p. 45). The team evolved into the LCDC's project manager. This was a captive role, and little work was done for other clients in the neighborhood. This occurred in part because of interlocking relationships among the principals in the HANDS program and the LCDC. The HANDS project's principal investigator did not want to alienate the LCDC's leadership, so he did not push them to change. The team could not move out and help build capacity in other nonprofit developers because it was captive to the LCDC. Several times, the team stressed to the principal investigator that the LCDC needed to work on its own. The team even offered to prepare grant applications to help the LCDC. These suggestions were to no avail.

This would not have been a serious shortcoming if the LCDC had chosen to use the team's talents and skills to train LCDC personnel to carry on the work of the nonprofit developer after completion of the grant. This would have allowed them and their development efforts to become self-sustaining. This did not occur. Rather than seek funds to pay for a small staff, or use funds from projects to pay them, and let the team train them, the LCDC used the no-cost (to the LCDC) expertise of the HANDS team to continue to accomplish the work. It had no incentive to hire or develop its own capacity as long as the HANDS project provided all project management and planning services for them. After the depletion of HANDS' funds, the LCDC was in the same position it was at the beginning of the grant—lacking expertise but requiring the same services. This is a serious failure. The LCDC did not have a sustainable base of expertise, other than a paper trail, to carry it far into the future.

Another failure of the community design team, and perhaps of the grant as a whole, was a failure to institutionalize the approach, methods, and attitude of the two key players on the team. Both were graduate students who arrived at the University of Louisville in the fall of 1992 for the doctoral program in urban and public affairs. This fortuitously coincided with the beginning of the HANDS grant. Both were licensed professionals with broad experience in the planning, design, and construction industry. The principal investigator drew both of these individuals into the HANDS program.

There was no attempt during the grant's duration to bring along other students to show them how things could be done. This could be attributable to several things. Only one other student had a similar technical background coming into the doctoral program and team members were so busy accomplishing the large workloads that there would have been little time for instruction without a significant reordering of priorities. Since they were both full-time professionals, they accomplished their work at odd hours, meeting with agencies and others on an as-needed basis, and they worked from their homes using electronic tools (i.e., e-mail, fax, etc.) to communicate with one another, the grant team, cooperating agencies and organizations, and clients. This was not conducive to passing on knowledge and lessons learned. Since things were going well, there was little incentive for the grant leadership to make a change or to try to force an institutionalization of this knowledge. This problem was noted by Jack Trawick, a member of the American Institute of Certified Planners (AICP), executive director of the Louisville Community Design Center. His statement follows:

> The notion of creating a . . . University of Louisville-based community development corporation that would basically take the methodology that you [R. L. Mullins Jr.] and Mark [Wright] developed to continue . . . , [t]he purpose of the CDC [would be] to train undergraduate and graduate-level students in particular community development methods. Otherwise, what you [the HANDS community design team] did will end up in a file drawer. The houses don't, but the process does.

Part of this concern was addressed in a follow-up grant, named "Sustainable Urban Neighborhoods." An applied research center involving the University of Kentucky's (UK) College of Architecture and the University of Louisville's School of Urban and Public Affairs was developed and studio classes were taught to focus on various real-life problems. It has not been fully successful as a long-term solution to institutionalizing the process. The U of L is now (2004) trying to hire a permanent director for the design center.

Another problem involved the technical knowledge level of the project managers in the planning and design arenas. There were two project managers over the life of the grant. They were not knowledgeable about the tasks and the technical accuracy of the team's efforts; they could not review or oversee the work because they did not understand it; and neither of the principals understood the processes that team members used to accomplish their work.

Reaction to the HANDS Program

Overall reaction to the HANDS program was mixed. Some nonprofit agencies with overlapping responsibilities were as enthusiastic about the program as the nonprofit developers and builders. They feared competition for scarce resources from local foundations that were needed for matching funds on many grants. Others believed that white planners, developers, and contractors should not be involved in African-American economic development efforts. Still others worried that the market demand for housing was not large and that the HANDS-assisted housing development might absorb the demand, leaving other housing developments without buyers. Finally, there was the pessimistic view of writers such as Rusk (1993), that it was a waste of resources to try to renew an inner city-neighborhood, and that African Americans should be encouraged to move to white, suburban areas.

Local government agencies were positive about the focus that the community design team brought to development efforts in the neighborhood. Because team members, although graduate students, were professionals working in the community, they brought a breadth of development knowledge and a cooperative approach to various projects that eased the administrative burden on government staff elements.

The HANDS program became an important partner in the Russell renewal effort and received national recognition. The editors of the *Harvard Journal of African-American Public Policy* declared that the program provided an "innovative approach" to solving inner-city problems. The HANDS project was the subject of a video documentary prepared by the U.S. Department of HUD. Former President Bill Clinton and HUD Secretary Henry Cisneros recognized the HANDS program as a potential national model for neighborhood revitalization. The program was also featured in the American Planning Association's *Planning* magazine and in a HUD video and book that promoted bottom-up planning.

About halfway through the grant, a negative piece appeared in the local newspaper. The gist of the article in *The Louisville Courier-Journal* was that the HANDS grant had become a vehicle for self-promotion by the principal investigator, whose motives were questioned, and that the effectiveness of the projects and programs was investigated because a lack of records made assessing the effects of the HANDS project hard to establish.

Partly due to the aforementioned newspaper article, and partly due to project leadership changes, the next nine months encouraged the HANDS staff to take an extensive look at where the project had been and where it was heading. This internal assessment culminated in the initial strategic management plan for the HANDS project. The plan that was developed identified measurable objectives for project components. There were questions about the balance of the article from both proponents and opponents, creating a local backlash against the grant. While this caused great pain for the principal investigator, university, and grant team, it also provided focus and reinforced the commitment of all parties to make it a success. This is discussed in greater detail in the section "Practical Problems of University Participation in Community Partnerships."

Evaluation of the HANDS Program

Evaluation is crucial in determining the success of grant programs. According to Osborne and Gaebler, in *Reinventing Government*, "[46] percent said inadequate measurement of agency performance created significant problems. If results were measured, however, think what effect it might have in every activity of government" (1992, p. 73). The evaluation component was intended to help the HANDS project stay focused on project and customer goals. As discussed earlier, evaluation was not as effective as it could have been.

The final evaluation of the HANDS program was completed in the summer of 1996. As noted earlier, one purpose for the grant was to develop effective "neighborhood revitalization strategies" (Gilderbloom 1992, p. 45). In discussions with HANDS evaluator, Dr. Reginald A. Bruce, only one real long-term strategy was developed during the grant; it concerned the home ownership fairs. The HANDS project provided the critical early financing and expertise to sustain this effort into the future. The sustainability of the other facets of the grant was questionable. The community design aspect continued as part of the SUN program, however, this does not mean that it is sustainable, as discussed earlier in the section "Community Design Team Failures." It turned out that it was totally dependent on the availability of soft grant money and the right mix of graduate students—two things that did not balance well.

Two independent groups, the Community Advisory Committee and the National Advisory Committee, supplemented the HANDS program's evaluation effort. The Community Advisory Committee was composed of neighborhood residents, community leaders, and former HANDS clients who worked with HANDS staff to identify the needs and problems of residents and assess planned program strategies and directions. Dr. Derek Bok, former president of Harvard University, Vincent Lane, former chairman of the Chicago Housing Authority, Marilyn Melkonian, president of the Telesis Corp., national investigative reporter Mark Dowie, and Don Terner, President of the BRIDGE Housing Corporation, are the members of the National Advisory Committee. One comment from Bok is particularly noteworthy.

> I very much support your comprehensive approach to community development. I have no doubt that there are many serious problems in blighted communities, that they are highly interdependent, and efforts to address one or two problems in isolation are virtually bound to fail.

> I also strongly approve of the attempt to enlist the University of Louisville, an urban university, in the effort to mount a comprehensive attack on a distressed community. There is no other institution other than a university that offers the variety of expertise and skills so necessary to a comprehensive, multifaceted program of revitalization. Properly managed, such a program can offer great benefits to both parties. The community will receive all sorts of assistance at remarkably low cost. The university will be able not only to discharge its obligation as a socially responsible urban institution; it will be in a position to offer its students from various faculties invaluable practical experience that can be integrated into their academic programs to enrich their education. (Personal correspondence to John I. Gilderbloom, 17 February 1996)

Some outcomes are difficult to quantify, but they are real and vital nonetheless. For example, a grandmother who lived her entire life in rental housing is now a home owner because of the HANDS program. "I just felt like God was going to bless me with a new [house]" (Rayburn 1995, p. 9).

The HANDS team prepared an initial assessment of the existing types and conditions of structures in the target area of the Russell Neighborhood. Various measures of housing quality and condition have been based on census and physical survey data. A post-grant assessment of the growth of new business, new housing construction, and related economic development measures was to be prepared but was not because of funding issues.

Distinguishing the HANDS Program from Previous Efforts

What makes the HANDS program different from top-down programs that have failed in the past? Such efforts seemed to fail because of some combination of the following factors: (1) inappropriate planning leadership to unrealistic program expectations; (2) failure to involve program recipients in a true partnership in the planning and execution phases; and (3) lack of foresight to plan for and an inability to contend with politics during implementation. The last factor may be the most important.

Expectations for the HANDS program were determined by community leaders, residents, local government officials, and members of the private and nonprofit sectors. While the goals were high, they were established by those responsible for achieving the goals. This included neighborhood residents and leaders. Contrastingly, presidential task forces evaluated the goals from endeavors such as the Community Action Program (CAP) and Model Cities. Their vision was for a nation, and the programs used large sums of federal money and minimal local investment. They covered large sections of cities or regions and tried to be flexible enough to suit every need, while remaining structured enough to ensure accountability.

HUD officials in Washington was not able to integrate the programs and functions of various agencies into a single, coherent program. In its new programmatic governance, the Department of HUD now advocates a local focus, planning from the bottom. It will work up through the system as opposed to imposing plans from the top down. This is the approach that the HANDS program has taken. As a result, goals can be realized and success can be more readily defined for a single neighborhood than for a national program.

Such planning is vital to the success of an undertaking such as the Russell Partnership. Too often individuals or small organizations have a desire to accomplish worthy goals such as revitalization of their neighborhood, but they lack the skills to put together a plan and the expertise to make it happen. The HANDS program was able to provide the necessary expertise.

A second factor that led to the failure of past programs was the lack of true partnerships involving program recipients in the planning and execution phases. Many grassroots organizations have difficulty determining the stakeholders in the process. Partnership consists of pulling together all of those with a stake in the enterprise and the resources to effect positive change.

The partnership that was one of the greatest strengths of the HANDS program, however, also may have been its most serious problem. The HANDS program relied on a fragile coalition for continuity and accomplishment. If the coalition falters, then the program falters as well. Constant nurturing is needed by the parties to keep the partnership vital, active, and responsive to the needs of the neighborhood and its residents. The Russell Partnership is evolving so that it can continue to be responsive to the needs of the neighborhood. New partners come, and old ones go; it is a process that ebbs and flows as needed. It is easier to integrate such a program at the local level, because most planners know each other. The university minimizes bureaucratic infighting among agencies by constantly attending to the needs of the various partnership groups.

The third factor that contributed to past failures was the lack of foresight to plan for and an inability to contend with the local political process during implementation.

The Ten "Ps" of Success

To the two "Ps" of success, planning and partnership, eight more can be added: perseverance, perspiration, passion, professionalism, politeness, prophet, people skills, and profit.

Perseverance is the ability to see an enterprise through to its logical, and hopefully successful, conclusion. It requires an empowered group to make things happen and to stay with the effort. The process of getting through the grants business is long and arduous, and many nonprofit organizations do not have the experience, nor do they believe that they have the power required to see these efforts through to completion. In many cases, they must seize the power themselves. The HANDS program charted a number of processes for partnership members to show them that all things take time.

Perspiration is often a forgotten ingredient. It is one's willingness to do the tedious, mundane, little things that make a project successful. It is one's willingness to work late nights, weekends, and holidays. Planning documents, house plans, planning and zoning approvals, and permits do not just magically appear. This requires a sustained, determined effort by many people, some paid, some volunteers, to make it happen.

Passion is woven through each of the other "Ps" and binds them together. It is that intense, burning belief that what one is doing is important. Without it, the revitalization effort is sure to die. Passion permeates and inspires the plan. It draws together groups of people and organizations into a partnership that has little prospect for a large profit, but the chance for a better life for residents. Passion gives one the energy to persevere when a key backer leaves the partnership or a promise is not kept. Passion gives the energy to continue to work and sweat, knowing that the cause is just, and that the effort is what will make it succeed.

Professionalism is learning to get products done on time, to return all e-mails and phone calls by the end of the day, to ensure that products have style and substance and that presentations look state of the art, and also that presenters always show respect for clients by dressing in business attire and meeting with everyone. One must treat others how one wants to be treated with good service. Several years ago, one of the authors (Dr. Gilderbloom) was asked to give a presentation in Washington. Because of a communications foul-up, nobody showed up at his scheduled time until a man dressed as a biker came in to hear the talk. Dr. Gilderbloom assumed that this man was not part of this professional organization but decided to give his best presentation. Several years later, this "biker" became one of the most powerful funders of housing programs in the United States, working as a top HUD aide and no longer looking like a biker. He called Dr. Gilderbloom to say that he wanted to fund SUN programs and thanked him for the memorable, professional presentation.

Politeness: Rude people will never be successful. Disarm folks with social skills. Using a mixture of humor and humanness will count a lot in getting the support of various community partners.

Prophet: Rebuilding a neighborhood means having a vision of what can be. Russell looked far meaner and tougher than South Central Los Angeles, which had the race riots at the same time. Successful builders have a "vision" of what can be, and they promote that vision. In Russell, the developers decided to redefine the neighborhood by renaming one development "Pioneer Park" and another "City View Park." The former neighborhood names were negative and had a history of crime and despair associated with them. Conventional wisdom was that nothing could be done and that it was wasteful to try anything. Partners fought against all odds, promoted a vision of revitalization, and helped rebuild the neighborhood.

People skills: Many times, whites are perceived to be phony when they deal with blacks, and that does not build trust. One needs to be who and what one is.

Profit: One cannot bring in capital without showing that profit can be made. Nonprofits need to be run as a business, not as a charity. People need good salaries, and a good return has to be made to finance future developments. Many successful suburban developers were willing to "give back" in Louisville's poor neighborhoods if they could have a go-between such as the HANDS or SUN program, which tried to ensure fairness for all parties.

The HANDS program is more than a cute acronym; it has a much deeper meaning, symbolizing partnerships of people (black and white, old and young, rich and poor) coming together and cooperating to serve the community good. When a partnership unites under a singular vision, lives and communities can be rebuilt. The goals, objectives, and dreams belong to the community. Goals are set to more realistic budgets, established at the local level. Local decision makers can quickly make changes to programs. The HANDS project demonstrates that incremental strategies are feasible and have the potential to make a real difference in the lives of neighborhood residents.

The HANDS project had a small but positive effect on housing supply by helping developers selectively add to the housing stock rather than endorsing the wholesale clearance of land and plowing under of neighborhoods. Design and construction are being accomplished by pooling the assets and wisdom of many actors, both inside and outside of government. Because of the nature of funding (a heavy reliance on private-sector capital for construction) and the partnership, the HANDS program used the discipline of the market to propel it. It also reduced adverse environmental impacts by using the existing infrastructure of roads, sewers, electricity, water, and gas lines and inhibiting ecologically unsound urban sprawl. One of the most interesting stories concerns Dr. Mark T. Wright, a member of the American Institute of Architects (AIA), one of the community design team members. He graduated from the program and founded a development company that has since built hundreds of affordable and market-rate housing units in Russell and all over western Louisville. While the HANDS and SUN programs were not directly responsible for this, they were a motivating force.

Sustainable Development

Renewal of the Russell inner-city neighborhood is providing a multitude of environmental benefits. The Louisville and Jefferson County Metropolitan Sewer District has applauded these revitalization efforts, because redevelopment of the Russell Neighborhood is halting out-migration and recycles the existing infrastructure of roads, sewage and other utilities, and buildings. It reduces the need for imprudent or premature development in outer metropolitan areas and the exorbitant attendant infrastructure investment. Brownfield sites are being identified and remediated, returning this land to productive use. This revitalization effort is promoting greater use of public transit facilities and has encouraged alternate forms of transportation to nearby jobs in the central business district, which is at the edge of the neighborhood. In addition, all housing designs developed by HANDS personnel have been reviewed and approved by the state historic preservation officer. They blend harmoniously with the existing housing stock to form a seamless whole, preserving the character of the area while providing many advantages of modern housing, including better insulation for reduced-energy consumption.

Renewal of this inner-city neighborhood is providing many environmental benefits. The Russell revitalization is halting out-migration and recycles the existing infrastructure. Abandoned houses and lots, which drain the city's tax base, can be recycled into family owned homes, allowing individuals to buy into the American dream while helping to relieve a sizable fiscal burden for local governments. Inner-city renewal promotes the use of public transportation and biking or walking to the downtown office district—still the largest concentration of employment opportunities in Louisville. Energy conservation in the rehabilitation and construction of homes also is being promoted.

Concluding Observations

Louisville mirrors many of the nation's urban ills with high homelessness rates, excessive rent-to-income ratios, neglected inner-city neighborhoods, and a large number of impoverished persons who are without the training and education skills to be employable. The HANDS strategy is to develop a partnership between the university, community, government, and business. The HANDS program worked with its partners to develop and secure the necessary resources to support the aspirations of residents in the target areas. Faith in the American dream needs to be restored by committing to renew inner cities. As resources become increasingly scarce, new paradigms must be forged. In an era of reinventing government, the Russell Partnership in Louisville demonstrates a viable, humanistic approach to renewing a blighted, inner-city neighborhood.

A wide spectrum of political leaders and policy experts argues that revitalizing inner-city neighborhoods is an almost impossible task. These critics point to failed federal programs that have done little to improve the conditions of the poor. Their policy prescription is simple: Since nothing works, nothing should be done.

Learning from the mistakes of the past, cities such as Louisville are designing programs that can successfully revitalize inner-city neighborhoods. A thread that links these programs is the creation of local partnerships uniting higher education, business, community, and government to create jobs, housing, and educational opportunities. Today Russell is undergoing a dramatic rebirth as a revitalized community. Jobs and housing opportunities are being created in this neighborhood.

What can the Russell Neighborhood become? Its destiny is limited only by the imagination and energy of its residents and the resources available to its leadership. It demonstrates that urban universities with planning programs can bring tremendous creative and technical resources to community leaders. Research universities with planning programs should take activist roles in helping their communities by supplying the knowledge and assistance that so many disenfranchised groups and organizations need so desperately. As resources become increasingly scarce, new paradigms must be implemented.

The HANDS program emphasized the important role that urban universities can play in partnership with local government private businesses and not-for-profit organizations to address community needs. U of L students involved with the program included representatives from the College of Business and Public Administration's MPA and MBA programs, Kent School of Social Work's MSSW program, the Speed School of Engineering, the School of Law, and the School of Education.

Universities need to have a scholarship, which Ernest Boyer calls an "application" of turning the vast university resources, which are connected to other institutions to help solve the most pressing urban problems of the day. The partnership that the HANDS program facilitated could be a model for the rest of the nation. In some ways, the HANDS project was similar to the agricultural component of traditional land-grant universities that provide state-of-the-art information to farmers or best practices. Universities need to give similar expertise to urban problems.

CHAPTER 4

Urban Revitalization Partnerships:
Perceptions of the University's Role[1]

Inner-city communities have severe problems with crime, homelessness, joblessness, illiteracy, environmental and infrastructure problems, and a host of other challenges. Universities can play important roles in partnership with the public, private, and nonprofit sectors in ameliorating these urban problems. There is not a vast body of literature on university-community partnerships. In fact, there has been little effort to rigorously evaluate the successes and failures of partnership ventures (Harkavy and Wiewel 1995; Nyden and Wiewel 1992). A few efforts have been made to connect with the surrounding community, and hopefully "[t]he ideal of the urban university rolling up its sleeves and getting involved in urban affairs will spread, because it is a tremendous opportunity to deal with real issues, the issues that are on people's minds every day of the year" (Stukel 1994, p. 21). There may be a role for universities to play and potential sources of funding.

Learning from Louisville:
A University-Community Partnership

No systematic evaluation or data set is available to examine the full scope and effectiveness of university involvement in community partnerships as they relate to the three aspects of university life: teaching, research, and service. The following describes reactions to the University of Louisville's HANDS program. It also discusses how these many different viewpoints blended and molded a follow-up program: the SUN program. The U.S. Department of Education and a host of local sponsors funded the HANDS program in 1992. The program included a comprehensive case management system, educational assistance, job, minority contractor, leadership, and home ownership training, community design and urban infrastructure assistance, and evaluation. Students, teachers, and professional staff were joined in this venture. The hope behind the grant was to develop effective

107

"neighborhood revitalization strategies" (Gilderbloom 1992, p. 45). The Russell Neighborhood is one of Louisville's poorest.

Land-use patterns are best described as "mixed." The neighborhood includes single and multifamily residences, commercial and industrial areas, and public uses such as community services and churches. Many structures have been razed, abandoned, or boarded up. Several blocks are without any viable structures. Pawnshops, liquor stores, and taverns abound, whereas supermarkets and pharmacies are nonexistent (Gilderbloom and Mullins 1995, p. 80).

A previous study (Gilderbloom and Wright 1993) discussed the proposed goals and outcomes of the HANDS program. The pages that follow will present the myriad viewpoints and attitudes of various partners representing business, government, community, and the university. Does the university have a role to play in the community? What kind of positive and negative outcomes can result from a university-community partnership? What is the future of university-community partnerships? What works, and what does not work?

Methodology

This was a qualitative case study that examined the effectiveness of a university-community partnership. The interview guide consisted of a mixture of closed-ended and open-ended questions. Broad categories were offered on several questions to facilitate discussion and to simplify analysis. All questions with categorical responses also had an "Other" or "Please Elaborate" section. This allowed the subject to not be confined to the author's perception of an appropriate response. The interviewer was a participant-observer in the HANDS program. His situation was similar to that of Liebow's (1967). The nature of the topic would have made development of all structured, closed-ended questions impractical. Since the scope of partnerships is so broad, it would be extremely difficult to develop a comprehensive list of responses. Interviews were initially requested from thirty-three different individuals. Of that number, twenty-four were interviewed. Interviewees were chosen "based on their knowledge and experience . . . using a purposive itinerary" (Andranovich and Riposa 1993, p. 77). The selected individuals had extensive experience in community partnerships for urban revitalization in Louisville. All were in responsible positions and provided a variety of viewpoints (see Table 4-1).

Actual interview times ranged from as little as twenty minutes to as long as two hours. On average, interviews lasted about one hour. During the interviews, further probing questions were improvised to expand the scope of inquiry or to clarify a subject's response. A few subjects did not have time to be interviewed and provided written responses to the questions on the interview guide. Some telephone follow-ups were necessary to gather further information on these responses.

Table 4-1
Distribution of Interview Subjects among Sectors

Sector	Number of Interviewees [1]
Public [2]	8
Private [3]	5
Nonprofit [4]	6
University [5]	5
Total	24

[1] Interviewees were predominantly male (20 of 24). Two-thirds were white, and the remaining were African American. Approximately one-half were heads of their organizations.
[2] Economic development officials, political appointees, and senior civil servants
[3] Developers, architects, and builders
[4] Primarily developers in 501(c)(3) corporations
[5] Senior administrators, faculty, and researchers

Source: Mullins (1996), p. 102.

Several questions related to university involvement in community partnerships are addressed herein. They include: Why should the university get involved? Who should involve them? What roles can the university play? Where can the university make a contribution? What practical problems arise from university involvement in community partnerships?

Reasons the University Should
Get Involved in Community Partnerships

Three responses were offered to interviewees to start the discussion in this area: academic inquiry, civic responsibility, and institutional survival. This question seeks to get at the underlying reason for a university's involvement with its community. Academic inquiry suggests that this area of applied research is a valid use of faculty and student time. Something will be contributed to the broader knowledge base of urban development, and both faculty and students will benefit from working and gaining experience in this area. Making the community the classroom enables the research to come alive and enhances the teaching and student learning experiences. Academic inquiry was mentioned in many different literature sources as a reason for university involvement in community revitalization (Hackney 1986; Klotsche 1966, Kerr 1968, 1972). The university is a corporate citizen. Civic responsibility and corporate citizenship also were favorites of many writers (Bartelt 1995; Bok 1982; Hall 1989; Ruch and Trani 1995; Wallerstein 1969; Winthrop 1975). Some believe the university has a duty to help institutions and individuals and is born of what Ruch and Trani (1995, p. 231) refer to as the university being not just "in the city, but of the city."

Many urban universities are being increasingly isolated and find that they must participate in partnerships with the surrounding communities if they are to survive, much less prosper, into the future. Marquette (Boyce 1994), Yale (Gilderbloom 1996; Kysiak 1986; Stukel 1994), and Northwestern (Kysiak 1986) are examples of universities concerned about their survival. The interviewees unanimously saw reasons that the university should get involved in community partnerships.

All public and nonprofit sector interviewees mentioned civic responsibility as a reason for university involvement in community partnerships. Most private-sector (four of five) and university (three of five) interviewees mentioned this reason. Academic inquiry was usually mentioned second by the interviewees. Most public-sector (seven of eight) interviewees believed that academic inquiry was a good reason to involve the university in revitalization partnerships. The private (three of five), nonprofit (three of six), and university (three of five) sectors were a bit less enthusiastic. They felt, as did members of the Chicago School of Sociology at the University of Chicago in the late nineteenth and early twentieth centuries (Glaab and Brown 1983, p. 244), that the city was a laboratory for the university, and that it should not turn its back on a marvelous teaching tool and the opportunities it provided.

The most intriguing discussion involved the "institutional survival" response. The response rate was very close to academic inquiry. Several interviewees noted that public and political support for the university would probably increase if members of the community could see it more actively involved with the many challenges facing the city.

Who Should Involve the University in Community Partnerships?

All persons interviewed indicated that they, or their organizations, participated in partnerships for urban revitalization. This reinforces the notion that no single organization can afford to go it alone (U.S. Department of Education 1992; U.S. Department of Housing and Urban Development 1994b; Cisneros 1995). Interviewees were asked to identify the types of organizations that were available to them as project partners. Six categories were most often cited as key organizational partners: business (twenty-two of twenty-four), community development corporations (twenty-two); federal government (twenty-one), state government (twenty-one), local government (twenty-two), and the university (twenty-one).

The university was cited for its twin abilities to access capital sources not available to local groups through large grants and its broad expertise.

Interviewees were asked if they saw a role for the university in community partnerships. The answer was a unanimous, resounding "Yes!" We tried to elicit their view of what entity should take the lead in involving the university. Many respondents said that the answer was situational. Given a particular problem, the lead responsibility could go to any sector. Often it would depend on who had the problem and whether they believed the university could assist in solving it.

An interesting aspect of the data collected is the almost unanimous (twenty-three of twenty-four) view that it is the university's responsibility to take the lead in getting involved. The most delightful result of these data is the response from the university sector, which was unified in its belief that the university had a responsibility to lead in this area. It echoed the thoughts of many in the other sectors, that the university was a starting point for much of the knowledge in the community.

Roles of the University in Community Partnerships

Interviewees' opinions were unanimous in seeing a role for the university in community partnerships for urban revitalization. Their opinions were not unanimous, however, in either the types of roles or the ease of bringing the university into partnerships. The question posed to interviewees was, "What roles do you see for the university in these partnerships?" A number of categories (i.e., facilitator, funding source, leadership, mediator, and technical assistance provider) were provided to structure responses, but there were also several responses that fell into the "Other" category. The most commonly cited roles appropriate for the university were the facilitator and technical assistance ones (see Table 4-2).

Table 4-2
Roles of the University in Community Partnerships

Roles	Number of Responses
Technical assistance	22
Mediator	14
Leadership	18
Funding	15
Facilitator	22

Source: Mullins (1996), p. 123.

The facilitator role was described by Mazey (1995). Briefly, the role of the facilitator is one of an honest broker: an individual whose integrity is unquestioned and who can remain unbiased throughout a decision-making process. Several interviewees indicated that the university's ability to rise above the fray and remain neutral was a key asset. A few, however, disagreed and stated that the university was a political creature and was incapable of rising above local politics. It was mired in the muck.

Technical assistance resulted in the broadest discussion. Most interviewees noted the breadth of expertise of the university's faculty. Assistance can potentially be provided from large urban universities in almost any field, from medicine to engineering to law to the social sciences. Some frustration was expressed over not knowing all that the university could offer or over being unable to access that expertise readily.

The leadership role engendered a great deal of discussion (eighteen of twenty-four). It was the second most cited role by interviewees. There was disagreement over the scope of the leadership role. What most interviewees agreed upon was that the university could provide leadership in keeping the partnership together by acting as a cohesive force. This could be an extension of the facilitative role described earlier. The university's strengths seem to be its ability to deliver expertise and to not engage in the local politics that can fetter the revitalization process. A comment heard from a few of the interviewees involved taking credit for work. They felt strongly that the university should not be concerned about receiving positive publicity or credit for the good that happens. They believed that if university officials focused on successful project completion, then the credit would come.

Areas for University Contributions

Interviewees were provided with a variety of potential responses to the question, "What products do you see the university producing as a member in these partnerships?" Responses provided for interviewees to consider included economic development, grade schools, secondary schools, environmental help, health care, housing, and job training (see Table 4-3). Dr. John Nelson, executive director of the University of Louisville's School of Economic and Public Affairs, pointed out a glaring omission in the choices available in response to the question. He noted that teaching is the university's primary mission.

"The first and foremost product the university produces is students who are prepared to take on real world problems in all of these areas. I would rather have five really great, quality students than hundreds of mediocre ones that can't solve any problems" (Newman 1913; Patton 1995). This response was popular and reflected the university's traditional mission and primary focus.

Economic development was the most common response (sixteen of twenty-four) and reflected a variety of viewpoints. This has been a critical focus of scholars as well. "[W]e lead most industrial democracies in ignorance and in many of the pathologies of modern civilization while lagging behind in the rate of economic progress" (Bok 1990, p. 6).

While mentioned by more than one-half of interviewees, environmental assistance generated very little discussion. Availability of the resource was often mentioned as an asset, but that was all. The students on the HANDS community design team, for example, assisted one nonprofit development corporation in obtaining funds for a housing development. They required an analysis of the environmental setting and an investigation of environmental infrastructure capacity (i.e., storm sewer, sanitary sewer, and water). This vaulted the nonprofit ahead of other groups that did not do the same thorough investigation. The team also prepared conceptual designs and related documents for two urban parks in the Russell Neighborhood. The work had a positive effect on the attitude of residents. Most interviewees did not see a role for the university in elementary (eight of twenty-four) and secondary education (eleven).

Assistance in the housing area was differently focused, depending on the sector responding. The public sector saw opportunities for technical assistance to struggling nonprofit developers (six of eight). Private-sector interests saw the university's contribution being assistance in overcoming regulatory barriers to development with some minor technical assistance (two of five). The nonprofit sector saw the university as a competitor; it did not see a housing role for the university (only two of six). The university saw its role as a combination of technical assistance, administrative coordination, and applying the latest research to these problems (three of five).

Table 4-3
Areas for University Contributions

Area	Number of Responses
Job training	15
Housing	13
Health care	15
Environmental help	13
Secondary education	11
Elementary education	8
Economic development	16

Source: Mullins (1996), p. 128.

Promise and Betrayal

Practical Problems of University
Participation in Community Partnerships

A number of practical problems keep universities, as entities, and individual faculty members from getting involved in community partnerships.

Money as a Limiting Factor

The university, like many other entities, is being pressed to do more with less in a tight fiscal world. The nature of the institution will make a difference in its freedom to use and seek funds. For example, private institutions are under less scrutiny than public colleges and universities. Three sources of funds were provided in the interview guide: grants, partners, and university budget. Of the three primary categories of responses, "grants" was the most favored response (twenty of twenty-four) followed closely by "partners" (nineteen of twenty-four).

Funding was a delicate subject with most of the nonprofit organizations, and it became a turf issue. A serious concern was that the university would compete with them for these local resources, leaving them with few funding options. One interviewee summed up the perceptions of many nonprofits by using the analogy of Wal-Mart and family businesses. A phenomenon that has been observed around the country is the loss of small and family businesses in rural areas when a Wal-Mart locates in the community. The local nonprofit groups fear the same thing from university involvement in their particular niche of the community development business.

One of the canniest responses was self-sustaining ventures. If the institution would adopt a more entrepreneurial approach to its urban revitalization mission, there would be many additional sources of funds. Other schools have spun-off nonprofit (Porter and Sweet 1984) and for-profit (Kysiak 1986) development corporations. The response was positive, under certain conditions. The primary concern of the interviewees was duplication of existing services. Interviewees did not believe that the university should come in and compete with existing organizations, but they did welcome university participation as an equal partner.

Adverse Publicity

In any applied research, there is a possibility that things will not go as intended. This can result in adverse publicity to the academic institution and constitute a mark upon its integrity. It also can have a severe impact on the career prospects of the affected faculty member(s).

In the HANDS project described elsewhere, there was significant adverse publicity in the middle of the second year. The real concern for those who champion university involvement in community partnerships is the possible chilling effect that such critical publicity, whether or not deserved, would have on others considering doing the same type of applied research. As one interviewee put it, "Have you ever heard of a rat swimming toward a sinking ship?" Individual researchers and the institution as a whole must be prepared to cope with the effects of adverse publicity.

Fear of Failure and Lack of Understanding

As Huth noted, "Most experts agree, however, that it takes at least 20 years to effect significant changes in urban development patterns" (1980, p. 118). Knowing that the time horizon to effect change is very long, and that funding to perform applied research is normally obtained for a short period, usually one to three years, many in the academy do not want to take the risk that they will have nothing to show for their investment of time and academic credibility. This credibility is a form of capital that some believe is diminished if the project is considered a failure.

There are potential ethical pitfalls, from the university's perspective, in every community partnership. It has a duty to tell the truth, but when? And how much to tell? The researcher has an obligation to avoid hurting anyone (or any organization) participating in the experiment. In applied research, however, there are failures. If, at a minimum, the results are not made public, then the academic integrity of the institution could be impugned.

Another concern is a lack of understanding by those outside of the academy of the meaning of experimentation and academic integrity. Often the media and the public at large do not value the learning that occurs as a result of failure as much as they value success. As one interviewee put it, the need to be true to scholarly principles can be at odds with political expediency and real-world requirements. Again, the fear of the perception of failure by those outside of the academy, especially on the part of a funding source, keeps many academics from taking a chance on applied research. Even with learning that occurs from failures, there is a concern that a good vita is not built on failures. Scholarly research is much safer, because failure is harder to define and is often described in the journals as merely a path taken that leads to another road ripe for investigation.

University Commitment

A question that many partners can ask concerns the depth of commitment of the university to the revitalization effort. In talking with senior officials at the University of Louisville, the discussion of who has the authority to make a commitment was interesting. The University's power structure is decentralized.

Promise and Betrayal

Actual commitments are not just made by deans and department chairs. Individual faculty members also make commitments. The discussion of what constitutes a commitment also was very interesting. The University of Illinois at Chicago's Great Cities Initiative constituted a university commitment to the community because a "hard" budget line was set up to support the initiative (Stukel 1994). Marquette and Yale universities committed their own funds to community revitalization efforts. In programs such as HANDS, the depth of commitment generally extended to the availability of "soft" grant or nonuniversity source funds. Was HANDS a commitment by the University of Louisville? Yes. But it was not a university-wide commitment.

Benefits of University
Participation in Community Partnerships

Benefits accrue to five different groups: students, faculty, the university, the community as a whole, and the overall body of literature benefiting researchers and practitioners everywhere. A brief discussion of each follows.

One of the beauties of applied research is that it gives students the opportunity to gain real-world experience and to develop skills in their professional practice or enhance their research and writing capabilities. The students working on the HANDS community design team gained valuable platform skills through a number of presentations of master plans, designs, and related products, to city officials, regulators, nonprofit groups, and the public. The project also provided them with funding opportunities and the chance to put what they learned to work. It helped them learn common workplace skills, build a resume, and have the opportunity to publish. Some of the HANDS students used their experience as a springboard for employment in their field, and one student used the contacts he developed to start his own very successful design and development business.

The faculty enjoys a wide range of benefits from this type of research. Funding is often available from nontraditional sources for salary and graduate student supplements. Applied research is grist for a variety of publications to build a faculty member's vita. A downside is that some top-tier publications seem to favor pure versus applied research papers. Community-based research can favorably raise a faculty member's profile with the university's administration.

A university's profile can rise in the community based on the good work done by faculty and students. This can increase public support for the school and improve chances for increased funding by the legislature. The community can receive a number of benefits from the university sharing its energy, expertise, and resources.

Finally, literature grows as a result of this type of research. By sharing both good and bad results, the learning curve of others is reduced, and positive community benefits can accrue faster. Life can get better more quickly by adding knowledge to the body.

Conclusion

The university has a role to play in community partnerships based on feedback from potential partners and on the record of this collaboration. The most and least attractive aspects of these partnerships follow.

Most Attractive Aspects

The university has the potential to provide resources, highly skilled faculty and staff, and assistance in other forms. The energy, creativity, and dedication of students can be a tremendous asset—overcoming a lack of training or skills that they may bring to a particular task. Some felt that the University of Louisville's willingness to get involved in community issues was very attractive. One individual said that the University's involvement in some areas had secondary and tertiary benefits that were not readily discernible by everyone. This person used the example of the HANDS community design team's work with a nonprofit developer, saying that the University's work in researching the design and development approval processes, providing example reports that had been approved by regulatory authorities, and so on was transferred to work for a separate, church-based community development corporation. Without the community design team's work, the time and cost to get it into construction would have been much greater.

Several individuals, particularly in the private and nonprofit sectors, discussed the advantages of obtaining no-cost assistance from the University. When they did not have to buy a service, it lowered their cost of doing business, made them more competitive, lowered barriers to entry into markets, and leveraged their resources to allow them to engage in projects that they might not otherwise entertain. For nonprofits, this involved projects they could not afford to do because of a lack of resources. For the private entities, University assistance allowed them to participate in projects that would not otherwise be profitable or fiscally attractive. This provides development opportunities for neighborhoods that might not otherwise qualify for them.

From the University's perspective, some of the commonly discussed benefits of participating in partnerships included providing opportunities for students and faculty to be involved with practical work, garnering goodwill in the community, getting positive publicity, creating public and political support for the institution as a whole, and causing funds to flow to the University to support a variety of programs. One senior University of Louisville administrator said: "[Participating in community partnerships] causes the general public to want to continue investing in the University of Louisville. It broadens our base of support." There was also a practical aspect of University involvement in these partnerships. Often, external "soft" funding is generated that allows the university to write down overhead costs, expand the scope of academic services by reallocating existing "hard" budget dollars, and expand the scope of academic inquiry by providing support to research that would not be attractive to external funding sources.

Least Attractive Aspects

Some people felt that there was no downside to the University's involvement in community partnerships. Others, however, had at least one item they believed could be improved upon. One individual, speaking about the University of Louisville, summarized the thoughts of a few others by saying that "the University does not know how to be a partner and is not responsive to its customers." As one individual said: "If you think you know it all, you don't need to ask."

One of the University's strengths is also its weakness in the eyes of potential partners. In the pragmatic world of community development, "too much focus on academic endeavors can be frustrating," said a Louisville development authority official. A companion comment, particularly from private-sector interviewees, concerned the bureaucracy or "red tape" associated with accessing University resources. Many felt that there was a queue and no consideration for the cost associated with waiting for someone to help.

Another pragmatic concern dealt with personnel turnover. Many praised student involvement because of the creativity and energy students brought to development projects. The flip side of the student coin is the length of time that students are available to work on a project. By the time they understand the process and are beginning to be effective, they are lost to graduation, the end of the semester, or another pursuit. This results in a loss of continuity and a lower level of service delivery.

Many mentioned concerns with University personnel being "too egotistic and media hungry." In this same vein, there were concerns that University personnel were playing politics and trying to improve their personal situation at the expense of projects or the people to be served. Some faculty members noted that the University tenure and rewards systems do not encourage individuals to get involved in the community.

Despite some of the aforementioned challenges, there are a lot of winners from this kind of research. Applied research enhances the teaching, research, and service aspects of a university's life, making better students and communities.

Reactions from National and Community Advisory Committees

As discussed in chapter 2, two groups were established to provide on going advice to the HANDS program, the Community Advisory Committee and the National Advisory Committee. The former was comprised of neighborhood residents, community leaders, and former HANDS clients who worked with staff to identify the needs and problems of residents and to assess planned program strategies and directions. In two separate visits, in teams of two, the latter offered advice and counsel to improve the HANDS programs.

Don Terner, a member of the HANDS National Advisory Team, stated in his evaluation:

> I was most favorably impressed with the HANDS program. It appears to be precedent setting in many ways, and I hope it can become a model for other communities and universities to adopt, including many of our own out here in California.
>
> Many political leaders and policy experts think that revitalizing inner city neighborhoods is an almost impossible task. Yet the HANDS program appears to provide an innovative model for how this can be done. As you have demonstrated, urban universities have a wide variety of technical resources, which can be effectively utilized to help solve many of our urban problems. I was particularly impressed with the various HANDS program components in community design, home ownership, case management, and education. The individuals involved appear to be talented and committed, and the various programs seemed to provide a real contribution to both the non-profit community development corporation (CDC) in the Russell Neighborhood and to the City of Louisville Housing and Urban Development Department (see Appendix A).

The project, and its activities, has been dedicated to the empowerment of the community. Its goal is to continue to assist the community in defining, articulating, and prioritizing neighborhood problems and solutions. The community development component and master planning efforts, as guided by the central involvement of the Community Advisory Committee, ensured the integration and coordination of the various components toward the realization of a shared community vision. The input of the National Advisory Committee and the wide-ranging expertise of the University provided a means for bringing fresh new ideas, perspective, and potential solutions to the neighborhood level. In conjunction with the practical know-how, financial experience, contributions, and investment of its partners, the HANDS program provided not only long-term confidence in the community but also some of the means and practical steps necessary to ensure the implementation of the shared vision.

The HANDS project received a great deal of national attention as a humanistic model for rebuilding the lives and neighborhoods of inner-city residents. Former President Clinton recognized this public-private partnership that worked to transform a distressed inner-city neighborhood. In his remarks before the U.S. Conference of Mayors (carried live on CNN and C-SPAN), Clinton pointed to the Russell Neighborhood in Louisville, Kentucky, as a model for revitalizing an impoverished neighborhood. He added that Russell demonstrates that tough situations can be turned around and commented that elsewhere HANDS is just the kind of comprehensive, community-based partnership effort that his administration was trying to stimulate in distressed communities across the country. Clinton also commented that he was convinced that the most effective ideas for local economic renewal come from the communities themselves. Partnerships such as the HANDS project that brought all community sectors together (state and local governments, businesses, universities, nonprofits, and community-based institutions and residents) around a comprehensive vision for change are critical in helping distressed communities join the economic mainstream. Similar praise for this unique and innovative public-private partnership also has come from former Vice President Albert Gore.

CHAPTER 5

The Urban University in the Community:
The Role of Boards and Presidents[1]

Colleges and universities are increasingly important partners in urban re-vitalization programs. While much good can come of these university-commu-nity partnerships, results to date generally have been inconsistent and marked by distrust or disinterest. While universities are seeking a role, they are unsure of what communities need or want. Moreover, despite a broad range of univer-sity-community involvement programs, there has been little agreement on who should be involved to ensure success, what their roles and responsibilities should be, and what the impact on the community could and should be.

In May 1995, the Association of Governing Boards of Universities and Colleges (AGB) hosted a roundtable discussion addressing these concerns. This chapter summarizes the discussion.

As many of the nation's inner cities continue to decline, taxpayers are be-coming increasingly frustrated by the lack of results produced by money spent on urban problems. The realities of scarce resources and increasing social prob-lems are becoming more apparent. The challenge facing the nation has become how to balance the competing demands of fostering an equitable society while running an efficient government.

Academics and community leaders alike are asking if the university can and should be a player in solving our most pressing urban problems. All too often, urban colleges and universities have grown and prospered by their acad-emic reputation, while their surrounding communities have suffered decline. It is as if the university and the city have been on separate tracks, their futures in-dependent of one another. As the late Ernest Boyer (1990) documented, the uni-versity has too frequently turned inward, focusing on research that has little use for the urban community at large.

Universities must now reverse their historically insular behavior by looking outward and developing a comprehensive strategy to address urban conditions.

121

More attention should be placed on teaching partnership strategies, faculty team-work, and community service. Students should have the opportunity for hands-on community service before they enter the job market. Young scholars should be encouraged to celebrate cultural diversity through action, not instruction. When these types of actions are taken, universities can play important roles in partnership with the public, private, and nonprofit sectors. As James J. Stukel, president of the University of Illinois System and former chancellor of the University of Illinois at Chicago, writes:

> The ideal of the urban university rolling up its sleeves and getting involved in urban affairs will spread, because it is a tremendous opportunity to deal with real issues—crime, taxes, the economy, and elementary and secondary education, the issues that are on people's minds every day of the year. This will generate public and political support, which will be increasingly necessary in this era of diminishing resources. And it will actually be doing some good for this country. (Stukel 1994, p. 21)

This is not to suggest that universities can, like superheroes, descend into disastrous circumstances and provide instant solutions. Rather, the coupling of fiscal austerity and increasing social challenges demands the creation of new paradigms. And a new paradigm of university involvement will hinge on the university's ability to ask how it can most effectively marshal its rich human resources and move from the ivory tower to confront the harsh realities of the streets. From these questions, appropriate and responsible actions can follow.

Historical Precedents

University involvement in addressing public issues is not a new idea. In the 1900s, Catholic and Jesuit schools played a role in serving the needs of the urban poor. Forty years ago, President Lyndon B. Johnson presented his vision of university-community partnerships in a speech at the opening of the University of California, Irvine. Recognizing that the twentieth century was witness to the transformation of the nation from a rural to an urban society, Johnson argued that universities should try to provide answers to the pressing problems of the cities "just as our colleges and universities changed the future of our farms a century ago. . . . Why not [create] an urban extension service, operated by universities across the country and similar to the Agricultural Extension

Service that assists rural areas?" (Klotsche 1966, p. 51). Six months later, Johnson urged Congress and universities to replicate the success in helping farmers by addressing the needs of the city. Klotsche describes the vision underlying this initiative:

> The role of the university must extend beyond the ordinary extension-type operation. Its research findings and talents must be made available to the community. Faculty must be called upon for consulting activities. Pilot projects, seminars, conferences, TV programs, and task forces drawing on many departments of the university should be brought into play. (Klotsche 1966, p. 60)

The ensuing period saw the development of many creative, bold, and innovative university-community partnerships. These efforts, however, had mixed results. Cities continued to be overwhelmed by a wide range of social, political, and economic forces, many of which remain to this day.

The Importance of a Comprehensive Urban Mission

As much of the literature on poverty indicates (Gilderbloom and Appelbaum 1988), urban issues are complex and interdependent. Because of this, initiatives that are not comprehensive in scope do little more than provide temporary relief. Recent federal programs support such comprehensive initiatives. These programs recommit the federal government as a central player in facilitating urban-university partnerships; they include HUD's Community Outreach Partnership Centers and Joint Community Development Program and the U.S. Department of Education's Urban Community Service Grant Program. Even though the future funding of these federal programs is uncertain, the programs have the potential to create sustainable relationships at the local level and to be more than just another Band-Aid placed on social problems.

With or without federal support and involvement, evidence suggests that increasing numbers of urban colleges and universities are willing to reexamine their missions and societal roles. Many are actively revitalizing relationships with their communities. Others are sharing ideas and models through such conferences and organizations as the Coalition of Urban and Metropolitan Universities. And others, which may not reside in an urban area but carry a statewide mission, are rethinking their responsibilities to major cities of the state.

Institutions with comprehensive urban missions should focus a significant portion of their teaching, research, and service efforts on the problems of their host cities. Many of these efforts include faculty research and the provision of technical expertise; some provide direct faculty and student service to the community. As Donald C. Swain, then president of the University of Louisville, said in his spring of 1995 farewell address to the university community:

> A comprehensive urban mission might consist of partnerships for attacking unemployment and housing shortages in low-income neighborhoods, and for economic development and technical assistance to small and minority-owned businesses. It might include relationships with local health care providers to improve the health care of the elderly and underprivileged, and with the local school system to improve the curriculum, supplement in-service training of teachers and school administrators, and provide mentoring by tenured faculty in specific academic disciplines.

A comprehensive urban mission will have an ongoing student community service and internship effort; programs for working with at-risk youth on issues of job training, self-esteem, drug abuse prevention, summer recreation and employment, and tutoring; and programs for working with city government and community leaders in low-income areas on neighborhood revitalization. The mission also may include the education of urban students. Admitting and graduating large numbers of inner-city students—many of them nontraditional, part time, or adults who are not able to relocate to find better jobs—is critical. Recognizing the obligation to prepare new generations of urban leaders to become teachers, officeholders, and organization heads, as well as to fill all kinds of other roles in the city, is part of the educational mission of an urban college or university.

The mission also may include the role of "corporate partner." This may mean that the university is one of the community's largest employers, is a developer of city improvement projects, is a planner of research parks to spur economic development with local manufacturing and high-tech industries, or works with not-for-profit or for-profit companies to ensure viable university health clinics and teaching hospitals. Finally, the mission may entail service to city government agencies for economic planning and research, analysis of crime statistics, evaluation of city services, or similar activities.

Before a university or college can embark on a new or an enhanced initiative or a university-community partnership, and before such partnerships can be fully realized, a number of major policy issues need to be debated by governing boards. Should the institutional mission be examined? What are the costs associated with community partnerships? How can the external urban environment be assessed? These and other policy issues are explored.

The Importance of Community Partnerships

Charles Ruch, president of Boise State University in Idaho, notes that "the interaction [between the university and community] should be mutually reinforcing, guided by institutional choice and strategy on the part of both parties, and viewed to be one of value and importance" (Ruch and Trani 1995). While this notion seems simple enough, it is complicated by the fact that each party typically has different customers, agendas, time lines and motivations. Even within the confines of the university, the roles of the president, the board, and the administrative and academic officers must be coordinated to produce a viable and realistic partnership between the urban university and the community in which it resides.

Furthermore, discussions of university-community partnerships frequently fail to recognize distinctions among the many different types of post-secondary institutions. Large multi-campus universities, junior colleges, private colleges, and research institutions all have different missions and ways of operating. When viewed as separate entities, the types of partnerships that are feasible and desirable under each type of structural arrangement can be addressed. Similarly, it is important to realize that relationships between universities and the communities in which they are located vary considerably from one place to another. Each community has its own specific set of needs and unique history and culture. In addition, universities have different amounts and kinds of resources and capacities. Without a clear vision that takes all of these factors into account, an urban mission will be fraught with ambiguity, and partnerships specifically tailored for a given community cannot be developed.

Each college and university first must address the nature of its own urban environment and determine how that environment relates to the campus. In so doing, it should not view cities as totally impaired or dysfunctional entities. Even with their multitude of problems, urban areas are still vibrant communities. They have much to offer as economic and cultural centers, and universities can benefit from their resources in very practical ways. As Wim Wiewel of the University of Illinois at Chicago writes in personal correspondence:

> If it is only from a sense of noblesse oblige that colleges and universities commence an urban agenda, their efforts will be viewed by their cities as condescending and fall short. Communities, even poor ones, are places of ethnic pride and heritage, of culture and art, of safety and acculturation, of creativity and vitality of political strength and resistance. If communities are only viewed as places of problems, what can they offer the university? In fact, problem definition, identification of solutions, implementation, and evaluation all have to be done jointly, because there is knowledge in the community that is different from, but

complementary to, the knowledge that universities have. (Gilderbloom 1996, p. 9)

Recognition that the relationship is indeed a two-way street provides further rationale for the establishment of partnerships. One of the AGB roundtable participants, Michael Garanzini, vice president for academic affairs of St. Louis University, pointed out that the university is a permanent part of the city: its fate is tied to the fate of the city, and it does not have the option of leaving, as a business or a corporation might.

Some universities have been forced into community partnerships purely out of a need for survival. Racial unrest, rioting, high crime, or a shocking murder in the surrounding community can devastate a university. These problems create the necessity for partnerships to help a community with innovative, responsive, and pragmatic programs. Without these vital partnerships, the fate of both the university and the community would be in peril.

The issue of institutional survival, described briefly in the last chapter, also depends in part on where students come from and where they go after graduation. Urban universities that attract mostly local students who remain in the community may be more motivated by practical reasons to forge partnerships than universities without a largely local student body. In tight-knit communities, it may be possible to create a symbiotic relationship between the university and community.

Institutional Leadership:
The Roles of Presidents and Governing Boards

College and university presidents and their governing boards must be agents of change, establishing and implementing policies that enable institutions to develop and strengthen university-community partnerships. They must provide the resources and incentives to move in the desired direction if an urban mission is to be more than rhetoric.

The President

The president has the largest role in a college or university in seeing that existing partnerships are continued, new ones are initiated, and success is rewarded. The role of the president is perhaps best addressed in the context of vision and leadership. Presidents set the direction in which their universities will change and grow. They do this through both their verbal messages and actions. As chief spokesperson for the institution, what a president says commands a great deal of attention. Speeches that are not backed up by commitment and substantive action—even when they are well intentioned—will make creating inroads into the community more difficult in the future. Unfulfilled promises undermine the element of trust that must be present if partnerships are to achieve their maximum potential. The transition from rhetoric to action, however, can be a difficult course to negotiate.

Fear of controversy may make some university presidents more reluctant to enter into new relationships and to assume new roles for themselves and the university. Presidents have many internal and external constituencies, and the risks associated with taking action on an issue (be the action substantive or symbolic) can disrupt a base of support and thus result in a reluctance to act. Addressing a major social problem in the community carries the risk of being unsuccessful and the added risk of damaged relations with the community. And even if an initiative is successful, community groups and city leaders may feel that their domain has been invaded. Universities also may have to contend with the criticism of community groups that were not brought into partnership roles.

Despite these constraints, university presidents must persuade others, and be convinced, that partnership efforts can strengthen their institutions. For example, the late Daniel H. Perlman, former president of Suffolk University, suggested a range of symbolic and substantive functions that university presidents can undertake to help build solid relations with a predominately minority community:

> By inviting the leaders of the various ethnic and racial minority communities to visit the campus and speak to student groups, by encouraging the parents and families of current and prospective minority students to visit the campus and share in the celebration of special holidays and festivals, by meeting with minority business groups and hiring their members, by becoming personally visible in the minority communities, and by showing that cultural diversity is not only tolerated but actively encouraged and cherished, presidents of metropolitan universities can promote a climate that will enhance the effectiveness of their institutions both in their function as neighbor, employer, and consumer. (Johnson and Bell 1995, p. 208)

Presidents at successful urban institutions have built ongoing, trusting relationships with city governments, communities, and business leaders. They meet frequently to discuss issues of mutual concern, such as community health care, crime, job training, and so forth. If such a forum did not exist when they arrived at the institution, they took steps to initiate informal meetings with these leaders. As part of these discussions, the role of the university as a service provider and resource to the community is explored.

Within the institution, the president must first assess the institutional mission to determine whether it clearly articulates the institution's desire to create urban partnerships. If it falls short or requires expansion, then the president must work with the board to see that it is revised. As the chief executive officer of the university, the president must next persuade and encourage deans, department chairs, and faculty to be responsive to community concerns. This may entail a change in the faculty reward structure; it also entails the encouragement of interdepartmental initiatives, interdisciplinary approaches, and a transdisciplinary approach, a bringing together of combinations of departments that might not otherwise communicate or cooperate with one another. This work is particularly important in dealing with multifaceted urban issues that cut across a wide spectrum of disciplines. Affordable housing can and should involve, for example, law, sociology, social work, architecture, and planning.

Regardless of the level of formal partnerships, faculty at urban-based institutions will have a number of points of contact and natural relationships with various elements of the community in such disciplines as education, business, social work, and community health. Just as the board must support the president in his or her efforts to build partnerships with the community, the president (and other senior academic administrators) must show support for these faculty members by meeting with them periodically to understand the issues they face and the relationships they have developed through their research and public service, and by working on meaningful expansion or replication of their efforts.

A president must determine the budget implications of new or potential partnerships and must advocate the funding needs of their institutions not only to the governing board but also to the governor, legislature, and other state boards and officials. Effective leadership will result if the president and governing board can work cooperatively.

It is critical that presidents bring before the board the policy options related to the institution's partnership program, and that the board support the president in the realization of the program once a policy is established. When boards are clear about the meaning of an urban mission, then the president will be better able to take meaningful action.

The Governing Board

If university-community partnerships are to last and succeed, then governing boards must play an enhanced role. Governing boards shoulder the immense responsibility of shaping institutions and their values. They must do this while maintaining fiscal discipline, raising funds, and fostering institutional growth and creativity. These various tasks position boards between the demands of the public, their founders, elected leaders, or other institutional stake-holders and the needs and desires of university administrators, faculty, staff, and students. Boards must play pivotal roles in pushing the administration to articulate and pursue an urban mission. However, some people assert that trustees and regents may be insulated from the very issues that serve as the im-petus for the creation of collaborative partnerships. This concern may be par-ticularly true for large multi-campus system boards (and less true for community college boards) that may not focus on the issues confronting their urban campuses. It also may apply to institutions whose board members typi-cally reside far from the city or outside of the state and who come to campus only for board meetings. Such institutions are missing valuable opportunities. As Joseph Harris of the National Center for Urban Partnerships said at the roundtable:

> There's a gap in the knowledge base of trustees—and very often [of] presidents—in terms of what is their role, what is their responsibility, when it comes to responding to their environment. (Gilderbloom 1996, p. 11)

POLICY ISSUES FOR GOVERNING BOARDS

In addition to a positive working relationship with the president, boards of trustees must be informed and aware of the policy issues involved in urban partnerships before they can develop a clear sense of how to proceed. What are the issues that boards and presidents together must consider? What questions should boards ask?

MISSION STATEMENTS

Surprisingly, only 12 percent of the urban universities have a mission statement that addresses urban needs (AASCU 1995). If fundamental change in the way universities relate to their communities is to occur, then an appro-priate place to begin is with institutional mission statements. With a mission statement that clearly articulates the institutional commitment to its host city, a college or university can begin to play a significant role in helping its com-munity understand and combat urban problems. During a period of con-strained resources and insistent demands for educational quality, many trustees may ask whether it is wise to expand the institutional mission to in-clude the community, or if it is better to concentrate on liberal arts education, teacher education, graduate education, or whatever the institution does, or should be doing, best.

Without question, institutions must be true to their primary mission. An urban mission can be an outgrowth of an institution's primary mission, but it can never drive it. Boards also must ensure that institutional ideals are not compromised—the education of their students and the collection, dissemination, and advancement of knowledge.

Whether its mission or reputation is regional, national, or international, an institution cannot allow assistance to its host city to drain resources or divide the university's attention. By planning strategically, boards can develop a commitment to the city without jeopardizing their institution's ideals, primary mission, or reputation. The following examples of board-approved urban mission statements from the University of Louisville and the University of Houston system demonstrate such commitments.

THE UNIVERSITY OF LOUISVILLE. The University of Louisville (U of L) serves as Kentucky's urban-metropolitan university. Located in the Commonwealth's largest metropolitan area, it shall serve the specific educational, intellectual, cultural, service, and research needs of a diverse population, including many ethnic minorities and place-bound, part-time, nontraditional students. The U of L is a research university that places special emphasis on the research and service needs of Kentucky's urban areas. Research is encouraged, in particular, as part of doctoral and high-priority programs. Through its research and service efforts, it contributes to economic development, educational reform, and problem-solving initiatives in the Commonwealth.

THE UNIVERSITY OF HOUSTON SYSTEM. The future of our state and nation depends as never before on the integrity of our cities—on their ability to forge a productive and integrated society, to provide an acceptable quality of life and standard of living, and to compete in global markets. As a consequence, a new imperative emerges for higher education, and the urban university takes on an unprecedented role in meeting the challenges of the future.

Driven by this imperative are the four universities of the University of Houston system. We attribute much of our structure and character to the people, institutions, and energy of urban life. We define ourselves not in isolated "academic" terms but in terms of the social and economic complexity of the city, and we are committed to developing and sharing our intellectual resources with the communities from which we draw our strength and purpose. This does not mean that we in any way jeopardize the core values and freedoms of the academy or compromise exacting standards of excellence. We steadfastly refuse to reduce the pursuits of intellect to mere utility or the academy to a service organization whose agenda is set by others. Instead, our task is to reawaken public consciousness in order to focus on pressing problems and challenges that we cannot solve alone but, equally true, cannot be solved without us.

OTHER POLICY ISSUES

While clarification of the mission is a critical beginning, many other policy issues also require board consideration, as follows:

HOW DO WE ASSESS THE GENERAL NATURE OF THE URBAN ENVIRONMENT AROUND THE CAMPUS? An occasional (perhaps annual) board meeting in the community with community leaders as guests can give the board a better understanding of and appreciation for the environment around the campus. If a number of students are from the community, the board could invite them to speak at a board meeting. Many faculty members probably have a community relationship for certain activities, and they, too, should be heard by the board.

WHAT ARE THE COSTS OF DEVELOPING PARTNERSHIPS? ARE PARTNERSHIPS SUSTAINABLE IN THE LONG RUN AFTER INITIAL FUNDING OR COMMITMENT DECLINES? The board is responsible for ensuring adequate resources to carry out the institutional mission, including aspects that apply to community partnership programs. Revising or expanding the mission will be meaningless unless dollars are placed behind it. The board and the president must determine which partnerships must be initiated, which sustained, and which terminated. Government and private support can underwrite the university's involvement with the city, but such funding is never guaranteed. Various departments or faculty members involved in partnerships may vie for the board's attention, and the board may need to develop priorities to help determine which program deserves greater funding. For example, board priorities may reward those programs serving the city's neediest, those serving the surrounding neighborhood, or those where the institution may have the largest impact. Long-term commitments to the idea of partnerships also may require a reallocation of internal funds as external funding ends. Although it may be very difficult for the board to do, a budget reallocation is always an option.

WHAT HAVE WE LEARNED FROM PAST EXPERIENCE IN WORKING WITH THE CITY? Many universities engaged in successful partnerships have realized that no single institution can turn around the inner city by itself. Other entities must be equal partners with the university in this effort. In some instances, this may require the resources and coordination of others, forcing the university to limit its role to that of a facilitator or broker. This realization is perhaps a change from the idealism of the 1960s and 1970s, when many felt universities could practically single-handedly solve urban problems with the aid of targeted federal money.

University leaders also may find that some entities, rather than collaborate, play political games because of power, status, money, or other concerns, and that it may be difficult to build bridges to particular groups. Universities must bring an honest and objective viewpoint to the table and in so doing must become an effective interface between the community and government.

It is critical for boards and presidents to learn from the experiences of other institutions in other cities. The most pressing problems of the inner city may appear overwhelming, the odds for meaningful change too remote, or the environment too unsafe to risk university money or personnel. Institutions seeking to engage in an urban mission may want to start in incremental ways and build a more comprehensive program later. They may wish to focus on one segment of the population, or they may wish to work with locally owned businesses—perhaps creating a "business incubator" that provides financing or consulting and technical assistance for economic development.

WITH WHOM SHOULD THE INSTITUTION COLLABORATE? Collaboration will depend on which activities are pursued and where a board believes its institution can make a difference. Boards should expect the administration to develop a plan that includes neighborhood groups (including organizations that represent the racial and ethnic diversity of the city), city government, the school system, local businesses and corporations, and possibly labor unions and not-for-profit organizations. Urban land-grant institutions also may collaborate with the cooperative extension service. Joining or forming a consortium with other universities in the metropolitan area may be desirable.

DOES THE INSTITUTION HAVE POLITICAL STRENGTHS AND CONTACTS THAT CAN HELP IT CREATE EFFECTIVE PARTNERSHIPS? It is in tackling this question that individual board members may be helpful to the full board, using their contacts with city, state, and federal government leaders either for resources or to cut through red tape. Trustees who are members of the community can serve as individual bridges to that community, perhaps through service on other community boards or through business links with the community.

IN WHAT PARTNERSHIPS ARE WE NOW ENGAGED? ARE THEY ALL THEY COULD BE? The board must have a full understanding of its institution's academic departments and be aware of the activities in which it is currently engaged. To gain an understanding of the potential of partnerships, boards may want to seek information on departments with natural links to the community (through social work, education, and urban studies, for example) or other programs with required student internship and practicum experience. Not to be overlooked are professional schools such as business, law, and medicine, which may be servicing hundreds of poor clients every year.

An institution developing a comprehensive urban mission, or at least a mission active on many fronts, attempts to bring visibility and support to these current activities and sees what can be learned from them. It also tries to see what university-wide partnerships can be initiated. As former Harvard University President Derek Bok (1996) notes, "The problem is that the whole often fails to equal the sum of its parts. Because no one knows what others are doing, important opportunities for collaboration and synergy are lost."

How Can A Coordinated Institution-wide Strategy Be Developed? The decision of where to locate partnerships within the university is more than just a question of logistics. The placement of an office can sometimes reflect stature. For example, an office located within the president's office may connote that a particular function is of special importance to the administration. The placement of an office also has important implications for the direction and control of the partnership.

The board, together with the president, is responsible for determining the priority given to the partnership initiative by approving and funding the partnership office. Some would argue that since the university is opening itself up for increased scrutiny when it enters into new relationships with the community, the partnership should be coordinated out of the offices of the president or senior administration. Others would argue that one who is actually on the "front line" (such as a faculty member) should direct the activities of the office. In any case, faculty expertise should be at the fingertips of the person staffing a coordinated strategy.

Where Are Our Students and Faculty in Terms of Commitment to the Community? What Is the Reward Structure for Faculty? Zelda Gamson (1995) of the University of Massachusetts at Boston, writing on the issue of community responsibilities of faculty, remarks, "For years, academic leaders . . . have argued that higher education has to become more engaged with societal issues. Student service barely scratches the surface. We need the expertise and involvement of our faculties if we are to make a difference." Changing faculty contracts to delineate community service as a requirement and a basis for evaluation may be a means to achieve the goal of increased faculty participation in community partnerships. After all, what gets measured gets done. The reward and incentive structure is critical within institutions with an urban mission. This important issue, as well as student community service, is addressed later.

CAN THE MEMBERSHIP OR STRUCTURE OF THE BOARD BETTER REFLECT THE NEEDS OF THE INSTITUTION? It is a challenge for board members who reside out of state or outside of the city to develop a full sense of the urban environment in which their institution is located beyond quick impressions and anecdotes. At one extreme are boards of prestigious independent institutions whose members find it understandably difficult to devote time and effort to potential or existing university partnership opportunities. In these cases, it is incumbent upon the university's president and senior administration to educate the board, and for board members themselves to commit time to staying in the city an extra day or afternoon to learn of institutional initiatives or community needs. Such boards may be served best by appointing a board subcommittee or task force—with members drawn from faculty, staff, and community leadership as well as from the board itself—to address the issues at hand. The board also may want to consider appointing one or two local community leaders as regular or ex-officio members of the board.

At the other extreme are boards that may be composed totally of members from the community. A community college president once warned that such a board must not become a "Trojan horse" for the desires of the community, that is, it must not see itself as a vehicle to carry all of the needs and concerns of the community to be suddenly unleashed on the president in the public forum of a board meeting. Even if chosen in a popular election, board members must understand that their duty is to balance equally the needs of the community with those of the institution.

The membership of most boards will fall in between these two extremes, with a balance of local membership and statewide or national membership. Public boards appointed by the governor should appeal for an appropriate balance of community and state leaders.

HOW DOES THE BOARD MEASURE SUCCESS? Evaluation should not be an afterthought. Each partnership program should have goals and objectives that attempt to improve the quality of life for the community that the program is designed to serve. The board should expect data that document the results of such programs so it can determine which programs to continue to fund or support in other ways. Progress within programs that address major social issues will be incremental at best. Also, the definition of success is more complicated in the field than in the laboratory. The definition of success often might depend more on the eye of the beholder than on any specific objective measure. One university reported, for example, in working with underachieving youth, that test scores were raised considerably but not enough to be considered "passing." Is this a success or a failure?

Politics also may affect evaluation. A change in city administration may have an influence over what types of information an agency is willing to collect and turn over to university evaluators. Tangential benefits from community-partnership programs also will occur for students and faculty involved in community service; these should be welcomed and acknowledged by the board.

SPECIAL CONSIDERATIONS FOR PUBLIC MULTI-CAMPUS GOVERNING BOARDS

State boards must assess their own track records to see how they encourage or discourage college and university participation in community partnerships. First, there should be an explicit expectation of an urban mission for either the system or its urban institutions. The University of Houston system statement is truly exemplary. It is from an agreed-upon mission statement and strategic plan that all activities flow.

Multi-campus system boards must serve simultaneously as the governing board for the system as well as for each component institution—admittedly a difficult assignment, especially in a system that may have both a long-established, well-regarded flagship university and a newer and less prestigious urban university vying for limited resources. System boards must strive to balance these tensions while seeking consistency in critical policy decisions, such as the distribution of academic programs and the allocation of dollars among institutions. The boards can accomplish this by educating themselves on the issues of their urban campuses so they are in a position to support and advocate urban campus needs adequately. When the board has a meeting on the campus, it should devote some time to understanding the urban environment by visiting the site of a partnership activity. Also, if there is no urban university in the system, or if urban areas are underserved, the board should ensure that one of its institution's missions extend (within reason) to major cities of the state.

A multi-campus board should consider the creation of a local governing or advisory board for its urban campus or campuses, especially if the system comprises institutions in various parts of the state. Local boards can help focus system board attention on local concerns while serving as a bridge to the community. Because local boards may serve many functions, institutional and system leaders must be careful that such boards never become captive to any local constituency. It is best if local boards are appointed with prescribed authority from the system board.

Multi-campus boards (and state coordinating boards as well) should set different and flexible expectations for faculty. System boards should ensure that faculty-reward structures at their urban campuses adequately recognize applied research and service to the community. Such guidelines may need to be different from those of other institutions in the system.

Similarly, expectations and performance evaluations of urban college presidents must take into consideration the job's unique requirements. Urban universities within multi-campus systems, or under statewide coordinating agencies with budget allocation authority, must be granted a level of flexibility in their budgeting process. Just as land-grant institutions need resources for outreach to rural communities, resource allocations that differ from preset funding formulas may be needed to establish or maintain incentives for community partnership activities.

Issues Related to Institutional Change

Universities cannot ignore the clamor of businesses that want college graduates retrained to maximize their effectiveness as employees. Nor can they ignore the value of research applied to community problems or the need for graduate students (who will become the faculty members of the future) to be trained in nontraditional ways to encourage creative contemplation of expanded functions of the university. Therefore, the curriculum must include the many lessons that currently are offered through partnership initiatives. Dissertation research in many fields should be directed toward more practical problems. Faculty and staff involved in community service must bring their experiences into the classroom. The traditional "teach and research" paradigm too often gives short shrift to public and community service. Other issues have been identified concerning the current training of researchers that need to be addressed. Christina Croark and Robert McCall (1996, p. 21) argue that talent, competence, trust, and respect are essential ingredients of effective collaborations. According to them, however,

> These requirements are often antithetical to the way we train researchers, for example, who typically are taught to work independently, to maintain control over every aspect of the research enterprise, and to achieve within a profession that rewards individual productivity and contribution.

In an interview on university-community partnerships, McCall, co-director of the University of Pittsburgh's Office of Child Development and Policy Evaluation Project, said, "We need to broaden our student audience beyond those enrolled in our classes and our scholarly audience beyond our academic colleagues. Our academic reward structure should encourage applied scholarship and education, broadly defined, on a par with basic, empirical research" (Gilberbloom 1996, p. 17). Similarly, Ernest Boyer (1992) argues that standards for measuring faculty scholarship must now include the potential application for meeting pressing societal problems.

Creating Incentives for Faculty

One of the biggest obstacles to successful community partnerships is the lack of expectations, rewards, and incentives for faculty. Derek Bok (1996) writes: "[O]nly if collaboration with the city is seen as part of one's professional development will such work survive and prosper. But even the most committed universities have often found this hard to do." Partnerships, community service, and applied research can be promoted by considering them more often when making tenure, promotion, and faculty contract decisions, and university presidents and governing boards can directly influence this process. To do so, however, requires an understanding of the issue.

The phrase "publish or perish" is all too familiar to those in and around academic circles. According to a national survey of faculty conducted by the Carnegie Foundation for the Advancement of Teaching, the granting of tenure has become increasingly dependent on publications over the last twenty-five years. The implications of this criterion for survival make applied research less attractive to researchers: since applied research is not as "clean" as controlled experimental research, it tends to be devalued by academic journals. In the worst-case scenario, meaningful research is sacrificed in the name of scientific excellence. Recent advances in the fields of research methods and policy evaluation have helped bring social research to more respectable levels in the academic community. Nevertheless, in university settings where tenure and promotion are dependent on publication, applied research is a risky route. Given the demanding and difficult nature of applied research, the most talented researchers should be engaged in it. Unless the reward structure is changed, however, many will be reluctant to spend their time doing applied research in the community.

Institutions also have been slow to develop criteria by which to rate community service. In a recent survey of 186 members of the American Association of State Colleges and Universities and the National Association of State Universities and Land Grant Colleges, more than a quarter of the respondents cited lack of recognition of community service as a scholarly activity as a significant barrier to meeting a metropolitan-urban mission (AASCU 1995).

The issue of the reward system as it applies to public service also is complicated by the fact that some fields lend themselves to community service more readily than do others. Institutions that are primarily research oriented may fear that changing the reward structure will drive away valuable researchers and weaken the organization's overall level of quality. Where to draw boundaries over what is acceptable public service is not always an easy call to make. Too often, faculty service is defined as internal department or committee work, and not service to the surrounding community. And while student community service and service learning are encouraged and supported by the faculty, the need to engage faculty as more than just facilitators of students—especially those who teach within communities with dire needs—has never been greater.

Boards and presidents of urban institutions have begun to see how university-wide expectations can be integrated into college and department expectations and the reward structure adjusted accordingly so that applied research and community service become explicit requirements for contract renewal, tenure, promotion, and post-tenure review. Department reward structures need not be monolithic; rather, they should recognize the differences among academic fields and even among individual faculty members within disciplines. In such a flexible system, fields that lend themselves to partnerships, public service, and applied research on community problems can be identified, and fields needing more "traditional" reward structures still can attract quality faculty. Diamond and Brownwyn (1993) have written extensively on the principles and practicalities of flexible faculty reward systems that urban institutions should examine.

Although the biggest incentive for involving faculty in appropriate community partnerships may be through reward structures for tenure and promotion, another way is to offer budgetary incentives. Such incentives can be created (in keeping with institutional and board priorities) within the university by the governing board. For an urban institution, this could be competitive grants or matching-challenge grants within departments as financial rewards for individual faculty. The University of Minnesota, for example, solicits requests for proposals from faculty members to conduct policy research on the pressing needs of the Twin Cities area. Selected proposals offer two-months' salary plus a part-time graduate research assistant for the year as support for carrying out the project. Dennis Jones (1995), president of the National Center for Higher Education Management Systems, has prescribed how governing boards can develop incentives within the budget through a process called "strategic budgeting." The principles and procedures of strategic budgeting are easily adaptable to urban institutions.

The Emergence of Service-Learning and Student Community Service

Campus Compact, Campus Outreach Opportunity League (COOL), the Partnership for Service Learning, and the Corporation for National and Community Service have placed student community service and service learning on the front burner for many institutions. Service learning has many benefits for community organizations. Students are working and providing needed assistance to the community in the name of the institution while obtaining the spiritual benefits that come from helping others along the way.

The involvement of universities in community partnerships gives students an opportunity to test the theories and techniques that are presented in their course work. The urban environment can be an effective classroom. Fieldwork offers students valuable lessons they can use later. In a conversation on the Internet, David Moore, from the University of New Orleans commented:

> Having given graduate students the opportunity to work in "cancer alley" has opened their eyes to a lot of issues and resulted in a deeper understanding of environmental justice. I have personally witnessed this initial work turn into a passion in one individual who I am sure will have an impact on the movement, (Gilderbloom 1996, p. 19)

Students are often on the front lines of many of the partnership activities of their institutions. They perform many of the actual activities that partnerships are formed to do, such as student teaching, helping staff a health clinic, or assisting on a demographic study, for example. Although students are invaluable to successful partnerships, there are three inherent dangers to avoid. First, students must not just "front" for the institution—that is, perform the bulk of the partnership activity—while faculty and other institutional administrators sit back disengaged from any meaningful level of community involvement. The second concern involves adequate safety precautions for the students who serve and the served, including institutional liability. Institutions must do their best to ensure that they are not jeopardizing students' well-being by placing them in unsafe situations or placing them in situations that require a higher level of competence than they currently possess. The third concern, raised by Nevin Brown, regards the nature of students' time commitments at a university. As Brown remarked, "In a long-term collaborative effort, students may come and go. This can take a toll in the development of long-term, personal, collegial relationships that often are critical to the success of the partnership" (Gilderbloom 1996, p. 19).

Barriers to Successful Partnerships

Several types of barriers affecting an institution's urban partnership need to be continually evaluated and discussed at the policy level by the board and president. Tensions between various community players can be detrimental to the success of partnership initiatives. For example, when a university is formulating a plan for grant dissemination among community organizations, it must be aware of the political consequences of excluding certain groups from the allocation. Another unfortunate aspect of partnerships involves the other end of the project—when success is achieved and disagreement erupts over who should get the credit.

Universities cannot force their way into the community; they must be invited. Buy-in costs frequently are associated with working with long-standing community groups, and inconsistent behavior by a university drives up these costs. Charitable acts and temporary "do-good" programs are not the foundation of durable relationships or the sign of a comprehensive strategy developed by the president and the governing board; they only serve to open the door.

Many barriers to success are rooted in mistrust of universities. Government institutions at the local, state, and federal levels, as well as quasi-public agencies and not-for-profit organizations, have set patterns for functioning in relation to one another. Some localities resist the entrance of universities into partnership roles for fear of upsetting the balance among existing players. Institutions need to be sensitive not to intrude upon already existing and effective partnerships. If a university has not previously demonstrated a commitment to the city, then community groups may mistrust the institution's motives. They may question whether the participation of university faculty would impede or duplicate work performed by private consultants or other paid employees. In a climate of scarce resources, some community organizations may fear that universities will infringe upon their base of financial support. This fear may be substantiated by the fact that many university-sponsored community initiatives frequently require matching funds from community organizations. Thus university and community entities may find themselves competing for the same funding sources.

Stereotypes and preconceived notions may hamper effective communication. For example, academics may be viewed as egotistical or out of touch with real-world conditions, and government employees may be victims of "bureaucrat bashing."

Symbolic partnerships such as blood drives, book collections, and delivering meals to the elderly offer little risk to either partner. If they fall apart, little is lost. It is the substantive partnerships such as discovering the causes of homelessness or creating jobs or affordable housing that are high-risk ventures—particularly for the university. Something more precious than money or resources is involved in its failure. The university risks its prestige and preeminent position in the community if the project fails.

One of the greatest strengths that many university programs provide might also be the most serious problem hindering these programs: partnership.

As related in this book, partnerships rely on a fragile coalition for continuity and accomplishment. If the coalition falters, then the program may falter as well. The involved parties must provide the partnership with constant nurturing to keep it vital, active, and responsive to the needs of the community and its residents.

Conclusion

As difficult as the current fiscal, social, and political environment is for our cities, it may become more problematic in the future. New fiscal pressures on cities are a certainty due to constrained local, state, and federal budgets and the potential major restructuring of such federal programs as Aid to Families with Dependent Children and Medicaid and other programs such as job training. The added fiscal pressures may, in turn, exacerbate current social problems.

Universities cannot physically flee the cities. They are part of the community infrastructure. But being a permanent part of the community carries an obligation to interact with the city and the surrounding neighborhoods. The boards and presidents of urban universities and colleges must lead their institutions into an appropriate level of community involvement, an involvement based on expanded notions of traditional educational missions and purposes that will be sustained through fiscal cycles and political change.

Universities and colleges generally command great public respect. They can bring ideas framed in the context of objective truths and moral persuasion, and they can take risks that others might try to avoid. Governing boards at all urban colleges and universities need to engage in a full discussion of the policy issues involved in developing university-community partnerships to help clarify what may or may not work for their particular institution. These partnerships are risky undertakings that can result in symbolic or substantive gains for the community at large or in failure and controversy. But by developing such partnerships, colleges and universities can turn the ivory tower into a bridge to the community.

CHAPTER 6

A Model for University-Community Partnerships

Introduction

Universities have not been key players in most community revitalization partnerships. As discussed earlier, the academy has much to offer the community in its efforts to move from despair to hope. The following discussion of the partnership process provides examples of how to assemble partnerships.

Creating a Community Partnership

The days of massive investments of federal funds in our inner cities are gone. The U.S. Treasury is broke (again) after the brief surpluses of the late 1990s disappeared, and there is little hope that the extensive urban spending of the 1960s and 1970s will ever be seen again. Our urban problems are worsening. Infrastructure continues to decay. New capital investment is primarily going to the satellite suburbs, where there is a greater return on investment.

Trying to reverse this decline is a formidable challenge. Residents of a neighborhood do not have the resources to revitalize the neighborhood themselves. In fact, there is no single person or organization with either the financial resources or the will to complete all tasks attendant to the physical revitalization of the neighborhood. Residents must turn to a variety of sources for the capital and expertise needed to rebuild their neighborhood.

Residents try to identify all of the individuals and organizations with the potential to contribute to their revitalization effort and then seek to draw them into an arrangement that will benefit all parties. The university can provide this coordinating function by acting as a facilitator (Mazey 1995). This is the heart of a leveraging strategy, a partnership. If the neighborhood can obtain some initial capital and leverage that investment through its partnership network, then the results of that investment can be multiplied many times.

One of the biggest problems in developing a community partnership is determining the nature and extent of the community. This is what Bengtson, Grigsby, Corry, and Hruby call the "classic dilemma of grassroots politics: What is the community, and how does one determine who represents it? If one particular group is recognized as being representative, is there not a risk of alienating several others?" (1977, p. 82).

Who Can Participate in the Partnership?

Partnership members can come from within the community or from outside of the community. For example, partners can come from all levels of government (i.e., federal, state, county, or city) and can include members of the business community (i.e., banks, small businesses, large corporations, etc.). Other organizations that can make significant contributions include nonprofit service delivery organizations and community development corporations. Nontraditional members can include the education establishment in the community from the public schools up through the colleges and universities in the area.

Each partner brings its own expertise to bear on the problems of the neighborhood. That is why there is no single list of partnership members to address the varied problems confronting our cities today. Within the loose affiliation of different individuals and organizations, there will be many partnerships working to solve the problems that they are best capable of handling.

Potential Partners for Revitalization

Many different organizations can participate in partnership efforts for urban revitalization. They have been classified into six categories: government, businesses, nonprofits, foundations, educational institutions, and residents. Each of these categories of potential partners is discussed later. This is not intended to be an all-inclusive list. In addition, there are no guarantees that any organization will participate in a particular project.

In order to make this realistic, example agencies from Louisville and Jefferson County, Kentucky, were used. Based on experiences in other cities, each jurisdiction has a counterpart organization that performs the functions ascribed by the various organizations discussed.

Government

Many people look at government agencies as obstacles, something to be overcome rather than an agency to work with, use as a resource, or learn from about matters under their purview. A number of different government partners can be approached for participation in partnership efforts. Representative agencies follow.

FEDERAL GOVERNMENT

There are several grant-making agencies within the federal government that can provide funding for revitalization efforts. Most federal agencies do not provide expertise. Their focus is on grant programs authorized by the U.S. Congress.

In the area of physical development, the most likely source of funds is the U.S. Department of HUD. HUD grant programs are announced on the Federal Business Opportunities (FedBizOpps) Web site. Most grant opportunities through HUD will either have to go through a nonprofit development corporation, a state or local government, or a college or university. One of these types of organizations will be a crucial member of the partnership *if* federal funds are a key part of the partnership's success.

Other agencies make grants or provide low-interest loans to various groups. They include the U.S. Department of Agriculture (not too likely in an urban area, but it does have specialized programs that touch on urban issues), the U.S. Department of Commerce, the Department of Defense (if a military installation is located in the area), the U.S. Department of Education, the U.S. Department of Energy (if there is such a facility in the area), the U.S. Environmental Protection Agency, the U.S. Department of the Interior, the U.S. Department of Transportation, the Small Business Administration, the Department of Homeland Security for specialized areas and, of course, the U.S. Congress. While senators or Congressional representatives are unlikely to provide direct funding for a revitalization effort, they can open the door to a multitude of opportunities.

STATE GOVERNMENT

Like the federal government, the state has a number of grant-making programs. In addition, many agencies provide specialized expertise when it is needed. Among the organizations that can help in a revitalization effort are the Bureau for Social Services, the Department of Agriculture, the Human Resources Cabinet, the Kentucky Army National Guard, the Kentucky Business Enterprises, the Kentucky Historical Society, the Natural Resources and Environmental Protection Cabinet, and the Transportation Cabinet.

Consider this example. A neighborhood group is contemplating a development project in a historic area designated under the provisions of Section 106 of the National Historic Preservation Act of 1966. The state historic preservation officer (SHPO) and/or the Advisory Council on Historic Preservation (ACHP) in Washington must approve its plans. In Kentucky, the ACHP delegated project approval authority to the SHPO at the Kentucky Historical Society. In Louisville, the SHPO works closely with the Louisville Development Authority (described in the following section).

LOCAL GOVERNMENT

Many local resources are available from local government. In the Louisville metropolitan area, there was concurrent jurisdiction for some issues between the city of Louisville and Jefferson County. In January 2003, the city and county merged into a metropolitan government. It is unclear how this will affect all of the agencies described next, but the functions will remain somewhere in the metro government structure, even if the names change. Support can be available from both the elected officials and from the civil service sector. The following list is not meant to be exhaustive but will provide an idea of the types of assistance available for development projects.

BOARD OF ZONING ADJUSTMENT (BOZA).

The BOZA is an arm of the planning commission. It is empowered to make decisions affecting the zoning and use of various properties. It can change the zoning and/or use of a particular lot or plat, add conditions to the rezoning, or disapprove the proposal. It is important to understand the board's priorities and concerns *before* making a proposal. The best approach is to work with the staff to ensure that their concerns are addressed prior to presentation to the board.

HOUSING AUTHORITY OF LOUISVILLE (HAL)

If the proposed redevelopment project will impact on public housing in the city of Louisville, the HAL must be consulted.

HOUSING AND URBAN DEVELOPMENT (HUD)

This agency performs a number of valuable services for developers. It contains the land bank for the city. It can make property available for less than market rates. It also can provide funds for other city agencies, such as the city engineer, to perform services that can reduce the cost of development. For example, if funds are available and the project meets the goals of HUD, it can direct the city engineer to prepare lot surveys, conduct traffic studies and analyses, and perform design and even construction services on city-owned properties. These can then be blended with a developer's project in a variety of ways to enhance the value of the combined development.

INSPECTIONS, LICENSES, AND PERMITS

Before a project can be constructed in the city, a variety of permits may be required. It is best to contact this department to understand the regulatory "hoops" that an organization will be required to jump through on the way to project completion. If the project does not meet the requirements of this agency, it could be stopped. A work stoppage can impact on not just public perceptions of the sponsoring organization as a service provider but also could endanger continued funding and support for the project.

LOUISVILLE DEVELOPMENT AUTHORITY (LDA)

The LDA is a multifaceted agency that is an invaluable resource to the prospective developer, especially if the project is located in an urban renewal area or a historic district (as described earlier). If the property is in an urban renewal area, then permission to develop must be obtained from the approved developer, or approved developer designation must be sought from the Urban Renewal Commission. The commission relies to a great extent on the recommendations of its staff, and the staff is located in the LDA. The developer should visit with the staff to gain a complete understanding of the designation process.

If a project is in a historic district, the developer must consult with the Urban Design Division of the LDA, which will work with the developer and the SHPO to ensure that all plans are compatible with the neighborhood and meet any guidelines that have been established for the development area. It has a good understanding of what the SHPO will approve and is willing to provide advice and support to design efforts within the limits of available staff resources.

LOUISVILLE AND JEFFERSON COUNTY PLANNING COMMISSION

This is a body with broad powers over land use in Jefferson County. Most small development decisions will go before the BOZA, an arm of the planning commission, described earlier.

LOUISVILLE AND JEFFERSON COUNTY OFFICE FOR ECONOMIC DEVELOPMENT

This joint city-county organization provides a variety of services to existing and new businesses. It provides information on the business climate, where and how to access capital for expansion, opportunities for investment, and so on. Again, it is very willing to help support revitalization efforts with advice, analysis, and guidance.

PLANNING AND ENVIRONMENTAL MANAGEMENT DEPARTMENT

This Jefferson County agency oversees a wide variety of services, particularly relating to planning and development, as well as to zoning and related issues.

PUBLIC WORKS AND COMMUNITY DEVELOPMENT DEPARTMENT

This Jefferson County agency is responsible for the broad spectrum of transportation, infrastructure, and community development issues in Jefferson County outside of the city of Louisville.

PUBLIC WORKS DEPARTMENT

This city agency contains the office of the city engineer as well as a number of other functions for the local government. It is available for consultation on a number of development issues, particularly as they impact on transportation and related infrastructure issues in the city. It performs a number of assessments for executive and legislative officials on the impacts of proposals that are being made by different developers. It also provides support to other agencies, such as HUD, on a reimbursable basis. At HUD's direction, public works has hired architect/engineer contractors to design neighborhood improvements and later constructed them in consonance with the plans of developers because they furthered an important government interest.

Businesses

A variety of businesses is involved in neighborhood revitalization efforts. The most common partners include banks, realty companies, small builders, and several different size developers.

ARCHITECT/ENGINEER (A/E) CONTRACTORS

A/E contractors typically provide most of the technical expertise for physical development projects. They can prepare master development plans, budgetary and bidding construction cost estimates, and construction documents (plans and specifications) and can provide construction management services. They are vital to the development effort and should be brought in at the earliest time.

BANKS

Banks often have community relation officers or a department devoted to community-oriented investing. These offices administer many different programs, including low-interest HUD rehabilitation and construction loans, below-market loans from other sources, or in-house products to assist developers with their efforts.

BUILDERS AND DEVELOPERS

Builders and developers can be found in both the for-profit and nonprofit sectors. There are advantages to having both types of organizations involved in a project. For-profit organizations tend to be larger, have significant lines of credit, and have access to lower-cost suppliers. Nonprofit organizations have access to special-rate financing that for-profit organizations cannot touch. Together they can create a strong partnership to renew the neighborhood.

REALTY COMPANIES

Realty companies typically perform work at their market rates but can provide lower rates when there is a package or block of properties to be marketed. Their efforts are not limited to selling property. They can also perform market analyses to determine the sizes and types of houses that can profitably be sold in the area. Negotiations should focus on what is advantageous to both organizations.

Nonprofits

A number of different nonprofit entities can play a role in helping a partnership's revitalization efforts. Some are traditional, while others are not. A brief list of potential nonprofit partners follows.

CHURCHES

These are the most powerful groups in the nonprofit world not because of their size, capital assets, or expertise but because of their beliefs. Undercapitalized believers can make things happen when the best-financed organizations cannot. Some inner-city churches are forming nonprofit community development corporations (CDC) as part of their outreach and service programs. In Louisville, St. Stephen and Canaan Christian, both African-American churches, have organized CDCs.

COMMUNITY CENTERS

These centers can be affiliated with churches or with other nonprofit organizations. Their missions can vary widely. They may be able to provide services ranging from child care to education programs to micro-business loans, to name a few. The Louisville Central Community Center and Plymouth Community Center, both in the Russell Neighborhood, provide a wide range of human services. If a community center is located in the project area, discuss the types of services it offers and determine whether or not it can make a contribution to the partnership.

COMMUNITY DEVELOPMENT CORPORATIONS (CDCS)

CDCs are nonprofit organizations. Their missions generally include housing and economic development. Most CDCs are cash poor and project oriented in the Louisville area. In other large metropolitan areas, CDCs do housing, business development, job training, and land development, manage large apartment complexes, and provide a host of social services. They can access pools of below-market-rate financing that for-profit organizations cannot. If the CDC in the project area does not presently provide some of the services needed for this project, it does not mean that it cannot provide the services later.

UNIONS

Many people forget that unions have much to offer in the area of revitalization. In addition to apprenticeship programs to provide job training and work experience for residents, unions also control vast amounts of funds through their pension plans. These plans can be a source of financing for revitalization efforts if it is to the union's advantage to work with the developer on the project. If partnership contractors are union shops or agree to enter into a wage agreement with the unions, then partial or complete financing may be available from the union's pension fund.

Foundations

Foundations do not normally provide expertise to the development effort. Rather, they tend to provide funding within the constraints of their bylaws or charters. Many different types of foundations fund community development activities. Some foundations specialize in a particular area (e.g., the Lila Wallace-Reader's Digest Foundation's Urban Parks Initiative). Others fund a variety of programs. Good sources of information include the *Annual Register of*

Grant Support and the *Foundations Index*. These and other foundation resources are available through local and university libraries and provide information on contacts, addresses, requirements, geographic scope, application formats, and so on.

Most foundations will not fund an entire initiative, but they will provide partial funding or challenge funding (i.e., they will pledge some amount of funding if the partnership can raise a specified amount from other sources).

Educational Institutions

A variety of educational institutions can help an organization achieve its objectives. It requires a great deal of investigation to determine the types and availability of services from educational institutions. Services can be acquired from secondary schools, colleges and universities, and technical schools.

Secondary schools may be able to help with literacy programs, assisting adults in acquiring GED certificates and providing specialized vocational training and a number of other services. For example, if a vocational program is training people for apprenticeship programs in the construction trades, then the partnership may be able to provide real-life training opportunities for these students and obtain reduced-rate labor.

Colleges and universities offer a variety of internships and practicums for their students. If the project's needs coincide with projected student placements, and the partnership is willing to provide the needed supervision, then college students can be a source of energetic, enthusiastic, and inexpensive assistance. Faculty also can provide assistance.

Technical schools also have a need to provide their students with "real-life" experience that makes their graduates more attractive to potential employers. If some part of a project will require skills available from this type of school, then contact the school and see what you can work out. It will also be a resume builder for the student. Again, these students can be a source of good, yet inexpensive, help.

Residents

Residents are the most undervalued assets in any revitalization effort, and they have the greatest stake in the success of the effort! Many skills can be found among neighborhood residents. Either through a case management process, marketing, or other means, partners can find a wealth of talent right in the neighborhood, catalogue it, and maintain contact with people who can contribute later on. A periodic newsletter is a good, inexpensive means of doing this.

Tying the Pieces Together

How does the partnership actually get the people or organizations to come together? How does it make the contacts? The following is a brief description of one approach (see Figure 6-1).

First, partnership members must clearly and concisely define the problem that they are trying to solve and the project that they are proposing to fix the problem. They must put this in writing along with any background data that are needed. Members should be able to summarize the project on a one-page fact sheet.

Second, a list should be developed of all potential people or organizations that project partners believe could be part of this partnership. In addition, they should try to determine the benefit(s) that could accrue to that person or organization. This is important because one of the basic tenets of interpersonal relations is that people, and organizations, participate in ventures in order to derive some benefit. This is not mercenary; it is human nature. There are many types of benefits—some monetary, some altruistic, and some spiritual. Before approaching a potential partner, the organizers should answer this fundamental question: "What benefit will this person (or organization) derive from participating in this partnership?" If the group cannot come up with some potential benefits, then it is unlikely that it can sell new partners on participating in the program.

Now the problem has been defined, and a list of potential partners has been developed that can help solve it. Start approaching the partners. Initial contacts can be made in any number of ways. The HANDS community design team found that one effective method is to send a brief letter of introduction to the responsible official to describe the problem, the proposed project, and why the potential partner's participation is vital to the project's success. Let this person know that a team member will follow up in one week to set up an appointment to discuss the project. If the team does not want money from the organization, then this should be stated.

When setting up the appointment, limit the initial contact to thirty minutes. Walk in with a structured agenda and a brief presentation covering the proposal. Be incisive. Be confident. Be thorough. Get a point of contact, and ask for referrals to others who might make good partners.

Follow up with a thank-you letter, and then start pursuing the organization's or person's participation in earnest with the appropriate point of contact. Set up a detailed schedule for project completion, and then implement it. Partners respect professional project execution.

Keep the partners interested, informed, and involved, even when they are not directly acting at the time. This can be done through periodic progress reports, newsletters, update briefings, and so on. A partner's interest must not wane during its idle periods.

Figure 6-1
Flowchart on Partnership Development

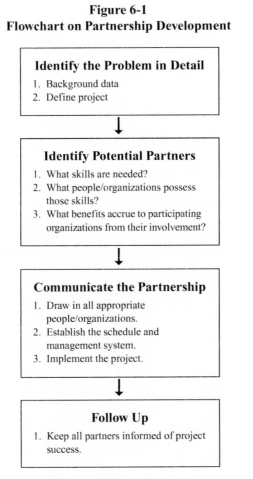

Identify the Problem in Detail
1. Background data
2. Define project

Identify Potential Partners
1. What skills are needed?
2. What people/organizations possess those skills?
3. What benefits accrue to participating organizations from their involvement?

Communicate the Partnership
1. Draw in all appropriate people/organizations.
2. Establish the schedule and management system.
3. Implement the project.

Follow Up
1. Keep all partners informed of project success.

Source: Mullins (1996), p. 168

Sample Typology for Partnerships

One of the greatest strengths of small, community-based programs may be their most serious problem: the partnership. The HANDS project, for example, relied on a fragile coalition for continuity and accomplishment. If the coalition falters, then the program may falter as well. Failure can come from a loss of resources or commitment, or from a loss of stature by a partner that affects its standing (and power base) in the neighborhood. Constant nurturing is needed by the parties to keep the partnership vital, active, and responsive to the needs of the neighborhood and its residents. A fundamental question concerns how one assesses a potential partner for an urban revitalization effort. Based on our research and the literature, we offer the following model as a starting point for future efforts (see Figure 6-2).

Figure 6-2
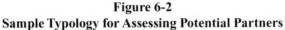
Sample Typology for Assessing Potential Partners

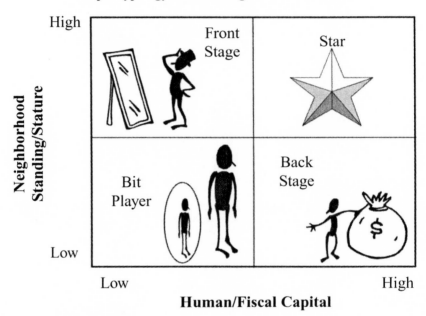

Source: Mullins (1996), p. 195.

The assumption underlying this model is that a good neighborhood revitalization partner is a function of its stature in the community and its resources, both human and fiscal. Another important dimension is the depth of commitment to the partnership. An assumption implicit in this model is that a "Star" will be committed to any effort it undertakes to maintain its standing in the neighborhood and high rate of return to maintain its fiscal resources. It could be stated as follows:

A Good Partner = f (Stature in Neighborhood, Capital/Resources)

Another concern with this type of model is the potential for gross over-simplification of complex interrelationships and ties among people and institutions. While this is a valid concern, this model is offered as a guidepost. This model does have explanatory power for what was observed in the Louisville revitalization partnership. In addition, it can be generalized for community partnerships across the nation.

Why should this model work? Let's examine it quadrant by quadrant. The "Bit Player" quadrant has low resources and little community stature. While an organization in this area would not be sought as a main player, it may be able to provide some small service to fill a special need. Generally, this type of player would approach the partners rather than be approached.

The "Backstage Player" is crucial. Capek and Gilderbloom (1992) discuss the backstage of politics and its role in community action, which may bring a lot of resources to the table but may not have much stature in the neighborhood. A university could easily fall into this category if it was working outside of its immediate vicinity, as was the University of Louisville in the HANDS and SUN portions of the Russell Partnership. The goal for this type of organization is to bring the fiscal and human resources necessary to make the partnership work, while not seeking to raise its visibility. As one senior U of L administrator stated, the university should be content to take credit in the coin of its realm—scholarly articles and the like.

The "Front-Stage Player" is necessary. It has a high profile and can provide an entrée into the community for the players who will make it happen. It can be the coordinator and provide dispute resolution services. In the HANDS and SUN portions of the Russell Partnership, the Louisville Central Development Corporation filled this role.

The "Star" is the ideal entity. It enjoys high status in the neighborhood and has the capital to make things happen. Louisville does not really have that kind of organization. Looking elsewhere, the New Community Corporation in Newark, New Jersey, is the type of organization that combines the best of both worlds. It is in the neighborhood, having risen from a small neighborhood group, and it now has the financial resources to significantly improve its locale.

What Should the Large Funders Change?

After an examination of the literature and working through the HANDS and SUN programs, things should change in the way in which large funders such as the U.S. Department of Education, the U.S. Department of Housing and Urban Development, and large private foundations dole out their funds. They need to focus their funds on the programs that are proven to work. However, it seems that many failed or failing programs continue to attract funding. The reasons are many and varied—from slick packaging to politics to lack of knowledge about what really does and does not work.

It seems that many of the human services programs that are implemented without a corresponding change in the neighborhood infrastructure are ineffective uses of funds. There is little measurable return on investment. Even if the programs were successful without the infrastructure upgrade, the residents would move out because the area would offer nothing to keep them in their new socioeconomic state. All that has done is further concentrate the truly poverty stricken in an area without hope. "To break the cycle of poverty, we need to address housing first" (Garr 1995, p. 76). An initial investment in upgrading housing, security, the physical environment, and making the area attractive to lower-middle and middle-class families is needed before true change occurs. "After a critical mass of new middle-class residents has been created at the center, growth will feed on itself." (Grigsby and Corl 1983, p. 91).

Conclusion

In programs such as HANDS and SUN, the university has been a player. It is making a difference in its community. As Peter Hall (1989 p. 282) noted, "Given a challenge of that order, there is not much justification for continuing to stand on the academic sidelines."

The University of Louisville, unlike Marquette, Yale, and Northwestern Universities, did not confine its activities to immediately adjacent geographic areas. It leapfrogged adjacent areas to help serve those with the greatest need. A further difference between the U of L's activities and those of Marquette, Yale, and Northwestern is that its future will not really be affected by the success or failure of the Russell Neighborhood. Its adjacent neighborhood, Old Louisville, is thriving having seen a great deal of investment to upgrade grand old houses and commercial structures. The University of Illinois at Chicago is taking the same approach of leapfrogging to those in greatest need through their university-community partnerships. The ultimate success of these partnerships will be measured in the future prosperity of these areas rather than in the mountain of reports being prepared today. Houses, jobs, and safe streets will be the true measure of success. Time will tell.

CHAPTER 7

Betrayal by the Universities

Universities can do a lot in their respective communities, but few really do. That is what we mean by "promise and betrayal" by our universities. The promise is great. Few of our nation's universities perform substantive community building. In 1992, approximately 100 out of 3,650 higher education institutions applied for the $1.5 million U.S. Department of Education Urban Community Service grants. Less than 200 universities received HUD Community Outreach Partnership grants. Traditionally, universities avoid substantive involvement in inner cities because success is difficult. Yet if universities are so knowledgeable, then one wonders why many surrounding neighborhoods of those institutions are filled with hopelessness and despair.

In ten years of community building in Louisville and elsewhere, we found that most academics fail to address, much less solve, inner-city problems. Conventional wisdom denotes that academicians miss the dynamics of the problem and fail to grasp the dynamics of gatekeepers, bureaucrats, and elected leaders that sociologist Max Weber discussed.

The public and private partnerships in the Russell Neighborhood in Louisville, Kentucky, are some of the most successful revitalization efforts in the country. The Russell Partnership is a progressive collaboration involving the University of Louisville's HANDS and successor SUN programs; local businesses; federal, state, and city governments; foundations and philanthropic groups; and community and not-for-profit organizations. The initiative incorporated holistic approach that addresses human, economic, and community development through case management, job training and creation, education, home ownership, community leadership, and community design services. "New urbanism" principles were introduced (Katz 1994). Houses were designed with porches, so that more eyes could be on the streets and alleys. The historic Victorian structures, magnet schools, YMCA, and library made the area suitable for gentfrication. People could walk to Louisville's downtown area, only five to ten blocks away.

Most "experts" believed that nothing could be done to change this inner-city neighborhood until a unique partnership was forged. In fact, several respected affordable housing advocates attempted to stop the University from assembling a $3.5 million federal grant package along with another $1.5 million in local non-federal support to facilitate the university-community partnership. They condemned the project before it even began with a letter to the University and subsequent letters to newspaper reporters, arguing that it was more sizzle than meat. The actions of these organizations were perhaps the most surprising, disappointing, and shocking part of leading a university-community partnership. The actions of these "gatekeepers" often are contrary to their stated goals. This is what sociologists call "goal displacement," where increasing affordable housing in the community is replaced by maintaining the funding, positions, and jobs of organizations by making sure that competing organizations are not successful. This is somewhat reminiscent of how certain organizations conduct business—cut us into the action, or we will cut you out. Before these programs came into existence, black and basement nonprofits did not have the capacity building or technical assistance to be successful. The HANDS and SUN programs changed that by making it possible for these groups to use approved drawings and guidance in getting necessary approvals. This created a whole lot of activity, competition, and homes.

Despite this work in a poor black neighborhood, assistance to black organizations, and with several gifted African-American faculty and graduate students who were part of the HANDS and SUN teams, two black leaders also attacked the programs privately. One made the false charge that the SUN program was taking "blood samples" from African Americans in the community and that program funding should be reviewed. This charge was derailed after a meeting with black leaders, and an apology was made. Another black leader was enraged when the HANDS project ended funding for a program that had only a few participants, while that organization proclaimed an enrollment of twenty-five students. This leader went to the president's office and claimed that the HANDS program was racist and that the University should cease its support. The claim was made that the program was treating residents like lab rats—giving aid to some and refusing it to others. It was more like giving assistance to effective and accountable organizations and ignoring sloppy, ineffective, and tired organizations.

The role of community gatekeepers is vastly underestimated in scholarly literature. In fact, it is nearly invisible. But it may be a big reason poor neighborhoods stay poor—because of middle-class gatekeepers who block and disrupt efforts that can cause meaningful change.

It also is this kind of backstage politics (Capek and Gilderbloom 1992) that pushes universities away from partnerships in poor neighborhoods. These programs demonstrate that whites and blacks working together from the neutral ground of the university can be effective. Good work trumps racism, gatekeepers, and bad press. One foundation stated that it was giving the SUN program money because it was still standing after taking so many punches and kicks.

The Russell Neighborhood is experiencing a revival. New houses have started going up there. Most of the houses resemble many of the older 100-year-old shotgun and camelback homes. With land donated from the city, and utilizing efficient stick-built design technology, hundreds of single-family houses have gone up in a neighborhood that for decades had no new construction and very few permits for remodeling. Moreover, the partnership helped renovate a boarded-up 1960s style housing project into an attractive, accessible, and affordable development of 500 units. It is estimated that over 600 housing units will be built in Muhammad Ali's old neighborhood. Many of these homes (three small bedrooms with one bathroom) were originally priced in the mid-1990s at around $49,000 to $55,000 with a soft second mortgage to encourage long-term commitment. Now these houses are being put back onto the market and being resold for $85,000 or more. For these urban pioneers, the houses they bought are real wealth generators, doubling in value in five years. Small businesses are starting to take root. A ten-screen movie theatre has been built. A once-abandoned shopping center is now filled with businesses. Banks are building new branches in Russell. A large, three-story African-American history museum is planned to occupy a historic trolley barn in the neighborhood. A once-down-and-out soul food restaurant has become one of the most popular restaurants in downtown Louisville. Nearby grocery stores are turning into supermarkets with prices comparable to suburban stores. Crime has fallen. Many of the pawnshops have closed down. Drug dealing and prostitution have dramatically decreased. Many of the crack houses have been closed down. Street gangs are no longer prevalent.

Individuals are restoring their neighborhood, their lives, and their dignity. And they are doing it themselves. The Russell Partnership is facilitating this revival. It is making tomorrow a source of hope rather than despair. Momentum is being fueled by citizen participation. For example, a fifty-seven-year-old grandmother is buying her first home; a homeless person now has a job and is continuing her education; and an older woman is teaching new generations of African-American children the meaning of pride and self-esteem. These success stories are being woven into the fabric of a new neighborhood. The Russell Partnership is a model that can teach the rest of the nation how to rebuild blighted inner-city neighborhoods. It is an excellent example of a university-community partnership.

Neighborhood residents, in concert with others in the community, reached out and formed a partnership with those who could help resurrect their neighborhood. The individuals working in the coalition believe that they have the power to make a difference and find, through themselves or their partners, people who can wield the necessary power to carry out their plans. Their plans are being developed and carried out by University of Louisville graduate students in the Urban and Public Affairs Department, with assistance from the University of Kentucky School of Architecture and other interested parties in the neighborhood. Russell demonstrates that if it can happen in what was once one of America's most desolate neighborhoods, it can happen anywhere.

While the success has been unprecedented, efforts are now being made to encourage more new urbanism concepts. East Russell remains 97 percent black. Black leaders had hoped to attract whites to achieve greater integration. On the upside, more working- and middle-class residents have moved back into Russell. In fact, even some rich families have built $400,000 houses. One-way streets had turned the neighborhood into the Indianapolis Motor Speedway during rush hour, but traffic calming techniques are being introduced, and certain streets will be converted to two-way. Bike lanes are being added, and hundreds of trees are being planted. These new urbanism concepts (Katz 1994) will raise the value of housing by reducing crime and creating a greater "wellness."

Some believe this may have happened without the partnership. But if this is so, why have the other historic neighborhoods surrounding the downtown seen so little change? It is about leadership, innovation, partnerships, and passion. East Russell had one ingredient that the other neighborhoods with "old guard" gate-keepers did not have: the HANDS and SUN programs. In the discussion that follows, we refer to the key programs as SUN, the successor of HANDS.

The SUN Program's Effect on the Local Community

The SUN program encourages national bank involvement in community and economic development activities to fulfill the goal of ensuring access to credit. To accomplish this goal, it provides policy guidance on community and economic development issues to national banks. In addition, it provides training in community development for examiners, performs research on timely topics related to community and economic development, and establishes community development projects. The SUN program also serves as an outreach resource for banks and their community development partners and offers technical assistance to organizers of community development financial institutions.

As part of its comprehensive approach, the SUN program provides oversight, monitoring, and technical assistance to the partners' network of programs, offering advocacy for low-income West Louisville residents and working closely with elected and appointed officials on budgetary and policy issues affecting the neighborhood. The revitalization of old urban neighborhoods is crucial to preserving Louisville's cultural heritage and helping it remain a beautiful city in which to live and work. Strengthening existing neighborhoods helps prevent sprawl, safeguards green spaces, and creates healthier environments while consuming fewer resources.

The SUN program assists housing developers and small business owners in locally designated revitalization areas, stimulates community revitalization activities that protect and enhance historic resources, and maintains and improves existing residential and commercial structures. Along with its partners, it supports initiatives to revitalize these neighborhoods through programs such as redevelopment assistance, business training for individuals, education and community crime prevention. It also identifies, studies, evaluates, and advocates the preservation and protection of significant historic sites, structures, cultural landscapes, and cultural artifacts of Louisville's inner city, as well as less tangible human and community traditions.

Possibilities of the SUN Program

The SUN program's vision goes beyond just the physical improvement of bricks and mortar. Through outreach-oriented partnerships, the program promotes human and economic development in the impoverished neighborhoods of West Louisville, with positive impacts rippling throughout the larger community. Its attempt to save a housing complex in one of Louisville's historic African-American neighborhoods from foreclosure and eventual demolition has been a comprehensive effort toward multifaceted growth achieved through revitalization as well as rebuilding.

The program's mission is to explore all strategies that foster the sense of community while empowering the individual, promoting neighborhood revitalization, individual self-sufficiency, and self-reliance through community partnerships. Its goal is to operationalize the concept of public-private partnerships in order to succeed in urban renovation and rehabilitation.

The SUN program has a successful track record of participation with community partnerships. There have been a few less-than-successful ventures along the way, but every activity has provided the faculty, staff, students, community agencies, local governmental and nongovernmental agencies, and neighborhood economic development groups with a wide variety of important information that can be directly applied to future endeavors.

SUN Community Participation

The needs of Louisville's inner city were determined in three ways. First, neighborhood organizations, CDCs and residents of the community provided input and information. Second, a community advisory team, consisting of community leaders and residents, was consulted. Last, data from the city of Louisville Consolidated Plan and Analysis of Impediments to Fair Housing, the 1990 U.S. Census, and the Community Profile for Jefferson County and related documents were examined.

Through the work and programs previously conducted in the community by the University and by SUN partners, an informal network for information sharing already existed to ensure that the proposed activities neither duplicated existing activities nor displaced them. Additionally, SUN partners were consulted directly during the development of the work plan, which complements and builds upon several activities already undertaken in the inner city. Working closely with the city of Louisville's Department of HUD, CDCs, a variety of neighborhood groups, and residents on a grassroots level, the SUN program has been an active participant in the inner-city revitalization efforts.

The SUN Program: Financing via Partnerships

This project, which started with funding largely by a U.S. Department of Education grant beginning in January 1992, and again in 1996, is part of a broader program sponsored by the U.S. Department of Education to encourage the establishment of partnerships between urban universities and the local communities they serve. As such, the project worked in conjunction with and relied on in-kind commitments and contributions from a variety of organizations, including the University of Louisville and other local colleges, government offices of the city of Louisville and Jefferson County, community development organizations, churches, and businesses.

The SUN program was also awarded another grant in 1998 through the U.S. Department of HUD. This grant established the Community Outreach Partnership Center, which is comprised of relationships between the University, CDCs, and local agencies, with a focus on four functional categories: housing, economic development, community organizing, and neighborhood revitalization. These funds are, in turn, partially matched by local churches, nonprofits, industries and businesses, local foundations, universities, and community groups.

Adopting the SUN Program to Other Urban Settings

The SUN program is essentially a goal model. Its goal-oriented successes could provide an example for future project guidance and accomplishments. Its strength is based on the comprehensive coordinated efforts of community and public partnerships to work with the neighborhood—not on it. Its vision to assist with West Louisville's efforts to build a healthy community, to create affordable homes, to provide better employment opportunities, and to promote family reunification with better education and the hope of achieving a bright future remains a goal model of private-public partnerships in urban rehabilitation.

The SUN program's successes are echoed throughout the urban development field and have received excellent reviews from specialists (see Additional Resources). It is a pioneer project, and its results have been positive, concrete, incremental, and measurable. Its successful programs illustrate the differences that are made when the university and community join in public and private partnerships to revitalize target areas. The SUN program has produced notable results. These results, significant though they may be for the local neighborhoods, also are important examples of tools that are available to cities throughout the nation that struggle with similar problems. The decision-making processes that have developed are being utilized as critical tools for successful urban rehabilitation.

Impact of the SUN Program on Students

Community service is good for students. Students who engage in service tend to have higher grade point averages and higher graduation rates, and they obtain better-paying jobs. It may be the challenge of working with diverse populations and having the nerve to go into a social setting that is different from anything students have ever experienced. Perhaps they learn empathy. Students who worked on this project achieved substantial amounts of success. The SUN program had a very positive impact on student leaders in terms of careers. Consider the following:

Michael Brazley, while earning his Ph.D., designed homes that were built for a nonprofit organization, worked on two separate HUD/HOPE VI project evaluations, and after graduation was offered teaching jobs at several universities before taking an assistant professor position at Southern Illinois University.

Mark Wright completed his Ph.D., but left the HANDS and SUN programs to become a highly profitable developer in the Russell Neighborhood and surrounding neighborhoods. He is one of a handful of builders working in predominantly African-American neighborhoods.

Bill Friedlander received his Ph.D., and built successful nonprofit housing developments in Louisville. He designed an innovative manufactured house that successfully matched the historic two-story camelback home. He completed what he started at SUN, sixty-five assisted living units from an old school building.

La Glenda Reed, who earned a bachelor's degree in education, developed Models and Self-Esteem, Inc., a nonprofit company that teaches inner-city children self-esteem.

Gloria Murray, while developing HANDS education programs, went on to become provost at another university.

Muthusami Kumaran earned his Ph.D., and became an assistant professor of public policy at the University of Hawaii. Previously he was a planning project supervisor for the Kentucky Commission on Human Rights, a consultant to African American Health, Incorporated, and worked for the Youth Policy Institute and Telesis Corp.

Karl Besel earned his Ph.D., and is now an assistant professor of public affairs at Indiana University, Kokomo.

John Martin Rutherford is finishing his Ph.D., and serving as acting director of the joint University of Louisville and University of Kentucky Urban Design Center in Louisville.

Hervel Cherubin is finishing his Ph.D., and works for the Louisville Economic Development Office. He hopes to return to Haiti to serve in a high political office.

Laura Chafin completed her master's degree in public administration and works for a private consulting company organizing programs for sustainable development.

La Tondra Jones completed her master's degree in urban planning and is now a planner working for the Louisville Planning Department.

Recognition

Successful housing developments are done in concert with media campaigns to change the perception of a poor black neighborhood: from down and out to up and coming; from a place of hopelessness to a place of hope; from a place from which to flee to a place from which to come back as a pioneer; from a place without prospects to a place of opportunity; from a place that is scary to a place that is a home. As the DVD shows, the SUN program used university resources to call for professional press conferences. Half-time pieces were made for football and basketball games highlighting HANDS and SUN accomplishments. We also were fortunate to get some of our work accepted into several scholarly publications, along with national press. Articles in the *Washington Post*, *New York Times*, local papers, and *Planning Magazine* presented a balanced picture of this unique, bold, innovative, and brash experiment in community rebuilding. The National Advisory Committee also shed more light on our accomplishments. But big media buildups are a double-edged sword. Once something is built up, it runs the risk of being torn down as well. A negative piece by a local reporter was attempted after less than seventeen months of HANDS's operation and was shown in the long run to be inaccurate—many of the goals of the HANDS program were met over the long run that looked impossible in the beginning. Even this negative piece resulted in a positive result—we improved the documentation efforts of the HANDS program and more effectively measured its accomplishments. It also encouraged us to show that the local paper was incorrect. This book *is* the record—it shows what is possible as we move into the twenty-first century.

The "SUN" Sets

We wanted to end this book on a happy note instead of a sad one, but that would have been dishonest. We wish to celebrate the victories while learning the lessons of our defeats. University leadership in the president's office allowed us to do a lot by making this program a priority. This support eroded over the years. Original supporters from the president's office to the department level were replaced with people who did not have the same priorities for the SUN program's approach to urban revitalization. The new administration had different priorities.

The SUN program helped create a whole new school of builders to revitalize the inner city, and it assisted builders in outperforming "old school" developers. This created a lot of anger, friction, and backstabbing. "Old school" players for ten years complained bitterly to University and city officials that the SUN program was unfair competition, arrogant, and an "outsider." We found that neighborhood residents were less concerned with the source of assistance than they were with innovative results.

In 2002 and 2003, the College of Business and Public Administration refused permission for the SUN program and its community partners to apply for designated funding from HUD to continue work. Letters were presented by black leaders both within and outside of the University in support of the SUN program. In 2001, twenty-five letters from various organizations were sent to the Gheens Foundation thanking SUN for partnering with them in the creation of twenty-seven computer centers in West Louisville. In 2002, representatives of nineteen community organizations (including two U of L vice presidents) wrote letters and signed petitions to the University administration, stating their strong support for the SUN program and asking the University to apply for a new SUN grant. These efforts were fruitless.

Letter Praising the SUN Program

In a December 16, 2002, letter by President Ramsey of the University of Louisville to Congress, asking for continued funding for HUD's Community Outreach Partnership Centers, he declares:

> One of the most successful COPC programs has been here at the University of Louisville's Sustainable Urban Neighborhoods (SUN) program. . . . U of L graduate students and faculty partnered up with government, builders, churches, and non-profits. SUN helped fund and teach programs which resulted in over 50 participants graduating from a contractor-training program for minorities. In addition, 27 computer centers were developed . . . Numerous architectural plans and approvals were done for non-profit community development corporations resulting in hundreds of new or renovated housing units in West Louisville. Non-profits were assisted with capacity building and technical assistance like the Neighborhood Development Corporation, which recently finished an assisted-living facility.

Even though Congress elected to fund these programs, the University of Louisville's College of Business and Public Administration denied permission to apply for these funds. Even with the passionate endorsement of the president of the University of Louisville, the leadership of the College of Business and Public Administration refused to continue the program. The University of Louisville is not only breaking its promise to the hard-working staff, students, and faculty of the University of Louisville but to the many disadvantaged communities that wanted a hand up, not a hand out. The University promised faculty that they would be rewarded, not punished, for these partnership efforts, yet community engagement apparently is looked down upon.

The University of Louisville's abrupt ending of university-community partnerships is not atypical but common of how universities operate. Better to play it safe than take risks by going into an inner-city neighborhood. Most professors complain that the rewards just do not exist for applied research, in general, and university-community partnerships, in particular. At one time, the University of Louisville was a leader in university-community partnerships; now it is a place of broken promises and broken dreams.

The SUN program now consists of just one faculty member and two graduate students. It has a small budget. Despite these setbacks, the program has become an inspiration to other universities around the world. We have made SUN
presentations in Holland, Cuba, Mexico, Costa Rica, Venezuela, and Canada, as
well as at numerous colleges around the United States. Moreover, the visits to
our Web sites <www.gilderbloom.org> and <www.louisville.edu/org/sun> have
been strong. Visitors coming to Louisville to witness the Russell renaissance—
delegations from the United Nations, the State Department, and housing advocacy—have been numerous and gratifying.

Other universities with whom we have consulted are planning to surpass
the University of Louisville SUN model. If Louisville sets the bar, then other
universities want to raise it even higher, and we encourage them. Friendly competition makes for a better environment. Of particular note is Arizona State
University (ASU), which raised $20 million from private donors to create af-
fordable family housing so that one of the nation's fast-growing cities can provide the housing necessary to keep the economy strong. At ASU, the new
director of the Affordable Housing Center will work directly for the president
of the university, have the title "vice president," and earn a hefty salary. Leaders at ASU believe that the foundation of positive economic growth in Phoenix
is building affordable family housing in "new urbanist" communities.

Universities have traditionally been a place of hope, a conduit to a better
future. We hope and pray that this book will change the minds of administrators
at the many colleges and universities that do not get involved in community
problems. We want to see a revolution, where colleges become partners with
communities via community service. If just one professor can make a difference in just one inner-city neighborhood, then imagine what 3,650 other places
of higher education could do in America's impoverished communities. Even
better, imagine what 1 percent of University of Louisville faculty, representing
sixteen faculty members could do in poor neighborhoods regionally if properly
rewarded. Universities hold a great deal of promise for poor communities, but
most have betrayed these communities by staying in the ivory tower.

We have seen the future, and it is a bright partnership between town and
gown. It is the ivory tower reaching out a helping hand across, not down, to its
neighbors. It is people helping people. One house at a time. One block at a
time. One neighborhood at a time. One city at a time. One university at a time.

Program Correspondence

BRIDGE HOUSING CORPORATION

January 14, 1993

Dr. John Gilderbloom
HANDS Project Director
Center for Urban and Economic Research
University of Louisville
Louisville, Kentucky 40292

Dear John,

Thank you for the invitation and the hospitality on my trip to Louisville on December 9th and 10th, 1993. I was most favorably impressed with the HANDS program. It appears to be precedent setting in many ways, and I hope it can become a model for other communities and universities to adopt, including many of our own out here in California.

Many political leaders and policy experts think that revitalizing inner city neighborhoods is an almost impossible task. Yet the HANDS program appears to provide an innovative model for how this can be done. As you have demonstrated, urban universities have a wide variety of technical resources, which can be effectually utilized to help solve many of our urban problems.

I was particularly impressed with the various HANDS program components in community design, homeownership, case management, and education. The individuals involved appear to be talented and committed, and the various programs seemed to provide a real contribution to both the non-profit community development corporation (CDC) in the Russell Neighborhood, and to the City of Louisville Housing and Urban Development Department.

I was also impressed by your leadership in putting together a partnership between the university, local government, developers, and a CDC. I know first-hand that such partnerships can be fragile coalitions that can easily fall apart, yet you have had the skills and perseverance to keep things together and moving forward at an impressive pace. I know of few other efforts that have done so well, and I think you have every reason to be optimistic as you look toward your second year of operations.

I have listed some specific observations below:

> **Community Design:** The design team was impressive, with strong credentials, which helps to explain its success. Mark Wright was an effective spokesman, and as a registered architect working on his Ph.D. in Urban Affairs, he seemed to offer many needed skills to the community. As usual, you were also articulate and charismatic, and you obviously bring extensive experience in low income housing to the program.

Wright's presentation was enlightening, particularly the neighborhood and housing design work which miraculously seemed to reconcile the diverse needs of the African American community with the City's historic preservation guidelines and the requirements of the local financial institutions. Although you've been in operation for only a year, it appears that about 100 new, attractive, and affordable homes will soon be started in the Russell neighborhood. It's hard to envision that this could have been possible were it not for HANDS, and the bridge it has created between the local non-profit and the private sectors. Both the private developer and director of the non-profit spoke to us about this point.

HANDS itself contributed to the process by obviously pushing the housing development plans through the usual maze of regulation and approvals. I believe that the community design team is a model for how educational institutions ought to provide more tangible services to non-profit housing groups, while offering the students meaningful education in the "real world."

> **Homeownership:** I was impressed with the apparent success of your first attempt at a homeownership fair. These fairs can be difficult to implement, and attracting 1,500 persons to the fair located in an inner city neighborhood is impressive, indeed. I admire the materials provided by the Homeownership team, and I hope to use some of this information in our own work.

As I mentioned, these fairs are quite popular in California, and they can be a great tool for networking. The price structure in your part of the country makes the promotion of lower-income homeownership all the more worthwhile, because it is perhaps more feasible in an economy such as yours which is less expensive. For your information I will send you some materials on similar fairs in California, operated by Brad Inman, tel. (510) 658-9252. Feel free to call him and mention my name. You might also try Fannie Mae. They may be more inclined to help you find the event this year, but you need to contact them early. I would recommend that you contact John Buckley in the Washington, D.C., office.

It also looked like your homeownership counseling is getting started. This is an important component of a well-rounded program, and deserves the resources to be strengthened and grow.

> **Education:** The relative importance of this component to the overall program is critical. The "esteem teams" seem to show considerable potential, and I recommend that you continue to develop this approach. Reaching out to children in their pre-teen years is important; they are the future of their respective communities. However, be patient. Education is a long-term commitment. It does not produce short-term results, except for the recruitment of more clients into the HANDS program.

GED training and tutoring are also essential to establishing self-sufficiency, and I was particularly impressed to learn of your efforts to get participants into the University of Louisville with scholarships.

I think integrating education into the leadership program and providing monthly educational outreach is a solid idea. Gloria Murray, the education team leader, was very impressive. She's both energetic and articulate.

> **Case Management:** This component also appears to be a success story within your program. It is the front line. I like the way that case managers are used to plug client-families into different HANDS components, and to refer them to other services. I would have liked to have met your case managers to have gotten their perspective. It looks like you have set up a system for documenting the work that is done in this area. I would be interested to see the output from your database and the kinds of things that you will do with this information.

One issue that does concern me is the issue of continuity. In general, I am concerned that having students interact for only a few months with a family, before the student moves on, is sufficient time to build a strong relationship with the family. We have tried without success to use students in our own company, and I don't have any concrete solutions to offer. However, I think you should take every possible measure to establish as much continuity as possible by finding the students who are most committed to the area, and who are, of course, reliable, enthusiastic, and capable.

> **Leadership Component:** I fully support your program of identifying potential leaders in the community, and then training them to be effective. However, I did not fully understand what the team leaders were doing from a programmatic standpoint. I concur with the decision to let the class choose the issues that it wants to address, but perhaps you should establish some boundaries and focus on a few predetermined topics.

Since this is a model program, the content of the leadership curriculum should be available for review and distribution. When it becomes available, I would be interested in seeing it. In the meantime, this is a weakness that needs to be addressed.

I was very impressed with Sam Watkins of the Louisville CDC, but less impressed by the representative of the Louisville Community Design Center. Perhaps in your second year, you might insert yourself and Gloria Murray into the curriculum. Murray can provide emphasis on education in the leadership class, while you might discuss your own extensive experience in community organizing.

I also liked your focus on entrepreneurship, and it looked as if you were having some limited successes in this area. From my perspective, this component could be stronger with a more detailed approach. You might consider bringing in more outside speakers who are power brokers in both the majority and minority communities. One of the things that are often overlooked is how difficult it is to network when one is out of the information loop. Bringing in speakers could help your participants connect the names and faces of people who they may need to know to get things done.

> **Job Training:** I know first-hand (unfortunately) that job training in a high-unemployment neighborhood where 60 percent of the households lack high school diplomas is very difficult. While job training is important, I think that you ought not fund programs, which are duplicative of those who are already in existence in the community. For example, the enrollment levels in the Urban League programs appeared to be low, and the job placement results also appeared to be low, and not particularly training-related. You might consider a needs assessment of what types of job training are needed but not offered. Find out which job training courses have been the most successful and which are advantageous to your clients in terms of location, transportation, meeting times, and childcare. Computer training, while important and useful, is quite commonplace. Perhaps you might focus on a different area, but have computer literacy as a sub-component of the larger program.

One such area to consider as a focal point is construction training. Given the hundreds of new houses planned for construction in the Russell neighborhood, job training in the construction trades may offer real employment opportunities and draw a great deal of participation. I was impressed to learn that Project Success, in collaboration with HANDS, was able to train seven women in construction jobs and get them placed with homebuilders.

Finally, thank you again for inviting me to visit and comment on the HANDS program. I found the experience stimulating, educational, and fun. The individuals we met with were excited and committed. I think that you and your obviously dedicated staff have the opportunity to form a national model that could showcase the effectiveness of university-community partnerships.

I think your plans for next year look very exciting, and as I mentioned at lunch, I hope to convince the housing delegation from Nelson Mandela's ANC party to visit HANDS when they come to the United States this coming spring.

Good luck with your fine work. I looked forward to our staying close in touch.

Sincerely,

I. Donald Terner
President

HARVARD UNIVERSITY
John F. Kennedy School of Government
Cambridge, MA 02138

February 17, 1994

Dr. John Gilderbloom
HANDS Project Director
Center for Urban and Economic Research
University of Louisville
Louisville, Kentucky 40202

Dear John,

Thanks so much for giving me the opportunity to come to Louisville to observe what you are doing [with the] HANDS program. It was a fascinating and rewarding experience, and I enjoyed it thoroughly. You should be congratulated for taking on such an ambitious project aimed at one of America's most severe and important domestic problems.

As it happens, I spent the next weekend in San Antonio observing the efforts of a 20-year-old grassroots organization in the Hispanic areas of the city, which has come to enjoy considerable influence in the city and surprising respect from the business community and City Hall. The work of that organization provided me with some interesting contrasts, which will color some of my observations below.

I very much support your comprehensive approach to community development. I have no doubt that there are many serious problems in blighted communities, that they are highly interdependent, and efforts to address one or two problems in isolation are virtually bound to fail.

I also strongly approve of the attempt to enlist the University of Louisville, an urban university, in the effort to mount a comprehensive attack on a distressed community. There is no other institution other than a university [that] offers the variety of expertise and skills so necessary to a comprehensive, multifaceted program of revitalization. Properly managed, such a program can offer great benefits to both parties. The community will receive all sorts of assistance at remarkably low cost. The university will be able not only to discharge its obligation as a socially responsible urban institution; it will be in a position to offer its students from various faculties invaluable practical experience that can be integrated into their academic programs to enrich their education.

Fortunately, your task in Louisville is easier. The Chamber of Commerce has already organized the local employers and identified the necessary job skills. The vocational education crowd has been taken care of so that the schools can provide state-of-the-art training geared to actual employer needs. I would certainly suggest that you firm up your ties with the Chamber and take advantage of all that has already been accomplished to allow better training to take place. In addition, I suspect that there is still an important role for HAND in creating mechanisms and programs to screen applicants, gain commitments from employers, and offer the initial preparation and continuing support to participants that will enable Russell residents to complete the training successfully.

These are very minor suggestions, at best, for what is obviously a well-conceived, ambitious effort that is already having an important impact on a community desperately in need of help. If you can preserve and make a real difference in Russell, you will have created an example, a model [that] has significance extending far beyond Louisville. Let me wish you every good fortune in that immensely important endeavor.

Sincerely,

Derek Bok, Former President
Harvard University

MARK DOWIE
Star Route. Point Reyes Station, California 94956
Telephone: 415 669-7117
Fax: 415 669-1255

January 16, 1995

John Gilderbloom
HANDS Project
University of Louisville
Louisville, KY

Dear John,

You have designed in HANDS an imaginative and innovative model for neighborhood revitalization. With a creative melding of public and private interests supporting proven and experimental strategies, you have formed the best application I have seen of true social investment. As a journalist long interested in the history and praxis of "social investigating" in the United States, and one who laments the contemporary misuse of the idea and the term, I find HANDS to be a shining example of what social investment should be, one that I intend to cite in future coverage of the subject. I can only hope that other universities and communities observe and mimic what you are doing, and that the White House, Congress, and appropriate agencies see fit to continue their support.

Of course I realize that the best designed programs amount to nothing without the imagination, creativity, and commitment of sound leaders. Inner city social programs particularly require an ability to work closely with people of every class and race, many of whom are competing over turf and resources, and to form coalitions of people and sectors of the community that tend to be distrustful of one another. Throughout my entire visit to Louisville, I was greatly impressed with your leadership, management style, communication skills, and compassion. Without those qualities, HANDS would surely founder.

Let me tell you first what impressed me most about the program. As I said, your persistent and patient diplomacy have brought and kept together people of enormous diversity, people who might otherwise be downright antagonistic to one another. This is the essence of good organizing. Without the kind of strong alliances and partnerships you have fostered, urban revitalization initiatives, no matter how imaginative or well funded, simply cannot succeed. I do believe that you are fortunate to have landed in Louisville, for there are, as you know, cities throughout the country that would present far greater, perhaps insurmountable, challenges to an initiative like HANDS. Nevertheless, if an urban renewal strategy can be made to work in Russell and La Salle, hope and inspiration will remain for similar neighborhoods across the country. I therefore wish you every success.

As you requested, I will now outline what I feel to be the assets and liabilities, strengths and weaknesses of the project. First the strengths:

- Your best asset, it seems to me, is the mutual commitment of city and university leaders to the possibility and feasibility of inner-city neighborhood revitalization. With so many academics and urban leaders throughout the country prepared to abandon the inner city and its residents, it is heartening to seen an urban university and its host city so committed to their mutual community. If the next president of the University of Louisville is as committed as Donald Swain to your project, you will be very fortunate. And if his commitment and sensitivity is emulated by metropolitan university presidents in Chicago, Cincinnati, Pittsburgh, and Los Angeles, those cities will be well served by him as well.

- Your clarity about the vital interrelationship between home ownership, education, responsible citizenship and economic development is inspiring. The positive feedback loop that HANDS creates by working on all four at once is, I am convinced, the reason for your success.

- The involvement of the religious community, so vital to and valued by African Americans, is another essential ingredient of your success.

- You have recruited and involved some impressive talent—particularly Mark Wright, Dolores Delahanty, Reg Bruce, Betsy Jacobs, Bill Friedlander, and Frank Clay. And you have formed vital community alliances at City Hall, the banking community, and at state and federal governments. With such bright and articulate associates, HANDS should flourish.

- The employment of university students in such socially worthy and rewarding pursuits will inure to the benefit of Louisville and the communities to which they eventually graduate.

- While ambitious in my view, your attempt to attract middle-class people back into Russell is a vital goal of the project. So many urban renewal projects have segregated the poor from the inspiration and hope they could derive from exposure to people who have made a go of it. It will in the end be from your more successful residents that leadership emerges.

- Patience with bureaucracy, regulation, and red tape is something I always admire (and lack). You have it.

- Your national advisory team is impressive. I am honored to serve with such people.

And now some criticisms, offered with great respect and affection for the HANDS idea and the HANDS reality. Generally my thoughts fall under one category: ambition. I had the feeling throughout my entire visit to Louisville that you are attempting to accomplish too much within the context and budget of a single initiative and organization.

The problem begins, I believe, with the wording of your mission. The sentence, replete with vague social buzzwords, could be used to produce a mission for almost any community program designed to assist a disadvantaged neighborhood. As currently written, it lacks a target and a philosophical premise. Since it is clearly your conviction that home ownership is the essential ingredient of neighborhood revitalization, shouldn't home ownership be your mission? Give yourself a specific number of owned homes to shoot for in [a] reasonable time period, and build your strategy around that target. This doesn't mean forsaking anything else HANDS is doing, it simply means giving case management, leadership training, esteem counseling, [and] job and home ownership training a clearer purpose: that being to foster the growth of home ownership in Russell and LaSalle. You and your staff say that is your purpose over and over in verbal conversion, speeches, and letters. Why not say so in your mission?

I would deemphasize economic development—in program, not aspiration. Housing is economic development, and its very construction will create additional enterprise in the form of new services and retail outlets that move in to serve a neighborhood where economic opportunity is perceived. If you end up with a lot of trained leaders, skilled workers, kids with self-esteem, potential home owners, and a dozen new homes on Pioneer Park, will you have succeeded?

Everything you do, it seems to me, should be aimed directly at the mission and central goal of increased single-family home ownership in Russell. The rest—leadership, job skills, employment, and personal esteem—will follow much more readily than if you attempt to achieve them in isolation, or absent the energy and promise exuded by a visible, ongoing housing boom. "More Homes" should be your mantra and "Building Homes" your motto. Empowerment is important, but you can't live in it. Since new single-family homes are the essence of your community design, [this] should be the essence of your mission.

This is not [to] suggest that you should stop doing anything HANDS is doing, although I must say I have a little difficulty seeing the direct link between esteem teamwork and home ownership and believe that training leadership may be a little premature. Build homes first, and it will be much easier to build leadership in Russell.

A few other tips and observations from my notes:

- Work on your pitch to middle-class people who you are trying to lure back to Russell and La Salle. Crime reduction is compelling, but broader social consequences are really only of interest to city planners and political leaders.

- Communicate your low loan-loss ratio. It's the best way to attract private capital into social investment.

- Explore shared appreciating lending.

- Seek tax breaks [for] all levels of government for commercial and industrial ventures.

- Case management is weakened by the foreshortening of relationships. I know this is difficult to remedy in an academic setting, where commitments are defined by terms and semesters. But it is clearly a problem, as is the fact that at present all your case managers and very few of your clients are white.

- Lobby for an ordinance to allow manufactured housing in Louisville. It's true that much of it is still substandard, but the industry is improving and economy of sale could produce real cost savings in the near future.

- HANDS should develop an innovative lending program with Fannie Mae, and Frank Clay should be at the table throughout the planning and negotiation processes.

- Take care not to create expectations and commitments you can't uphold if a substantial portion of your funding is lost.

- Your job skills program should teach basic skills—getting to work on time, following basic instructions, and getting along with fellow workers. Training should also include proficiency in English and avoidance of street slang in job interviews.

- Name recognition could be improved in the community with additional outreach and a bolder logo.

- There is, it seems to me, an inherent conflict between social work (case management) and the empowerment model of community development. Case management, with its psychological provider/patient relationship, can and often does create dependency rather than empowerment. I know there have been books written on this dilemma. I'm sure you've read your share. Just wanted you to know that even a lowly journalist noticed the contradiction.

- You might want to reconsider or reevaluate your leadership training component. As it exists, it doesn't seem to relate directly to your goal of home ownership. I know there is a crisis of leadership in America's inner cities, but I do wonder which will come first, leadership or physical neighborhood rehabilitation. Perhaps they come together, in which case they should be more closely interrelated.

- Carefully study the assertion made by Reed Bollinger, that "for profit development creates less cost to [the] ultimate buyer than non-profit development." It's difficult to believe, but if it is true and can be clearly documented it could encourage more public/private partnerships in Louisville and elsewhere. And private developers are more likely to encourage commercial interests to construct their infrastructure in neighborhoods where they have built than are non-profits.

Thank you again, John, for inviting me to join your national advisory board. It is both an honor and pleasure to assist such inspiring and worthy work. I hope my advice and feedback are useful. Call on me at any time.

In the meantime stay close to your mission no matter what you get hit with. It's very worth and very important [to] the entire country.

Highest regards,

Mark Dowie

U.S. DEPARTMENT OF HOUSING AND URBAN DEVELOPMENT
THE SECRETARY
Washington, D.C. 20410-0050

February 23, 1995

Dr. John I. Gilderbloom
Chair, Center for Sustainable Communities
University of Louisville
Louisville, KY 40292

Dear Dr. Gilderbloom:

Your presentation during the University Roundtable on February 9, 1995, was most significant, and necessary to the discussion we hope to generate around the subject of the university and its commitment to the greater community.

Because of the work the Center for Sustainable Communities is doing, the University of Louisville continues to emerge as an unparalleled example of the good things that happen when a university becomes vested in its community. We were all impressed by your successes and by the possibilities you offered in your presentation.

I look forward to continuing this dialogue. Thank you for having made time on your schedule for this important meeting of ideas.

Best personal regards.

Sincerely,

Henry G. Cisneros

UNITED STATES SENATE
COMMENDING THE CENTER FOR SUSTAINABLE
URBAN NEIGHBORHOODS

Mr. FORD: Mr. President, all across America, people from every walk of life carry a vision in their heads and in their hearts of the perfect community—of the kind of place where they can raise their children and their children can in turn raise their children.

There's no doubt that everyone's picture would look different, based on our own experience. But I feel certain they would have many elements in common. We want safe neighborhoods. We want to be economically secure. And we want to keep our families healthy. These are the building blocks of a liveable community, and the City of Louisville has played an important role in helping to put them into place, serving as a model for inner-city revitalization.

The city has rehabilitated and built hundreds of housing units, they've created new jobs and businesses, and more families are building stable, productive lives. East Russell, an inner-city Louisville neighborhood, has seized the nation's attention by creating a renaissance in that part of the city, bringing it new life and vitality. Rightfully so, this revitalization project has received attention by mayors and elected officials all over the United States.

The University of Louisville's Sustainable Urban Neighborhoods (SUN) is devoted to making inner-city neighborhoods healthy and safe places to live. The project is located at the Center for Urban and Economic Research at the University of Louisville. One of the biggest accomplishments of this project has been building affordable houses for residents with a strong cooperative effort by the entire staff, including the University of Louisville, City Bank, and Telesis, along with many community organizations.

Mr. President, the SUN staff—including its director, Dr. John Gilderbloom, and students from the University of Louisville—and SUN community partners have already done so much to strengthen our inner-city communities and boost the hopes and spirits of the people living there.

I would ask that my colleagues join me today in commending their work to make our cities "dream places" to live and for their continued commitment to the greater community. And as they host their conference the week of October 15th through the 17th, we wish them the best of luck in their continued efforts.

June 16, 1997

John I. Gilderbloom, Ph.D.
Director, Urban Studies Institute
Sustainable Urban Neighborhoods
University of Louisville
Louisville, KY 40292

Dear Dr. Gilderbloom:

We are pleased to report that the 1995 University of Louisville Sustainable Urban Neighborhoods (SUN) grant of $55,155 has provided us with the capacity to improve and expand our service delivery to residents of the City of Louisville's Empowerment Zone.

Our housing and neighborhood development program, with assistance from SUN, through the work of Mark Wright, Architect, and the University of Kentucky School of Architecture Downtown Design Center, completed nine affordable houses and sold four completed plans for the construction of four model homes. The cost of these houses ranged from $35,000 to $120,000. The program also completed preliminary plans for the renovation of a child-care center and started the plans for a development of the first "town square" facility in the empowerment zone for a multi-purpose commercial, cultural, and family services center of over 45,000 square feet.

The crime prevention efforts have provided mixed results thus far. We have been instrumental in helping to mobilize neighborhood and corporate leaders around the community. The initial planning and organization work should be complete by the middle of 1997. This planning process will include the expansion of the crime watch program committed to last year.

Using the 1995 evaluation by the University, and with support of other organizations, we have been able to increase the number of micro enterprise business loans, both start-up and expansion and technical assistance. In addition, with able assistance from Dr. Tom Lyons, Co-Principal Investigator of SUN, our Business Plus program has made $330,000 worth of loans to 18 individuals. We also have provided entrepreneurship training and assistance to scores of individuals.

We have reached out and encouraged resident participation by providing social services and referral services to over 1,300 persons living in the empowerment zone. These services have included small business training, crisis intervention, emergency assistance, homeownership, educational assistance (GED, tutoring, and career development), transportation to work and interviews for work, and time limited child care to support working families and parents and training.

Sincerely,

Sam Watkins, Jr.
Executive Director

PERSPECTIVES ON HANDS

By Roger E. Hamlin, National Advisory Team Member

HANDS is a fascinating and imaginative project. It is one of the most comprehensive efforts I have seen to attack the problems of an urban neighborhood. One bit of knowledge gleaned from 30 years of experience with central city redevelopment is that comprehensive interventions focused on clients and citizens are necessary to significantly effect the complex and interrelated problems faced by disadvantaged people. Attempts to improve just housing, or infrastructure, or schools, or just provide social services or just provide tax incentives do not have the power to turn a neighborhood around. The manner in which the HANDS project pivots on a case management system that refers clients to such diverse social, economic, and physical services as esteem training, a micro loan program, and housing is truly unusual. The visible effects of HANDS on the Russell Neighborhood are impressive.

The following random thoughts are not meant to be criticisms of HANDS but rather a "for what it's worth" outsider's view of the project, offered with the hope that insights may benefit HANDS and related projects in the future.

A typical question of a project like HANDS is whether it tries to do too much. Could limited time and resources be better focused? This is a valid question, since neither the $1.5 million funding nor the three-year term are large relative to the problems being addressed. Whether the project is spread too thinly depends on how the project was conceived and is perceived. Whether stated or unstated, the project has at least three goals. One is to build institutions and systems in Louisville that will produce results for many years. A second goal is to test intervention models and strategies. A third goal is to have a direct and immediate effect on the quality of life of the residents of the Russell Neighborhood. These goals may sometimes be in conflict. An understanding of the value of the project might be promoted by viewing HANDS from each of these three perspectives.

As institution builder and partnership creator. An institution building project's primary goal is to strengthen organizations and organizational linkages so that a set of desirable activities continues long after the original funding ceases. An institution building strategy calls for maximum utilization of existing service deliverers and focuses on promoting coordination between existing community NGOs and governmental agencies. An institution building strategy bestows credit for accomplishments upon those permanent community institutions rather than the project.

Institution building has been a great success of HANDS. It is clear that the project director has great skill in motivating talented and committed people in all relevant organizations and giving them credit for projects' successes. The project director has also attempted to maximize involvement of community organizations and other service deliverers rather than keep tasks internal to the project staff. Partly because of the imaginative comprehensive design of the program and partly because of the personalities and skills of key actors, positive effects of HANDS have exceeded what was originally intended or imagined. As a result of some project activities and actors city, state, and federal agencies are working together better. The benefits of institution building have gone beyond the Russell Neighborhood.

Building the partnership between the university and the community is also a major accomplishment of the leadership of HANDS. The success of this partnership can be held out as an example for other universities. Yet, because of the vicissitudes of university politics and the difficulties associated with faculty evaluation systems, establishing a university-community partnership cannot be accomplished in three years. It takes a series of successful projects over more than a decade to change the university's culture.

As experiment. One view of a brief federally funded project of this kind is that it is a test of an innovative intervention system. To call it an experiment often elicits negative connotations of a populous being used as guinea pigs. The evaluate perspective does not mean that a control group exercise must be conducted, or that assistance to neighborhood residents is less sensitive or humane. Rather, it recognizes that three years is too short to dramatically effect a complex situation. Yet, by implementing a comprehensive intervention system, and by documenting results, we can learn a great deal.

To some degree this experimental perspective should be a part of all federally funded projects. The nation needs to stop reinventing the wheel and repeating past mistakes. We need to learn which intervention strategies work and in which situations. In this way, future projects in Louisville and elsewhere can begin with a better understanding of what must be done.

In the case of HANDS, the original proposal did not put heavy emphasis, but enough client data has been collected through the case management system that a great deal can be learned through a final evaluation. A longitudinal study of HANDS clients, city blocks, and community organizations could provide valuable knowledge about the long-term effects of this innovation effort. Viewed as an experiment, the HANDS project is not spread too thinly. The comprehensive nature of the project is important for the test.

As immediate impact. A reality of any project of this kind is that it must show tangible results during the project period. This is true for external political reasons. Visible accomplishments also insure internal project momentum, establish client trust, and build local credibility. Hypothetically, if the HANDS project's only goal were to have the greatest possible positive impact on the neighborhood in three years with $1.5 million, then the project's strategy would be to focus on activities that produce maximum short-term benefits. Using this hypothetical yardstick, the HANDS project would be spread too thinly.

A beauty of the HANDS project's design and current management is the client-focused scenario of events, which intertwines social, physical, and economic development. According to the design, the case management system comprehensively addresses the social needs of a family, moves family members toward stable employment, and ultimately toward home ownership. While [this] scenario is beautifully incorporated into the project design and well managed by the project's leadership, it is very complicated and difficult to accomplish in a short time. For a troubled family in a troubled neighborhood, such a scenario might take a decade to carry from the beginning point to the end.

If viewed simply as a three-year, direct-intervention project, HANDS would look bifurcated. The education and social services side of the project functions well, as does the housing and community design team. However, since three years is not enough time to carry many clients from the beginning of the service scenario to the end, maintaining client, staff, or psychological connection between the two parts of the project is difficult.

Success is driving the two aspects of the project in different directions as well. Even though few houses have yet been built, the home ownership program shows signs of great success. A system is unfolding which combines free land, quality low cost design, and construction, lot preparation, neighborhood design, and HUD subsidies to provide quality homes at a marketable price. An exciting outgrowth of the project is that people who left the neighborhood but are still connected with local churches may now be willing to come back and buy a house. While this is an exciting development, it may mean that existing residents, suffering severe social problems, are less likely to be home owners in the short run.

Where to go from here. What should the strategy be for the final year of the project? The answer to this depends on how much and what kind of follow-up funding will be forthcoming. The following comments are based [on] the assumption that CUER will receive some future project funding for its work in the Russell Neighborhood, but future funding may come from a different funding source and have different goals. In other words, the HANDS project in its current form will end in 1996. The following comments also assume that the project is a mixture of experimental design and institution building and must show significant impact on the neighborhood during the term of the project. Based on these assumptions and my limited contact with the project, I suggest the following:

1. **During its final year, HANDS should focus on promoting house construction and rehabilitation.** HANDS is clearly not a weak project but is most vulnerable to outside criticism because only ten homes have been built. A strong system for building houses is now in place, and up to 30 more houses can be built and sold in the next year. To accomplish this, HANDS should focus on opening bottlenecks associated with preparing lots of construction, building spec homes on those lots, and using HANDS, LCDC and L&T resources to market those houses.

The Russell neighborhood appears to be on the verge of economic takeoff, a point where middle-class families will feel comfortable returning to live in newly built houses.

One evidence of this is that crime rates in Russell have not followed the upward spiral of surrounding neighborhoods. HANDS can have its greatest impact in the project's final year by promoting construction of 30 homes and assuring that takeoff is achieved.

2. **Conversely, HANDS should begin to reduce the education and social services aspect of the project.** While these services have been worthwhile, little time remains for the project to achieve its objective of bringing families with social, educational, and psychological need to the point of home ownership. The case management system should continue, but greater emphasis should be placed on referring clients to other social service agencies. If HANDS funds are in short supply, less should go to client support in social and educational services such as esteem training and leadership training and more allocated to community design and development. The link between these two parts of the project may naturally weaken as the project nears the end.

3. **As the project winds down, less funding and time should be devoted to central office support** and more devoted to direct and neighborhood services, particularly those related to house construction and home ownership.

4. **One central office function which needs to continue or be strengthened is project evaluation.** At the least, good data should continue to be collected by case management on all client contacts. Some ongoing effort should be made to document institution building by the project and capture before-and-after information on all project funded activities.

5. **To accomplish these things, the project director should be given a free hand to reorganize the divisions of the project.** Clearly the project leadership has done an excellent job of pulling together a complicated set of interrelated activities, finding key individuals to head up these activities, and motivating them to contribute significantly to project success. Yet the project is complicated, and time and resources are short. There is little room for slow, bureaucratic responses to changing project conditions.

Conclusion. HANDS is a fascinating project which needs about five more years of funding to fully develop its structure, it institutional partnerships, and its momentum to positively effect the lives of Russell Neighborhood residents. The project is well managed and functions well in the face of rapidly changing situations and challenging project goals. HANDS is well positioned to contribute significantly to the rejuvenation of an inner-city neighborhood, a rare national success story.

THE WHITE HOUSE
WASHINGTON

April 26, 1994

Dr. John I. Gilderbloom
HANDS Project Director
College of Business and Public Administration
University of Louisville
Louisville, Kentucky 40292

Dear John:

Thank you for your letter of March 17 and the copy of HANDS On!

I hope your participation in the National Housing and Community Development Conference was successful.

I applaud the work of the Housing and Neighborhood Development Strategies (HANDS) project. It is just this kind of comprehensive, community-based partnership effort that my Administration is trying to stimulate in distressed communities across the country. I am convinced that the most effective ideas for local economic renewal will come from the communities themselves.

Partnerships like the HANDS project that bring all community sectors together—state and local government, business, universities, non-profits, community-based institutions, and residents themselves—around a comprehensive vision for change are critical to helping distressed communities join the economic mainstream. Again, I applaud the HANDS project for its successes thus far and wish you continued success in the future.

Sincerely,

Bill Clinton

Village West Press Conference
Tuesday, June 18, 1996, 11:00 A.M.
Village West

Mayor Abramson's Speech

Finally, after ten and a half long years of challenge and for many frustration; finally after going through one failed attempt to find a developer after another; finally after watching Village West continue to decline, even as our city plans to revitalize the Russell Neighborhood around it, [it] has met with such tremendous success. Finally we are here today to announce that we do have a deal, and that Village West will be revitalized and restored.

Today, I take great pride in announcing that construction will begin soon on the complete restoration of Village West thanks to the dedication and hard work of so many people. The banking industry in this community, the non-profit sector in this community, the private sector in this community, the education community, and people at the federal, state, and local levels of our government. What you see around you [and] around me, behind me to my right and left will be completely transformed some time in my last year in office. We will be back here showing off a complex that will be a model of privately owned affordable housing rather than an eyesore.

Our "angel" and I underline angel in this deal in Marilyn Melkonian, who is President of Telesis Corporation of Washington, D.C., a company which specializes in rebuilding neighborhoods and building affordable housing.

I first met Marilyn in December 1994 (I hope you remember that) at the airport when she was getting off a plane to attend a meeting with my good friend, Dr. John Gilderbloom, [of the] U of L HANDS program, [who] had invited her in. In fact, John Gilderbloom then continued to call and to focus my attention on how Marilyn had done such outstanding work in other communities that we really needed to try to attract her back into this community to invest in Village West. In early 1995, we contacted her to see if she was interested. And putting together the financing and working out the details was no easy task.

Did I say it was no easy task to put together? The financing and all the details? Fourteen months we have been working on this project. Fourteen months to put this deal together as compared to the ten and a half years to put other deals together. But it's because it's such a big deal. Not only in terms of what it will mean to this community and to the revitalization of the Russell Neighborhood but also in terms of the money involved.

The total cost of the redevelopment is $33.7 million, and working out the financing and the details of such a large financial undertaking was complex and arduous to say the least. It took incredible cooperation, especially among the banks in the community, exhaustive patience, and very hard work on the part of so many folks. The federal Department of Housing and Urban Development played a key role [in] being willing to buy down the old $6 million mortgage and then to advance $10 million under the HUD 241 program. Morgan Stanley, Urban Horizons, is the equity limited partner, putting up $21 million in equity tax credits, and the City of Louisville is contributing loans of $1.8 million from our federal home loan program. But the most difficult and complicated piece of this package was the construction financing, which put $9.8 million of construction bridge loan money together from the banks in our community.

We specifically want to thank Bank One for taking the lead as the lead bank in putting together a consortium of Louisville lenders, for providing the structure and structuring expertise, and for putting up, also, the largest amount of loan money, $2.25 million.

We thank the Kentucky Housing Corporation for the construction loan of $2.2 million. The city, in addition to the million-eight we've put in the deal, we're giving another million of our community development block grant funds for the construction.

And finally, we want to thank the consortium of banks who really stepped up on this project, stepped up to the plate with loan funding to make the important renovation happen. PNC Bank and National City Bank each putting up $1.5 million, Great Financial, $600,000, Fifth/Third, $550,000, Citizen Union Bank, $300,000, Citizen Bank of Kentucky, $250,000, Republic Bank and Trust, $150,000, Stock Yards Bank, $100,000, and Jefferson Bank, $100,000. Now, as part of the renovation plans, Village West will be downsized from presently 663 units that exist today, to 503 units in the future. Since Village West is now about 50 percent vacant, we won't be losing any of our low income housing units that we have today that have people within them. The good news is that the new units will provide what is now in very short supply affordable housing for larger families. The new complex will have thirty-one four-bedroom apartment units to accommodate larger families along with the one, two, and three bedroom units, and I'll let Marilyn tell you more about the details, but I can tell you I'm very excited about the plans.

I'm very grateful to the University of Louisville. The University of Louisville has been actively involved through the leadership of John Gilderbloom. As part of a $1 million grant, the University's Sustainable Urban Neighborhoods program will continue to provide assistance. John $1 million will continue to provide assistance to Village West with crime prevention, community planning, and other needs. And we want to thank (President) John Shumaker and we also want to thank Patrick Flanagan. I saw Dr. Flanagan here representing the President along with John Gilderbloom.

I want to make special mention of Bob Astorino and Bob Horton with the Housing Partnership because of their help in facilitating this project. It would not have been done had it not been for Bob Horton, who is the banker with Great Financial, but more importantly is the chairman of the finance group within the housing partnerships that kept the banks around the table and kept working with them to develop the package that would ultimately give us the $9.8 million of construction loan funds and with Bob Astorino and his staff we owe the Housing Partnership a great deal of gratitude. Thank you.

I also want to thank Jim Allen with the City Housing Department who, also with his staff, has been working in a great, aggressive way to ensure that our $3 million, give or take, will be invested appropriately and properly. And let me thank the residents and tenants of Village West for their patience. Deborah Todd, who is here and you'll hear from her, is the president of the Tenants' Association, and I just want to say, Deborah, it's been a long, hard road but you've kept the faith and finally we've reached our destination.

As you can see, an awful lot of people have contributed to the success of this project, and I want to close by paying tribute to the spirit that exists in Louisville to work together to make this community a better place to live. It's a fact that so many people are willing to not only contribute their time and their talent, but to stick with it. To stick with it through the entire fourteen months of getting us to this point through whatever it takes and however long it takes that allowed us to successfully tackle this very difficult problem. From bringing back the downtown, we've had commitments all over this community from the business folks that have joined with us right here in the project. And as I said, it's been a long, hard road, and when you travel it with people who are willing to go the extra mile for their city, it's definitely a journey worth making. This project, with all its delays and with all its frustrations, is certainly proof that together we can make a difference in a positive way for the future of our hometown.

June 27, 1996

Dr. John I. Gilderbloom
University of Louisville
SUN Project
426 W. Bloom Street
Louisville, KY 40292

Dear John:

Thanks for all your assistance with the Village West project. I want to thank you for your dedication and the hundreds of hours you put into this project. The beginning of the reconstruction effort is a testament to the commitment of the residents, the city, the university, federal and state governments, and the business community to the success of Village West and the Russell Nighborhood.

Completion of the renovated homes will offer affordable housing, with the goal of homeownership, to over 500 households. The investment of more than $33 million for the renovation and saving of Village West is an investment in families and futures. The redevelopment was supported by the Sustainable Urban Neighborhood team, the University of Louisville, Mayor Abramson of the city of Louisville, and the residents of Village West, in partnership with local and national lending and investment institutions. It is the serious commitment of all these organizations and individuals which brought about this accomplishment.

The University of Louisville was instrumental in bringing Telesis to Louisville. From the perspective of my involvement on the HANDS National Advisory Board and recent events, the partnership of university and community at work in the city of Louisville has been impressive. I look forward to continuing work on this neighborhood redevelopment and thank you for your hard work, commitment, and sincerity.

Sincerely,

Marilyn Melkonian

Marilyn Melkonian, President of Telesis

Thank you very much. Casey Stengel once said that ability is the art of getting the credit for all the home runs other people hit, and there certainly are a lot of home run hitters in Louisville who made Village West possible. I cannot repeat some of the thanks the mayor has already touched on for this very, very special community.

I don't think there is another city in America that would possibly have been able to organize the partnership, the public/private partnership that came together in order to carry out this very unique urban renovation.

The communities that came together, beginning with the mayor himself and this government, this local government, the federal government, the state government, the Kentucky Housing Corporation, without their faith in this process and particularly then director Bob Adams and now director LuAllen would never have committed the major investment potential to this project, the banking community, in organizing so many financial institutions into a coordinated whole to invest million of dollars into this community's neighborhood. I want to recognize not only Bob Horton, because I think he does deserve very special recognition for holding together a coalition, along with the lead banker, Bill Hinga, represented here today, Fred Horneffer, Bank One, their colleague Julie Johnson, who really was a catalyst for the banks becoming involved, who I knew in Washington, D.C., and then finally of course the people of Village West themselves, along with their former owner, really of Village West, which was the Department of Housing and Urban Development.

This unique relationship between the federal government, the Department of Housing and Urban Development, and the people who live here and their supporters, the Legal Aid Society, for example, Sam Watkins, who runs the Louisville Central Community organization, this is a combination of people that is without parallel in America, believing, I think, in one particular thing, and that is that a city cannot be great unless all of its neighborhoods and its communities are great, and that we all should work together to make every place in this city a great place, and that's what we're dedicated to doing here at Village West.

The other partner of course was the University of Louisville. The first person I met in Louisville was John Gilderbloom, who brought me here, as the mayor mentioned, in 1994. And then the partnership with the University is continuing for the benefit of this community, bringing a whole range of activities and services to bear.

The vision for Village West goes beyond just the physical improvements of the bricks and mortar. This is a community vision that goes to homeownership, which is built into the plan for this community, employment we have here today—residents of this community who are already at work building the new Village West. And with the opportunity for jobs, and there'll be many of them here, will come the opportunity for family reunification—for bringing men back into this community who are part of the community and should be working here and helping to build it. We're also looking forward to education opportunities, meaning that every single child can look forward to graduation from high school and going to college. These are the goals that the residents of this community have set for themselves, and we are here to help bring about these dreams and to help bring about these aspirations as their partners in achieving what I think will be a very bright future. Thank you very much.

MEMORANDUM

July 15, 1997

To: **SUN Partners and Other Interested Parties**

From: **John I. Gilderbloom, Ph.D., with Muthusami Kumaran, Ph.D.**

Subject: Estimating Job Creation by Housing Developers in West Louisville

A positive outcome of housing development is the creation of jobs. The goal of this memorandum is to report the estimated economic impacts of housing developers SUN has been associated with.

In order to determine the economic effects of the partners who have worked with SUN, various estimating models were considered. The model which was the most appropriate, defensible, and rigorous was determined to [be] the economic base multiplier model. The essential idea underlying this model is that certain activities in a locality or region are basic in the sense that their activity leads and determines the region's overall economic development by exporting and bringing outside money into the community.

Growth in basic industry has a multiplier effect on non-basic employment. Other (non-basic) activities circulate money informally and are simply consequences of the region's local development (such as markets serving local consumers). If such an identification of basic activities can be made, then an explanation of regional growth can be accomplished by explaining the location of basic activities and identifying the processes by which basic activities in any region give rise to further development of non-basic activities. Usually, economic base theory identifies basic activities as those that bring in money from the outside world, generally by producing goods or services for "export," that is, goods or services consumed outside of the region or locality, or those activities which attract outsiders and their expenditures (such as tourism).

Once the export base multiplier model was selected, the next step was to obtain access to a database to establish the economic effects of the programs. Once various possible databases were examined, it was decided that the most comprehensive, rigorous, and comparative database was the U.S. Army Corps of Engineers' Economic Impact Forecasting System (EIFS).

[The] Economic Impact Forecast System is the most accurate, valid, and comprehensive model for short-run forecasts and estimation. Because of its ability to generate multipliers for any county or metropolitan statistical area (MSA) within the United States, [the] EIFS is one of the most far-reaching economic modeling programs ever created. [The] EIFS provides a standardized model that allows for comparisons across cities, counties, and regions in the United States. [The] EIFS can simultaneously examine and hold constant anywhere from 600 to 1,500 variables in developing its estimations. The

EIFS provides a consistent estimate, which is an improvement over existing customized economic forecasting. Moreover, the comprehensiveness of the model far exceeds the local models; depending on the county, the number of variables put into the model ranges from 600 to 2,000, with larger metropolitan areas having more variables. [The] EIFS uses both governmental and privately generated data like the Census Bureau's County Business Patterns, Census of Population and Housing, and other current data. Congress has used it as a bipartisan means to examine the impact of military bases closing on cities. Although originally developed as a means to forecast the economic effect of closing army forts and other military bases upon cities, the EIFS model is also used to predict the economic consequences of an exogenous infusion of funds into an area. [The] EIFS is able to provide as good an approximation of new jobs created or new money put into circulation into a local economy as a non-survey model possibly can.

The EIFS model can predict the consequences of an external infusion of money with a variety of measures. These indicators include sales volume, employment, income, the change in the local population, school enrollment, demand for housing, changes in governmental expenditures, and changes in governmental revenues. As the focus of this report is the economic consequences of federal funding, the measured sales volume, that is, the amount of money spent by individuals on goods and services, and employment (the number of jobs created) were chosen as the most appropriate.

Thus when the federal government spends a certain amount of money in a county, metropolitan area, or other region, [the] EIFS forecasts approximately how many new jobs and sales are created in the local area. As discussed in the EIFS manual:

> The economic base model assumes that external changes resulting in increases in export activity cause increases in the payroll of export firms, which are then transmitted to the local service sector establishments. Also, the inflow or outflow of money causes activity in local services to changes by a multiple of the original change (i.e., the multiplier effect) as the influx of funds is spent and respent in the local economy. A large infusion of money into a local economy will either directly and/or indirectly cause the sales of basic industries to rise just by the fact that many basic industries sell to both the local economy and export to other regions. As the sales of export-based (basic) industries rise, these industries will demand more workers. As these basic industries do more hiring, more jobs will be created in non-basic (non-exporting) industries.

For example, the construction of housing in an area would create a certain number of new construction jobs. Contractors who work on the project would also place orders with suppliers and manufacturers who would be considered in a basic industry. Orders placed with local suppliers would be expected to increase the sales and subsequently the employment of those suppliers. Since these suppliers are part of a basic industry, economic base theory predicts that there will be additional hiring in non-basic industries. The employment impact of the expenditures on the new construction project should go beyond those of just building the bridge.

For this report, [the] EIFS was utilized to estimate the sales volume generated and the number of jobs created. The EIFS model identifies and then quantifies economic activities in a regional economic area which are basic, in the sense that their performance leads and determines the region's overall economic development.

Central to [the] EIFS is the multiplier effect. The multiplier effect refers to how many times one dollar is circulated. That is, when one dollar is spent by a consumer, a portion of that dollar is in turn spent by other persons. The EIFS model quantifies this effect and thereby determines the direct, indirect, and total effects of an external infusion of funds. By using the information in the database on each city and by entering the amount of the Empowerment Zone award into this database as an external influx of funds, the sales volume and jobs generated are determined.

Summary of Findings

The housing developers who have worked closely with [the] SUN project in the years 1996 and 1997 were plugged in using the standard EIFS Forecasting model to estimate their economic impacts.

1. Telesis Corporation's Village West Redevelopment Project:
Telesis Corporation was successful in getting 33.7 million dollars in funds to rehab 500 units in the deteriorated Village West low/moderate income housing complex. According to the standard EIFS model forecast, this 33.7 million has resulted in a direct sales volume of $22,349,000 in the city. The EIFS has also estimated that the investment has induced sales to the tune of $44,000,000 in the locality. On the whole, the economic impact in terms of total sales as the result of [the] Village West redevelopment project is $66,349,000.

As to new job creations, Telesis [Corporation's] investment [in] Village West has generated 155 new direct jobs in the community. Including the 305 jobs created through inducement, the EIFS estimates that the project has created an impressive 460 jobs in the impoverished West End Louisville.[1]

2. 1996 Home Ownership Projects of SUN's Nonprofit Partners:
In 1996, SUN assisted its various partners in their home ownership projects. The following are SUN's partners that received direct helps in their projects: Canaan Community Development Corporation (5 units), Neighborhood Development Corporation (3 units), Louisville Central Development Corporation (9 units), Neighborhood Housing Services (8 units), Saint Steven's Economic Development Corporation (5 units). SUN has assisted these organizations in 30 houses being built in West Louisville. Assuming an average cost of $60,000 per house, the total investment for the year 1996 was to the tune of $1, 800,000. According to the standard EIFS forecast model, this investment has resulted in the direct sales/consumer spending of $1,193,400 and another $2,350,800 in induced sales. Thus the total sales volume resulted by the investment in $3,444,200. The investment has also created an estimated number of 9 direct jobs and 11 indirect jobs, bringing a total of 20 new jobs into the community.

3. 1997 Home Ownership Projects of SUN's Partners:
By the end of the year 1997, SUN will have assisted its partners in building 48 housing units. The projected housing projects of SUN's partners are as follows: Canaan Community Development Corporation (3 units), Neighborhood Development Corporation (15 units), Louisville Central Development Corporation (14 units), Neighborhood Housing Services (8 units), and Saint Steven's Economic Development Corporation (8 units). Assuming an average cost of $60,000 per unit, the EIFS model predicts that the total investment of $2,880,000 in these housing projects will result in an increase of $1,243,400 in direct sales and $2,455,280 in induced sales—a total of $3,698,680 in increased sales in the local economy. This investment [in] new houses also is estimated to create 40 new jobs: 14 direct jobs as the result of the investment and 26 jobs through inducement.

SUMMARY

In summary, SUN's partners have helped mobilize $38.38 million towards urban renewal projects in West Louisville. This investment, besides rejuvenating the lives of hundreds of poor households, has resulted in an impressive development in the local economy. [The] EIFS, the most accurate economic forecasting system so far, has estimated that in 1996, 97 new housing developments created $74,835,280 in total sales ($24,785,800 in direct sales and $50,049,480 in induced sales) and 520 new jobs (178 direct jobs and 342 indirect jobs).

Note:
1. The efforts of housing developers (Telesis, Canaan Community Development Corporation, Louisville Central Development Corporation) to target development of affordable housing in East Russell have seen a corresponding decrease in crime between 8th and 13th Streets. Data from the City of Louisville Police Department shows that crime fell sharply in 1996.

HANDS Strategic Management Plan

A major initiative was the development and implementation of a strategic management planning process for HANDS, which was led by HANDS Acting Project Director Steve Zimmer, a certified strategic management facilitation consultant. When the original HANDS grant was conceived, the planning team defined six goals, which were really objectives, to be accomplished by the end of the three-year grant period:

1. **Case management:** Place and counsel 400 residents in the HANDS program;

2. **Job training:** Provide job training and placement for 60 target area residents who currently receive government assistance;

3. **Education training:** 108 students complete high school equivalency diplomas, 225 persons receive assistance for higher education scholarship, and 150 families obtain literacy training;

4. **Leadership training:** 150 residents will learn community organizing skills, entrepreneurship, and self-help strategies;

5. **Home ownership:** Turn 180 low-income families into home owners;

6. **Community design:** Design a neighborhood master plan, create a nonprofit housing corporation, and teach defensible space design.

HANDS project staff began the development of the strategic management process, which caused the reevaluation and expansion of those original six goals. As is true with any project, the process demonstrated that the original plans had to be modified to fit the reality of the experience of the actual operation of the grant program. Therefore, some of the original goals were scaled back and others were expanded. Some were eliminated when new ones emerged. New strategies were designed to replace old ones, resulting in new goals and objectives. Planning is simply the continuous process of identifying needs and designing strategies to address those needs, abandoning old strategies, and embracing new ones.

The strategic management process began with the establishment of values, vision, and mission statements. Based on these statements, the original six goals were replaced with seven goals with a series of measurable objectives for each one, resulting in a total of forty-two. What follows are the values, visions, mission statement, situational analysis, goals, and objectives.

HANDS' Core Values Statement:

HANDS' core values were the *fundamental, ethical, moral, and professional beliefs of the organization, which served as the guide for decision making.* HANDS believed that the conditions that manifested poverty could be ameliorated. Empowerment of residents and the neighborhood, through strategies, promoted neighborhood revitalization, led to self-sufficiency, and promoted individual self-determination and self-expression.

HANDS' Vision Statement:
HANDS' *vision was a description of the preferred future of the organization with respect to its structure and purpose, role in the community, and relationships.* HANDS helped renew the historic Russell Neighborhood, worked to help alleviate poverty, and was a catalyst for empowerment. HANDS celebrated and valued the distinct ethnic culture of the neighborhood.

Role:
HANDS was a significant neighborhood partner as evidenced by a strong grass-roots philosophy. Neighborhood residents and neighborhood-based organizations helped define the community's vision, and neighborhood residents were empowered to achieve their preferred future with the support of all partners.

Reputation:
HANDS was seen as the premier component of the U of L's urban mission. The program stood as a national model of a university-community partnership. HANDS represented the future of what universities need to do to maintain relevancy. The HANDS project demonstrated that that U of L could provide services to help renew the American dream of hope and opportunity at the neighborhood level.

Relationships:
HANDS was an organization that promoted direction and focus through team-work to enhance cooperation and communication. Hence, HANDS helped its several partner organizations and used input from neighborhood organizations to empower using U of L's resources.

HANDS' Mission Statement:
HANDS' mission was a *broad but directed description of the six vices provided, geographic area of operation, and clients served.* The mission of HANDS was to explore strategies to foster community and individual empowerment in order to promote neighborhood revitalization and individual self-sufficiency.

Services:
HANDS provided neighborhood design and affordable housing design services, home ownership promotion and support, case management and referral services, and education and training for jobs and leadership.

Geography:
HANDS served the historic Russell Neighborhood and the La Salle housing development.

Clients:
HANDS' clients were organizations that served the Russell Neighborhood and the La Salle housing development. They were individuals who were residents of Russell and La Salle and persons who expressed interest in owning a home, operating a business, or taking steps to establish residency in Russell or LaSalle.

HANDS' Objectives

HANDS' objectives were measurable statements of achievement that led to the accomplishment of its goals.

GOAL 1: For HANDS to provide quality services to clients (people).

What were the objectives?

1. To enroll and provide referral, placement, and counseling services to 400 clients. (Case management)

2. To provide job development training services to 90 clients, 40 percent of whom would be public assistance recipients, and of the 90 clients, 45 to obtain employment after training. (Job development)

3. To provide leadership training to 60 clients. (Leadership)

4. To provide grant writing training to 15 people. (Leadership)

5. To participate in the process of 180 low- and moderate-income families becoming homeowners. (Home ownership)

6. To provide home ownership orientation to 75 clients. (Home ownership)

7. To bring 50 housing vendors together with potential home owners/clients. HANDS must fill out Agreement to Participate form. (Home ownership)

8. To make available home ownership counseling and support services to 150 past and present La Salle residents. (Home ownership)

GOAL 2: For HANDS to help rebuild the physical Russell community.

What were the objectives?

1. To complete the Louisville Central Development Corporation's (LCDC) nine prototype housing designs to meet the mandates of the Historic Preservation District. (Community design)

2. To complete a neighborhood design plan. (Community design)

3. To develop a plan and cost estimate to upgrade Western Cemetery for a passive park. This may enable the appropriate parties to move this project forward and make the balance for the Pioneer Park development more attractive to potential home owners. (Community design)

4. To prepare a report to obtain approved development designation for another tract in the Russell urban renewal area. (Community design)

5. To work with L&T Properties on the Phase I-B development. (Community design)

6. To assist with advertising additional CHDO houses if the LCDC board wishes to pursue this course. (Community design)

7. To participate in the Bruner Foundation competition submittal. (Community design)

GOAL 3: For HANDS to assist Russell to become a community of learning.

What were the objectives?

1. To refer 60 clients for educational assessment through the Metroversity Educational Opportunity Center (EOC) Program/Jefferson County Public Schools (JCPS). Out of this number, to ensure 20 clients will have received assistance for higher education scholarships, 20 will have received a high school equivalency diploma, 20 will have been enrolled in a family literacy/Adult Basic Education program, and 10 of these will have received a high school equivalency diploma. (Education)

2. To assist 100 children attending schools in the Russell Neighborhood through participation in the HANDS esteem team activities. Ten parents are to be actively involved in esteem team training. Specific definition of active parental involvement is participation in Parent Advisory Team. (Education)

3. To obtain an additional external grant to support HANDS' educational activities to serve clients in the Russell Neighborhood. (Education)

4. To work to obtain an environmental education program. (Education)

5. To work with JCPS to implement a family literacy center at Coleridge-Taylor in Village West. (Education)

GOAL 4: For HANDS to become a model of community partnerships.

What were the objectives?

1. To help create a nonprofit housing corporation and provide ongoing technical assistance and support to that organization. (Community design)

2. To assist the city of Louisville with the preparation and submission of at least two grant proposals, which would benefit the Russell Neighborhood. (Administration)

3. To assist two nonprofit organizations with grant proposals that would benefit Russell. (Administration)

4. To continue to write and submit at least one article a year for national publication, having a total of at least three articles generated. (Communications)

5. To encourage other departments of the University of Louisville to become involved in the community. (Administration)

6. To help teach other universities how to build university-community partnerships.

GOAL 5: For HANDS to promote economic development in and for the Russell neighborhood.

What were the objectives?

1. To help implement a micro-business development program at the Louisville Central Community Center (LCCC). (Job development)

2. To institute a micro-business loan program as part of the micro-business development program at the LCCC. (Job development)

3. To identify and target 20 retail and service-oriented companies to approach and convince them to locate their businesses in Russell. To locate an operation in Russell. (Job development)

4. To recruit 30 clients for the micro-business program of which 20 will have completed training and 10 will have received business loans. (Job development)

5. To approach four banks to create innovative loan programs for business development and to ensure that a bank will have implemented one program. (Job development)

6. To recruit eight clients for minority contractor development training. (Job development)

7. To assist the city of Louisville with the preparation and submission of at least two grant proposals that will benefit the Russell Neighborhood. (Administration)

8. To assist two nonprofit organizations in or which serve the Russell Neighborhood in writing and submitting of grant proposals. (Administration)

9. To accomplish an integrated model for the University to respond to the-community. (Administration)

10. To develop a matrix to identify categories of clients and tie specific-demographics to each specific component of HANDS. (Administration)

GOAL 6: For HANDS to be a high-performance work organization.

What were the objectives?

1. To implement a strategic management plan, which will facilitate direction and purpose to the HANDS organization. (Administration)

GOAL 7: For HANDS to achieve funding stability.

What were the objectives?

1. To develop a work plan for soliciting private companies and other organizations to provide matching funds to HANDS. (Administration)

2. To negotiate and execute a written agreement with the Louisville Central Development Corporation (LCDC) for a set contribution to HANDS on a per home basis. (Administration)

3. To submit a proposal to the city of Louisville for matching funding for a U of L/City Center for Community Partnerships. (Administration)

4. To prepare for submission to the Department of Education a grant for a five-year extension of HANDS. (Administration)

5. To submit a request to the University of Louisville for ongoing core funding for the HANDS project to include permanent funding to support core administrative staff positions. (Administration)

6. To identify and submit grant applications for annual funding of at least $100,000 to four funding sources. (Administration)

Notes

Chapter 1

1. The view expressed is inconsistent with Peterson's (1981) assertion that a unitary interest controls development decisions in the city. The essence of the unitary interest paradigm is that all players in local development decisions, the local elites, must focus on "the long-term economic welfare of their community" (Peterson 1981, p. 65). The elites that control decision making will agree on what is right for the city and act on that shared belief. There is an absence of conflict among the elites, in Peterson's view, because of their focus on the common good. This assigns a higher level of motives to the diverse interests, even among the elites, competing for scarce resources than is merited by the many entities competing for power, position, or other items. Some support for this view of unified elites making decisions can be found in Molotch's (1976) discussion of "boosterism" and the city as a "growth machine" (1976; in Cummings 1988). He does, however, acknowledge some of the obstacles that the elites must overcome to implement their agenda.

Chapter 2

1. This section was co-authored by John I. Gilderbloom and Reginald Bruce.

Chapter 4

1. This chapter is the revised version of an article, "Urban Revitalization Partnerships: Perceptions of the University's Role in Louisville, Kentucky," By R. L. Mullins Jr. and John I. Gilderbloom, in *Local Environment*, vol. 7, no. 2. We appreciate the permission from *Local Environment* to use portions of the original article.

Chapter 5

1. This chapter is drawn from a report conducted by Gilderbloom for the Association of Governing Boards: "The Urban University in the Community: The Roles of Boards and Residents," published in 1996. A revised version of this report was published by Gilderbloom (2002) in *Metropolitan Universities*, vol. 13, no. 2 . This chapter is a revised version of the original report. We thank the Association of Governing Boards and *Metropolitan Universities* for permission to use parts of these reports for this chapter.

References

American Association of State Colleges and Universities (AASCU). 1995. *AASCU and NASULGC Survey of Urban Universities.* Washington, D.C.: American Association of State Colleges and Universities.

Andranovich, G. D., and G. Riposa. 1993. *Doing Urban Research: Applied Social Research Methods Series,* vol. 33. Newbury Park, Calif.: SAGE.

Bartelt, D. 1995. "The University and Community Development." *Metropolitan Universities* 6 (3): 15–28.

Bender, T. 1988. *The University and the City: From Medieval Origins to the Present.* New York: Oxford University Press.

Bengtson, V. L., E. Grigsby, E. M. Corry, and M. Hruby. 1977. "Relating Academic Research to Community Concerns: A Case Study in Collaborative Effort." *Journal of Social Issues* 33 (4): 75–92.

Bok, D. 1982. *Beyond the Ivory Tower: Social Responsibilities of the Modern University.* Cambridge: Harvard University Press.

Bok, D. 1990. *Universities and the Future of America.* Durham, N.C.: Duke University Press.

Bok, D. 1996. Personal correspondence to John I. Gilderbloom, February 17.

Bookchin, M. 1986. *The Limits of the City.* Montreal: Black Rose Books.

Boyce, J. N. 1994 (February 1). "Campus Movement: Marquette University Leads Urban Revival of Blighted Environs." *The Wall Street Journal,* p. A1.

Boyer, E. L. 1992. *Scholarship Reconsidered: Priorities of the Professoriate.* Princeton, N.J.: The Carnegie Foundation for the Advancement of Teaching.

Boyer, E. L. 1994. "Creating a New American College." *The Chronicle of Higher Education* 40 (27): A48.

209

Campus Circle. 1994. *Campus Circle Review.* Milwaukee, Wisc.: Campus Circle.

Capek, S. M., and J. I. Gilderbloom. 1992. *Community versus Commodity: Tenants and the American City.* Albany: State University of New York Press.

The Chronicle of Higher Education. 1993. "UCLA, IBM Rededicates Partnership with Opening of Academic Technology Center." *The Chronicle of Higher Education* 40 (9): S10.

Cisneros, H. G. 1995. *The University and the Urban Challenge.* Washington, D.C.: U.S. Government Printing Office.

Cummings, S., ed. 1988. *Business Elites and Urban Development: Case Studies and Critical Perspectives.* Albany: State University of New York Press.

Dahl, R. A. 1967. "The City in the Future of Democracy." *The American Political Science Review* 21 (4): 953–70.

Diamond, R. M. and E. A. Brownwyn, eds. 1993. *Recognizing Faculty Work: Reward Systems for the Year 2000.* San Francisco: Jossey-Bass.

Eulau, H. 1968. "Values and Behavioral Science: Neutrality Revisited." *Antioch Review* 28 (3): 160–67, In H. P. Friesema, 1971. "Urban Studies and Action Research." *Urban Affairs Quarterly* 7 (1): 3–12.

Farbstein, J., and R. Wener. 1993. *Rebuilding Communities: Re-creating Urban Excellence.* New York: The Bruner Foundation.

Feagin J. 1998. *The Free Enterprise City: Houston in Political Economic Perspective.* New Brunswick, N.J.: Rutgers University Press.

Ford Foundation. 1965. "Ford Fund Backs Community Studies." *The American Journal of Economics and Sociology* 24 (1): 111.

Friesema, H. P. 1971. "Urban Studies and Action Research." *Urban Affairs Quarterly* 7 (1): 3–12.

Gamson, Z. 1995. "Faculty and Service." *Change* 27 (1): 4.

Garr, R. 1995. *Reinvesting in America: The Grassroots Movements That Are Feeding the Hungry, Housing the Homeless, and Putting Americans Back to Work.* Reading, Mass.: Addison-Wesley.

Gilderbloom, J. I. 1992. *Urban Community Service Grant Proposal: HANDS: Housing and Neighborhood Development Strategies.* Louisville, Ky.: Urban Research Institute.

Gilderbloom, J. I. 1996. "The Urban University in the Community: The Roles of Boards and Presidents." *Association of Governing Boards Occasional Paper No. 30.*

Gilderbloom, J. I., and J. P. Markham. 1995. "The Impact of Homeownership on Political Beliefs." *Social Forces* 18 (3): 350–64.

Gilderbloom, J. I., and M. T. Wright. 1993. "Empowerment Strategies for Low-Income African-American Neighborhoods." *Harvard Journal of African American Public Policy* 2: 77–95.

Gilderbloom, J. I., and R. Appelbaum. 1988. *Rethinking Rental Housing.* Philadelphia: Temple University Press.

Gilderbloom, J. I., and R. L. Mullins Jr. 1995. "The University as a Partner: Rebuilding an Inner City Neighborhood." *Metropolitan Universities* 6 (3): 79–96.

Glaab, C. N., and A. T. Brown. 1983. *A History of Urban America.* New York: Macmillan.

Goldsteen, J. B., and C. D. Elliott. 1994. *Designing America: Creating Urban Identity.* New York: Van Nostrand Reinhold.

Goldstein, H., and M. Luger. 1992. *Impact Carolina: The University of North Carolina at Chapel Hill and the State's Economy.* Chapel Hill: University of North Carolina Press.

Greiner, W. R. 1994. "In the Total of All These Acts: How Can American Universities Address the Urban Agenda?" *Teachers College Record* 95 (3): 317–23.

Grigsby, W., and T. Corl. 1983. "Declining Neighborhoods: Problem or Opportunity?" *The Annals of the American Academy of Political and Social Science* 465: 86–97.

Groark, C. J., and R. B. McCall. 1996. "Building Successful University-Community Human Service Agency Collaborations." In C. P. Fisher, J. P. Murray, and I. E. Siegel, eds., *Applied Developmental Science: Graduate Training for Diverse Disciplines and Educational Settings.* Norwood, N.J.: Ablex.

Hackney, S. 1986. "The University and Its Community: Past and Present." *The Annals of the American Academy of Political and Social Science* 488: 135–47.

Hall, P. 1989. "The Turbulent Eighth Decade: Challenges to American City Planning." *Journal of the American Planning Association* 55 (3): 275–82.

Harkavy, I., and W. Wiewel. 1995. "University-Community Partnerships: Current State and Future Issues." *Metropolitan Universities* 6 (3): 7–14.

Hathaway, C. E., P. E. Mulhollan, and K. A. White. 1990. "Metropolitan Universities: Models for the Twenty-first Century." *Metropolitan Universities* 1 (1): 1–12.

Haughton, G., and C. Hunter. 1994. *Sustainable Cities.* Melksham, Wiltshire, England: Cromwell Press.

Hester, J. M. 1970. "Some Observations on the Urban Involvement of Universities." *Urban Affairs Quarterly* 6 (1): 88–93.

Horowitz, F. D. 1990. "The Multiple Partnership: Scientist, University, Agency, and Government." *The American Psychologist* 45 (1): 51–53.

Huth, M. 1980. "New Hope for Revival of America's Central Cities." *The Annals of the American Academy of Political and Social Science* 451: 118–29.

Illman, D. 1994. "NSF Celebrates 20 Years of Industry-University Cooperative Research." *Chemical & Engineering News* 72 (4): 25–28.

Johnson, D., and D. Bell, eds. 1995. *Metropolitan Universities: An Emerging Model in American Higher Education.* Denton: University of North Texas Press.

Jones, D. P. 1995. Strategic Budgeting: *The Board's Role in Public Colleges and Universities.* Washington, D.C.: Association of Governing Boards of Universities and Colleges.

Katz, P. 1994. *The New Urbanism: Toward Architecture of Community.* New York: McGraw-Hill.

Kerr, C. 1968. *The Urban-Grant University: A Model for the Future. The City College Papers,* 8. New York: City College of New York.

Kerr, C. 1972. *The Uses of the University: With a Postscript—1972.* Cambridge: Harvard University Press.

Klotsche, J. 1966. *The Urban University and the Future of our Cities.* New York: Harper and Row.

Kysiak, R. 1986. "The Role of the University in Public-Private Partnerships." *Proceedings of the Academy of Political Science* 36 (2): 47–59.

Liebow, E. 1967. *Tally's Corner.* Boston: Little, Brown.

Lissner, W. 1980. "A 'Town-and-Gown' Assault on Urban Problems." *The American Journal of Economics and Sociology* 39 (4): 319–20.

Louisville Central Development Corporation (LCDC) 1993. (March). *Russell Neighborhood Development Plan.* Louisville, KY: LCDC.

Lyons, T. S., and R. E. Hamlin, 1991. *Creating an Economic Development Action Plan: A Guide for Development Professionals.* New York: Praeger.

Markham, J., and J. I. Gilderbloom. 1996. *An Analysis and Description of the Russell Neighborhood.* Unpublished manuscript.

Mazey, M. E. 1995. "The Role of a Metropolitan University in Facilitating Regional Cooperation." Pp. 195–205 *Metropolitan Universities: An Emerging Model in American Higher Education,* ed. D. M. Johnson and D. A. Bell. Denton: University of North Texas Press.

Medoff, P., and H. Sklar. 1994. *Streets of Hope: The Fall and Rise of an Urban Neighborhood.* Boston: South End Press.

Microsoft Corp. 1995. *Microsoft Bookshelf.* Redmond, Wash.: Microsoft Corp.

Molotch, H. 1976. "The City as a Growth Machine." *American Journal of Sociology* 82: 309–32.

Mullins, R. L. Jr. 1996. The University in the Community: Town and Crown Partnerships for Renewiing America's Neighborhoods. Louisville, Ky. UMI.

Mullins, R. L. Jr., and J. I. Gilderbloom. 2002. "Urban Revitalization Partnerships: Perceptions of the University's Role in Louisville, KY." *Local Environment* 7 (2): 163–176.

Newman, J. 1913. *University Subjects.* Cambridge, Mass.: Riverside Press.

Nyden, P., and W. Wiewel. 1992. "Collaborative Research: Harnessing the Tensions between Researcher and Practitioner." *The American Sociologist* 23 (3): 43–55.

Osborne, D., and T. Gaebler. 1992. *Reinventing Government.* Reading, Mass.: Addison-Wesley.

Patton, C. 1995. "Incorporating Public Service into the University Mind-set." *Metropolitan Universities* 6 (3): 45–54.

Peirce, N. R., and R. Guskind. 1993. *Breakthroughs: Re-creating the American City.* New Brunswick, N.J.: Center for Urban Policy Research, Rutgers, the State University of New Jersey.

Perlman, D. H. 1990. "Diverse Communities: Diverse Involvements." *Metropolitan Universities* 1 (1): 89–100.

Peterson, P. E. 1981. *City Limits.* Chicago: University of Chicago Press.

Pitts, J. P. 1977. "The Community Service Voucher Program: An Experiment in Community Access to University Resources." *Urban Affairs Quarterly* 13 (2): 181–206.

Popenoe, D. 1969. "Urban Studies Centers in Institutions of Higher Education." *Urban Affairs Quarterly* 5 (2): 143–50.

Porter, P. R., and D.C. Sweet, eds. 1984. *Rebuilding America's Cities: Roads to Recovery.* New Brunswick, N.J.: Center for Urban Policy Research, Rutgers, the State University of New Jersey.

Rayburn, K. 1995. "Helping HANDS." *University of Louisville Alumni Magazine* 13 (2): 8–10.

Rohe, William M., and M. A. Stegman. 1992. "Public Housing Homeownership: Will It Work and for Whom?" *Journal of the American Planning Association* 58: 144–57.

Rohe, W., and M. A. Stegman. 1994. "The Effects of Homeownership on the Self-Esteem, Perceived Control, and Life Satisfaction of Low-Income People." *Journal of the American Planning Association* 60 (2): 173–84.

Rossi, P. H., and E. Weber. 1995. "The Social Benefits of Homeownership: Empirical Evidence from National Surveys." *Proceedings of the Fannie Mae Annual Housing Conference 1995.* Washington, D.C.: Fannie Mae.

Ruch, C. P., and E. P. Trani. 1995. "Scope and Limitations of Community Interactions." Pp. 231–43 in *Metropolitan Universities: An Emerging Model in American Higher Education,* ed. D. M. Johnson and D. A. Bell. Denton: University of North Texas Press.

Rusk, D. 1993. *Cities without Suburbs.* Washington, D.C.: Woodrow Wilson Press.

Shore, W. B. 1995. "Recentralization: The Single Answer to More Than a Dozen United States Problems and a Major Answer to Poverty." *Journal of the American Planning Association* 61 (4): 496–503.

Shumaker, J. W. 1995. President, University of Louisville. *Continuity, Change, and Community.* Speech. 28 September.

Silver, C. 1985. "Neighborhood Planning in Historical Perspective." *Journal of the American Planning Association* 51 (2): 161–74.

Squires, G. D., ed. 1989. *Unequal Partnerships: The Political Economy of Urban Redevelopment in Postwar America.* New Brunswick, N.J.: Rutgers University Press.

Stegman, Michael A. 1991. *More Housing, More Fairly: Report of the Twentieth Century Fund Task Force on Affordable Housing.* New York: Twentieth Century Fund.

Stegman, Michael. A. 1995. "HUD's University Partnerships: HUD Shapes a New Role as Partner with Universities in Rebuilding Urban America." *Metropolitan Universities* 6 (3): 97–107.

Stone, C. N., and H. T. Sanders. 1987. *The Politics of Urban Development.* Lawrence: University Press of Kansas.

Stukel, J. J. 1994. "The Urban University Attacks Real Urban Issues." *Government Finance Review* 21: 19–21.

Tannenbaum, J. 1948. "The Neighborhood: A Socio-Psychological Analysis." *Land Economics* 24 (4): 358–69.

Tornatzky, L. G., Y. Batts, N. E. McCrea, M. L. Shook, and L. M. Quittman. 1996. *The Art and Craft of Technology Business Incubation: Best Practices, Strategies, and Tools from 50 Programs.* Southern Technology Council and National Busines Incubation Association

U.S. Department of Commerce, Bureau of the Census. 1990. *1990 Census of Population.* Washington, D.C.: U.S. Government Printing Office.

U.S. Department of Education. 1992. *Urban Community Service Program.* Washington, D.C.: U.S. Government Printing Office.

U.S. Department of Housing and Urban Development. 1994a. *Community Outreach Partnership Centers Program.* Washington, D.C.: U.S. Government Printing Office.

U.S. Department of Housing and Urban Development. 1994b. *Vision/Reality: Strategies for Community Change.* Washington, D.C.: U.S. Government Printing Office.

Walfoort, N. 1994. "Hyping HANDS." *The Louisville Courier-Journal,* 1 June, p. A10.

Wallerstein, I. 1969. "University in Turmoil: The Politics of Change." New York: Aeneum.

Winthrop, H. 1975. "Policy and Planning Programs as Goals of Scientific Work: Interdisciplinary Training for Social Planning as a Case Study in Applied Social Science." *The American Journal of Economics and Sociology* 34 (3): 225–45.

Young, W. B. 1995. "University-Community Partnerships: Why Bother?" *Metropolitan Universities* 6 (3): 71–78.

About the Authors

John I. Gilderbloom, Ph.D., 1983, University of California, Santa Barbara, is a tenured professor of urban and public affairs in the graduate program in urban and public affairs at the University of Louisville. He currently directs the Center for Sustainable Urban Neighborhoods (SUN) at the University of Louisville. Since 1992, his competitive, federally funded grants have totaled nearly $4 million. He has brought in from non-federal sources over $1 million from private foundations, churches, and local government. Since he earned his Ph.D., Gilderbloom's economic policy research has appeared in twenty-three refereed journals, twenty chapters in edited books, eleven monographs, and twenty-five opinion pieces in newspapers and magazines. He is the editor of a book on housing policy; co-author of *Rethinking Rental Housing,* and co-author of *Community versus Commodity: Tenants and the American City.* His book *Rethinking Rental Housing* was declared "the most significant piece on housing policy written in the last 30 years" by the *Journal of the American Planning Association.* A survey of college housing courses by the national Housing Institute found it to be the most widely chosen book. *Community versus Commodity: Tenants and the American City* has been hailed as "fascinating . . . a model of qualitative research . . . nearly flawless . . . a masterful combination of historical information, fieldwork, and theoretical analysis . . . it is worthwhile reading for urban scholars, social movement scholars, and methodologists," according to the *American Journal of Sociology.* Gilderbloom is finishing a new manuscript, *Invisible Cities: Planning, Housing and New Urbanism.*

Gilderbloom is also part of a progressive speaker's bureau for the Institute for America's Future (http://www.ourfuture.org/sb/sb.asp) in Washington, D.C. and is also the director of the SUN program <http://www.louisville.edu/org/sun>. His private consulting firm's Web site is: <www.gilderbloom.org>.

Gilderbloom's public policy research has appeared in the leading urban and public affairs periodicals in academia, including: *Journal of the American Planning Association, Social Forces, Urban Affairs Quarterly, Journal of Housing, Planning, Social Problems, American Journal of Economics and Sociology, National Civic Review, Environment and Planning, Environment and Behavior, Journal of Urban Affairs, Social Policy, Local Environment, Metropolitan Universities, Sociology and Social Research,*

Harvard Journal of African American Public Policy, International Journal of Aging, Teaching Sociology, Urban Analysis, Housing and Society, and *Journal of Applied Behavioral Science.* His opinion pieces have appeared in *USA Today, The Wall Street Journal,* the *Washington Post, Governing Magazine,* the *Los Angeles Times,* the *San Francisco Chronicle,* the *Houston Post, Business First,* the *Atlanta Journal and Constitution,* the *Texas Observer,* and the *Houston Chronicle.*

As an undergraduate, Gilderbloom graduated with highest honors at the University of California at Santa Barbara. He has been recognized for his research on public policy by the American Society of Landscape Engineers, the Western Governmental Research Association, the American Planning Association, the *Journal of Applied Behavioral Science,* the mayor of Houston, the Sierra Club, Harvard Innovations in Government, and the American Institute for Architects. In 1987 and 1990, he received two "teacher-of-the-year" awards at the University of Houston and University of Louisville, respectively. The College of Business and Public Administration presented Gilderbloom with the 1993 award for outstanding researcher and the 1997 award for "superior achievements in grant activity." In 1994, Governor (Brereton) Jones commissioned him the status of "Kentucky Colonel." Gilderbloom has provided research assistance for President Clinton's Council on Sustainable Development and the National Economic Council. Gilderbloom also has provided assistance to *National Geographic* magazine, the city of Houston, the city of Los Angeles, the city of Louisville, the Social Science Research Council, Shatil of Israel, Ontario-Canada, the U.S. Congress, the U.S. Department of Housing and Urban Development, and the State of California Department of Housing and Community Development. The White House Chief of Staff Office and National Economic Council consulted Gilderbloom on President Bill Clinton's 1993 state-of-the-union address. Ten years later, Gilderbloom was given the "Businessman of the Year" award and asked to be honorary chair of the Business Advisory Council.

During the Clinton administration, Gilderbloom was hired to estimate the economic impacts of the empowerment zone, enterprise community, and Section 108 programs for Vice President Albert Gore and the Department of HUD. In January 1994, in an address to the U.S. Conference of Mayors, President Clinton gave "a special word of thanks" for an op/ed article that Gilderbloom co-authored in the *Washington Post* on the successful "Russell project" in Louisville. President Clinton told the mayors in the White House: "You made the point that I have seen in Louisville, Cleveland, and Chicago and many other places that there really are things we can do if we have the right sort of partnerships. There are ways to use the relatively modest amount of federal money now available, to match with local funds and private-sector funds to really do things to get a lot of our troubled areas going again, and that was a very important point because there is a lot of cynicism about that around town; and you have helped to put a fresh note of reality in our discussion, and I appreciate that very much. . . . Our community empowerment agenda is the beginning of that work, and it can lead to a lot more projects like the one discussed in your fine op/ed piece."

Currently Gilderbloom is conducting a $210,000 evaluation of the Hope VI program in Newport, Kentucky. The Republican National Committee recently honored

Gilderbloom by delaring him "2003 Businessman of the Year" and making him honorary chair of the Business Advisory Council. Gilderbloom has lectured at Harvard, MIT, Stanford, Cornell, the University of California (Los Angeles, Santa Barbara, and Berkeley), the University of Southern California, Princeton, Yale, and Pennsylvania State Universities, and the University of Virginia, Rice, and Michigan. He also has lectured in Canada, France, the Netherlands, Venezuela, Mexico, Costa Rica, and Cuba.

R. L. Mullins Jr. is a vice president for Science Applications International Corporation (SAIC), in Falls Church, VA. He works on homeland security, infrastructure, environmental planning, and program management issues. Mullins spent twenty-five years in leadership positions for the U.S. Army Corps of Engineers before joining SAIC. His final posting was the senior civilian, Deputy District Engineer, in Louisville, Kentucky, where he was responsible for a more than one-half billion-dollar program annually consisting of civil works, military construction, family and unaccompanied housing, environmental remediation, and support to other federal agencies. Mullins was awarded 10 Department of Army medals and many other citations for service to the nation. In addition, he has received numerous awards and citations from local governments, agencies, and non-profit organizations. Over the years, Mullins has taught a variety of subjects, including project management and leadership development for a number of diverse organizations. He has authored several research and professional papers on infrastructure, water resources, environmental engineering, housing, and urban planning. He also is a licensed professional engineer and an attorney-at-law in Kentucky, and he is certified as a planner (the American Institute of Certified Planners) and a project management professional (the Project Management Institute). Mullins received his Ph.D., Juris Doctor, master of engineering, and bachelor of science degrees from the University of Louisville. In addition, he received a master of business administration degree from Vanderbilt University.

Name Index

Subject Index